Also by
DR. WINNIFRED B. CUTLER

Menopause: A Guide for Women and the Men Who Love Them,
1983, co-authored by C. R. García, M.D.,
and D. A. Edwards, Ph.D.

The Medical Management of Menopause and Premenopause:
Their Endocrinologic Basis,
1984, co-authored by C. R. García, M.D.

Hysterectomy Before and After,
1988

Love Cycles: The Science of Intimacy,
1991

Menopause: A Guide for Women and the Men Who Love Them,
1992, completely revised and expanded edition,
co-authored by C. R. García, M.D.

Searching for Courtship

Searching ❦ for ❦ Courtship

THE SMART WOMAN'S GUIDE TO FINDING A GOOD HUSBAND

Winnifred B. Cutler, Ph.D.

VILLARD BOOKS
New York
1993

Villard Books is a registered trademark of Random House, Inc.

All inquiries regarding motion-picture, dramatic, translation, and other
related rights should be addressed to the author's representative:
Loretta Barrett Books
121 West 27th Street—Suite 601
New York, NY 10001

Library of Congress Cataloging-in-Publication Data
Cutler, Winnifred Berg.
Searching for courtship : the smart woman's guide to
finding a good husband / by Winnifred B. Cutler.
p.   cm.
ISBN 0-679-41079-1 (alk. paper)
1. Courtship.   I. Title.
HQ801.C87   1993
646.7'7—dc20   92-50489

Manufactured in the United States of America on acid-free paper

9 8 7 6 5 4 3 2

First edition

This book was set in Berkeley Old Style Medium
Book design by Charlotte Staub

P30532000   5/93

To all who want
The joy of courtship,

Thoughtfully seek
And you shall find.

Preface

What single woman wouldn't like to be courted? Courtship is a remarkable experience in which a man gracefully pursues a woman, getting to know her on dates, treating her as though she were a prize and not a possession to be won, restraining his sexuality and allowing both of them the pleasure of anticipating sexual intimacy. Courtship is not a romantic ideal. It is a reality that you can experience if you are single and want to search for it.

In this book I will show you a proven and enjoyable way to search for courtship. Not only has it worked for me but for the many friends, relatives, acquaintances, and women who have attended my workshops. After some six years of trial and error, contemplation and study, through friendship and research, I was able to make these important discoveries.

When I became single unexpectedly in my late thirties, finding a good man to love became a top priority. Because I am a scientist, it was natural for me to use scientific methods when meeting men. My education and training in experimental psychology and reproductive biology made me realize how important a monogamous, loving relationship is to a woman's health and well-being. And like other women, I wanted to be in love and to get married again.

I approached courtship with the same discipline that I brought to my other scientific work. I would spend as much energy as it took until I discovered how things work. I recorded my emotions and experiences in a journal and tried to keep an open mind. I kept records of my experiences so that I would begin to learn what principles work (because they increased my ability to predict outcomes) and really figure out what it takes to find a good man to marry. Eventually I compiled a set of principles that I call the Code of Courtship.

I'll show you how to search for courtship in a way that will add grace to your evenings, dignity to your days, and a great sense of fun and richness to your life. If you're willing to learn what it takes and to try these principles, courtship can be yours this year.

I know because I have seen it happen all around me again and again: Women from all walks of life—lawyers, physicians, artists, housewives, corporate executives, small-business owners—have gone on to marry and build buoyant and loving relationships. The stories in this book are all true. Only the names and minor details of people's lives have been changed to protect their privacy.

You can find a desirable man to court you. Consider Ronnie, who at forty-four felt there were no good men left in
Philadelphia. She and I serve on the board of directors of
the Philadelphia chapter of the National Association of
Women Business Owners (NAWBO). Ronnie owns a gift
business serving corporate executives. She was convinced
she already knew what was out there—lots of lying and
cheating, albeit seemingly successful businessmen. However, she trusted me when I assured her that I could help
her find good men. She attended a workshop on May 3,
1992. Three months later when I saw Ronnie at a NAWBO
lunch meeting, she was dating four exciting men. She was
beginning her search for courtship, accepting formal dates
from men who were lining up to be put on her schedule.
"So many men," she said with a smile. "Winnifred, I am
having the time of my life!" Ronnie was experiencing what I
believe you, too, can find.

Or consider Scarlett who, at twenty-eight, was involved
with a man who was "in love" with her but had no desire to
marry her. He was annoyed by her insistence on an egalitarian relationship. He didn't think it appropriate for a man to
wash dishes or cook for women. He recognized that some
would consider him selfish, but he had a long history, at
thirty-four, of choosing compliant women. Scarlett loved
him and was on a roller coaster ride of highs and lows. Then
she attended a workshop and told me six months later that
her life had been turned around. Reluctantly, she ended her
unhealthy relationship, telling him that she wanted to marry
and begin a family.

Scarlett was now in charge of what happened to her. She
became involved with a man who brought flowers and
talked of love and marriage. She took her time, allowing the

friendship to unfold. She informed me that this new way of encountering men began for her when she decided to embrace the Code. During this process, although she made mistakes, she corrected them and discovered how much fun being single and searching for the right man could be.

And then there is Hilary, whose wedding I attended in March. At the wedding reception she seated my husband next to her, and me next to the groom. The bridal couple toasted me because of the beauty they had experienced— they considered themselves lucky to have enjoyed such a courtship. I expect to hear great things from them as the years unfold because they have established a marriage based on joy, respect, and fair play.

Searching for Courtship can serve as your own guide to success. It begins with a review of the principles involving biology, psychology, and human relationships that are relevant to finding love and marriage. It shows you how to apply these principles and make the journey every bit as pleasurable as the reward you will find—your wedding day.

I hope you will write to me with your questions and your success stories. Perhaps I will be able to bring a workshop to your neighborhood.

—WINNIFRED CUTLER, PH.D.
President
Athena Institute for
Women's Wellness Research
30 Coopertown Road
Haverford, PA 19041

Contents

Searching for Courtship

ONE

Setting Out on the Journey

Australian finches live in flocks, from which they choose their lifelong partner. Typically an unmated male initiates pair bonding with his song and stylized courtship displays. If he sings to an already mated female and is so bold as to approach her, he is rebuffed. The female will either fly away or he will be attacked. If the female he approaches is unattached and ready for mating, she may respond with a gentle greeting or a modest courtship movement. Her restraint and his enthusiasm set the tone for his pursuit.

In the beginning
One cannot see the path ahead . . .

THE START OF MY SEARCH FOR COURTSHIP

After having been married long enough to forget what a lonely Saturday night felt like, I found myself suddenly single in 1981 with a new and bewildering social life. The sexual revolution seemed to have wiped out the old rigid rules between men and women. The codes of conduct I'd learned in adolescence no longer seemed to apply. If new rules had replaced the old ones, I could not see any evidence of them.

3

When it came to reentering the dating scene, I had many questions. Where would I find suitable dates? Who pursued whom? When was it appropriate to act out a sexual attraction? How would I know whether the man who said "I love you" really meant "I want your body (and then I will want to go on to someone else)"? Who should pay for dinner? What about opening doors? Should I call when he said he would and didn't? What had happened to good manners? It seemed that men no longer knew the choreography of the romantic dance. And I knew I wanted to dance.

As a biologist, I was trained to look for an underlying order within the seeming chaos of life. In the course of my professional work, I had studied and made discoveries about the beautiful harmony of female biology: how our patterns of sexuality dramatically alter our health and well-being; how dangerous to our health and life span an unhealthy sexual relationship could be; and how beneficial a good one was.[1] Now I was the one living the data, not just discovering them!

From my objective perspective as a scientist as well as my intuitive feelings as a woman, I knew I needed a good man to love. Optimistically, and systematically, I set out to find him. I kept records (as any good scientist would do), read every available book about dating for adult single women, and compared notes with my "colleagues," a growing group of single friends. I made mistakes and corrected them. I

[1] My colleagues and I had discovered that women who have regular sex have better health, hormones, and well-being, and that sporadic sexual relationships—feast or famine—have the power to disrupt the endocrine system. My book *Love Cycles: The Science of Intimacy,* published by Villard Books (New York) in 1991, describes these sexual patterns.

listened to the successes, excesses, and failures of my friends and learned from them. And I pored over my written notes.

In all these ways I began to learn what worked. As I started to figure out a code of conduct, my single life began to get better. And better. Eventually, my social life became so full that I had to find ways to cut it back. It was not unusual for me to come home from a date to find three or four messages from other men who wanted to get together. By then I had discovered how to balance my energies and was limiting myself to dating three times a week.

Four years later, when I met the man whose marriage proposal I eventually accepted, I was amazed to realize that I had dated 160 different men. These were real dates: set in advance, initiated by the man, accepted by me. I was enjoying myself, too. I would often spend the late-night hours on the phone with my single women friends and discuss the issues we were facing. Sometimes I made suggestions that were greeted by responsive laughter. My single friends kept telling me I should write a book because the ideas and tactics I was proposing were not only effective but they were also fun to do.

Gradually, more and more of these wonderful women took command of their social lives, setting standards and living by them. All but one of the original fifteen are now married. Between the showers and the weddings, dating and searching, I was having a great time. And so can you!

Now, after three years of courtship and three more happily married, I can share what I learned. With the benefit of hindsight and the experience of teaching a number of courses to college students, as well as workshops to mature women, I offer the reader her own private at-home course.

Searching for Courtship is its name. Its goal is to show you a way to discover and enjoy the pleasures of courtship; to reap its rewards—a joyous marriage between lovers.

WELCOME TO COURTSHIP

Soon you can be experiencing the pleasures that go with a beautifully choreographed single "time of your life" as you move out to search for your own courtship.

Like twenty-five-year-old Peg, who came to a workshop and decided that she could take charge of her single life once she thought through what she wanted and what she needed to do differently to get it. Six months later she was enjoying the adventure of going out several times a week. She had a glowing confidence in herself and a feeling of goodwill that attracted good men to her.

Like Angela, who after six years of "going with the flow," dating whenever an interesting man showed interest, on whatever terms he set, took charge of her calendar and gently educated her pursuers so they would know what kinds of courtesy they had to show her before she could set aside time for them.

Like Barbara, who at fifty-five thought that fifteen years of being single was a fate that would continue forever into her future. Then she learned she could have a better life, was willing to go for it, and did. Fifteen months later she was sending invitations to her postnuptial celebration.

This first chapter gives you a brief overview of the guiding principles that helped me, my women friends, and workshop students. The rest of the chapters explore these principles in greater detail, providing examples and opportunities for practice. The book is designed to guide your journey in a systematic way. If you decide to follow its course, it will take you from your current state (single and un-courted), to getting yourself ready, to discovering where the good men can be found, to being a woman who is going out to play, to accepting some offers for dates, to being courted by one man you have selected, and finally to accepting a proposal of marriage from the man you love. *At every phase you will be in charge of what happens to you!*

The women who have had the most success with their search for courtship were the ones who worked at it systematically. They:

1. Worked at it on a regular basis. I recommend committing yourself to three weekly sessions of about two hours' duration. In order to learn, you need repeated exposure as you devote disciplined energy to the task at hand. Trust me, it will be fun once you get started.
2. Worked through the strategies in order. Read ahead if you like, but then come back and execute the campaign.
3. Took notes to record their progress. I suggest purchasing a loose-leaf notebook, twelve section dividers, and filler paper to keep your notes in place for later use and review.

If you are willing to be guided by what I call the ground rules, I can promise that as you do the suggested activities, you will find you are enjoying yourself as you travel through the path to courtship. This may be quite a switch from your present dating experience! If you don't want to spend this much time in your search for a man to love, then I cannot promise success. Yet even if you aren't ready to start the course, it might be useful to read about it. Maybe you will be ready to engage in the process sometime later. If you *are* ready to search for courtship, start right here and right now.

YOUR FIRST STEP

Look at your calendar and set aside the time this week for three separate two-hour sessions. This first week will be reserved for reading this book and reviewing the first four chapters for what you will need to do to get started. This is *not* time lost. Spending time on nurturing a love life (or searching for it) is as important a life activity as any other you will ever choose. *Searching for Courtship* offers a road map to guide you. T. S. Eliot said it beautifully:

> In order to arrive at a place you have not been, you must go by a way you do not know. (*Four Quartets*)

Courtship in the 1990s is unlike it ever was before. You are heading for a new place, with a new set of guideposts. If you are

- a woman who is single but doesn't want to be
- a woman who wants a quality relationship, whether experienced in relationships or not
- a woman who wants commitment and marriage
- a woman who has made all the "right moves" but still finds herself alone
- a woman who has had many sexual relationships but no feasible proposals of marriage

- a woman who has achieved success in other areas of her life and now wants success in courtship
- a woman who has enjoyed a long-term marriage and now finds herself single and bewildered

you are in the right place now. I have seen these principles work with many women. Age doesn't seem to matter. From nineteen to sixty-five, each used them successfully to find a good man and build a solid love relationship with him. After age sixty-five, the supply of men dwindles and you will probably need to go out to play four or five times a week if you want to be engaged within fifteen months. And every woman that I have seen practice these rules was engaged to be married within fifteen months. Really! You are neither too young nor too old to make use of its teachings.

What makes *Searching for Courtship* different from other how-to-find-a-man books or classes? First, it uses a scientist's focus on biological research to back up its principles. Second, it tells you exactly what you need to do to search for courtship and win. Sprinkled throughout the chapters, you will find scientific studies that underpin the principles I have devised and tested. Science is systematic. It tests and it measures results. Whether or not you have loved science before, you're going to love it now.

Searching for Courtship shows you the high road to intimacy. *You are* worthy of intimacy, no matter what your past relationship history. Are you ready? Ready to try a course that will elevate your dignity, preserve your health, provide a sense of decency in your relations with men and women, and engender a wholesome sense of well-being? Then take my challenge: Learn and live by the eleven principles listed below. I call them the Code of Courtship because they provide a framework to guide all your searching activities. Once you internalize these eleven principles, you will find that you are in charge of your love life. The journey of the search, as it is laid out here, will require your courage but reward you with high spirits (and good men). If you follow my suggestions now, I am certain that three years from now you will look back with a smile and a sense of accomplishment at how far you have journeyed. And you will probably feel a secret pleasure for all the good times you had.

THE CODE OF COURTSHIP
(The Eleven Principles)

1. You acknowledge biology's rules and use his sexual attraction for you to negotiate for courtship.
2. You accept the legitimacy of your own needs.
3. You recognize the value of balance: on the one hand, the merit of positive solitude and reflection; on the other, the importance of maintaining an active social life.
4. You communicate what you want.
5. You strengthen your capacity for self-control and your dignity by taking command of your calendar.
6. You develop your capacity for honesty and your ability to detect deception.
7. You acquire basic hormonal and sexual facts.
8. You understand and live the dignity of good manners.
9. You recognize that a positive attitude engenders personal magnetism for attracting legitimate courtship candidates.
10. You understand the importance of projecting a good impression, but nevertheless are slow to judge others.
11. You realize that there are many good men searching and muster the courage to end all romantic relationships that are not leading to courtship.

In one way or another, every part of this book and the course refers back to these eleven principles. Take a moment now just to consider what each has to say. Later, if integrated into your life, they will provide the basis to change the way you see men and the way they see you. Together these eleven principles work to bring you toward your goal: an intimacy that blooms into a successful marriage. This goal should be crystal clear in your mind as you start your search. It's the goal that propelled me forward in my search for courtship and intimacy.

THE RICHES OF INTIMACY

INTIMACY: A relationship between two people characterized by conscious vulnerability, sharing of confidences and privacy, extreme trust, and sensuality.

Intimacy is fundamental to life, and its rewards are worth listing[2] (see page 12). The rewards are worth remembering, particularly in moments of weakness when you are tempted to settle for less. These intimate rewards are the reason for searching for courtship. They are the reason to avoid the quick fix of a "hot weekend" or spending intimate time with a man who is not fully available because he is publicly committed to another woman.

---

[2] Men and women, from dating couples to newlyweds, from younger to elderly people, all list a similar range of benefits that they gain through a committed, intimate bond. In 1990, publishing a scholarly chapter in a new book, *Emotions and the Family* (Hillsdale, N.J.: Lawrence Erlbaum Assoc., Inc., 1990), psychologists Elaine Hatfield and Richard Rapson reported on their studies of thousands of individuals.

THE REWARDS OF INTIMACY

Personal

Having a partner who:

- Is an asset in social settings
- Provides intellectual stimulation
- Provides an attractive image to enjoy day after day

Emotional

- Liking and being liked
- Loving and being loved
- Understanding and concern
- Acceptance by a partner (which leads to the freedom to grow)
- Being appreciated
- Physical affection (touching, hugging, and kissing)
- Sex
- Security
- The pleasure of sharing plans and goals

Day-to-day

- Financial stability
- Sociability
- A partner to share decision making and accept a fair share of the daily responsibilities
- Being remembered on special occasions

The need for loving, supportive, caring relationships is as vital now as it ever was, but many young as well as mature singles suffer from a confusion of roles. This confusion leads to uncertainty about how to behave to achieve the rewards of intimacy. Does holding the door open for a woman diminish her "equality"? Who asks who on a date, and who pays? These uncertainties occur because the fight for sexual equality eliminated many of the old rules but failed to offer viable new rules. To shed some light on this matter, let's take a look at the science that backs up the reality.

THE BIOLOGICAL BASIS OF COURTSHIP

Why do we want intimacy? At its most basic level, there is a biological "urge to merge"—to be among our own kind, to get close to someone else. Isolation and its resulting emotional state, loneliness, is a painful experience because it causes a biochemical imbalance in the body. For this reason, as you begin your search, you will need to go out regularly. Going out gets you seeing people in casual settings for fun and recreation. Socializing alters the chemical reactions produced by being alone too much or working too hard. Biologists have recently discovered how social isolation affects the chemical secretions of the neuro-endocrine system. This research provides the background to show why you *need* to go out regularly in order to prevent social isolation.

Biological research in monkeys has a message for single men and women. In 1989, researchers in Atlanta, Georgia, conducted an experiment that proved how devastating social isolation is to body chemistry. They also showed that by restoring social contact, the internal chemistry of lonely creatures rapidly recovers.

To understand how such research might apply to people, some knowledge of "monkey business" is useful. Adult monkeys groom each other as a part of their normal social interaction. They show both a characteristic "grooming invitation" and "grooming response." The *invitation* involves one monkey approaching another and either (1) spreading its arms wide and offering its chest or (2) bending over and, in a similarly vulnerable manner, presenting its rear end. The *reaction to this invitation* varies. When the reaction is positive, the invited animal responds by petting and stroking the offered body part. When the reaction is negative, the invited animal turns and walks away—rejecting the invitation. What single person wouldn't recognize this body language?

After a monkey has been alone and then allowed to have social contact, the animal attempts to make up for loneliness by a dramatic increase in invitations. Watching it, you might label what you saw as "promiscuity"! More invitations lead to more contact—just what the monkey craves. With more grooming responses, the blood chemistry of the animal receiving the petting changes. The endogenous opiates, or pleasure chemicals, start to rise. In other words, the animals use specific "please touch me" behaviors to alter their inner emotional state.

The Message of Monkey Biology for Singles

This monkey research offers insight into the "singles scene." When people who feel lonely seek physical contact through "one-night stands," they are displaying an understandable attempt to make up for their isolation. But humans are not monkeys. The price for impulsive behavior can be outrageously high for a woman: from deadly disease and long-lived trauma to the lesser woes of despair and feelings of rejection.

Quick fixes usually fizzle out and quickly fade away. Stable relationships rarely follow from such random shots in the dark. As those who jumped too fast often learn, taking a chance was not worth the risk.

Stable relationships can follow when a man who wants to establish intimacy discovers that he is not the only one in charge. When a man is in pursuit, you can take charge of what happens. You can decide what you want to do with his expression of interest. In other words, the choices you make when a man approaches you help determine the kind of relationship that will unfold. When you are really ready for courtship, you need to make correct choices, the ones that will bring you what you want—a good marriage.

WHY COURTSHIP NOW?

Courtship sounds like an old-fashioned idea, but it has survived because it works.[3] A man pursues a woman as though she were a prize to be won. His actions produce the specific romantic relationship that leads to commitment, marriage, and cohesive family life. Courtship provides an art form in which both the man and the woman experience a sense of personal dignity, high value, and mutual respect as they move toward intimacy.

Courtship is not without some flaws. The culture of the fifties and sixties encouraged game-playing in courtship. Women often accepted a false role, a dishonest "weak persona." At one time, women were taught to pretend to be less competent than they really were. That pretense, like all lies, came back to haunt them later, compromising their growth and development. The rebellion against and liberation from such stunted growth was inevitable.

In the last thirty years, female roles have changed dramat-

[3] It still works in the animal kingdom. Think of all the courtship dances and displays of peacocks, roosters, ring doves, deer, etc. Nature rarely discards a winning strategy.

15

ically. The feminist movement has been an important factor
in changing both the behavior and the assumptions about
behavior of women and men in much of the developed
world. With that movement came the very reasonable assumption that women had as much right as men to develop
their talents, to be educated, to choose how to use their
education, and thereby to enjoy the fruits of such a life
journey—the potential for a rich, meaningful life.

The feminist movement also led many women to change
their sexual behavior, to be more open to sexual experience,
sometimes taking the lead where they would not have dared
to before. Feminism often suggested that we should feel free
to do whatever we wanted to do. Bedding many men seemed
like "freedom." I think it was another form of entrapment. It
exposed women to disease (bonding them permanently to
the internal scarring of the sexually transmitted diseases)
and it wiped out the power that women used to have: to
command respectful treatment by gentlemen.

For the woman who is already sexually experienced, there
may have been a time in her life when gathering experience
had its benefits in spite of the costs. Whenever you decide
that you are ready for courtship, the rules of effective conduct change. When you want courtship, you need to reserve
and preserve your intimate being. The time of freely and
spontaneously expressed sexual connection is over. Now is
the time of safe sex with a known and trusted partner, one
whose goal of marriage clearly involves *you*.

Why such vigilance? Why my stand on saving sex? You
don't have to be a biologist to know that sexually transmitted diseases (chlamydia, herpes, gonorrhea, HIV, genital
warts, and so on) are rampant and increasing. Many of these

diseases can permanently impair your fertility, but there is yet another reason to protect yourself from exposure to these diseases. They also impair the flow of sensuality because they damage nerve endings and often leave painful internal scarring behind them.

Consider Kirstin, a thirty-five-year-old beauty who considered herself a romantic and loved the eros that went with the early stages of a new love affair. It was only after she got herpes from a man who did not have an active lesion that she began to question and discover a better way to enjoy her passion and preserve her health. She is fine now, enjoying the three men she is dating and taking her time to see how she finds each friendship unfold before she even considers the possibility of getting sexually intimate with one of them. She has discovered how much power celibacy offers.

What I am suggesting is that you be more analytical. Take charge. Do not flow with the sexual requests of the new man in your life. Do not be impulsive. The price is too high. To search for courtship, I suggest you reserve sexual expression until you find a candidate for courtship, a man you will accept only after he has met your standards, a man whose ethical values are acceptable to you, a man with the capacity to treat you with great respect. For those who aren't sure what your standards should be, I suggest some later on.

Each man you date will learn from the start to treat you well or you won't go out with him. Chapter 6, "Formal Dating: Rules and Roles," provides the details. You can be in charge when you take control and exert your own restraints. If you think this will take energy, you are right. Being in charge takes work; but it sure feels good. It gives you a glow of confidence that will attract men to you.

I think it's time for women to reinstate courtship because it will lead to commitment and marriage. Courtship magnifies the well-being of women and men who are pursuing a loving, committed relationship. Courtship can be elegant when the woman dances—guided by her male partner, a partner she has given permission to lead her in the dance. When you decide courtship is what you want and restrain yourself from sensual pleasure before you have examined the man's character and intentions, you will win the prize.

COURTSHIP:
WHAT IT IS AND WHAT IT IS NOT

I define courtship as a process in which a man pursues a woman, asking her in advance for dates, treating her as though she were a prize (but not a "possession"). A man pursues a woman with the intention and the hope that his efforts will lead to intimacy, and with the expectation that, should the relationship flourish, his proposal of marriage will inevitably follow.

It is *not* courtship when a man pursues a woman for a sexual relationship while he is sexual with others as well. Neither is it courtship when he calls Friday afternoon hoping to get together over the weekend. Four days' advance notice is courteous behavior.

Nor is it courtship when a woman asks a man out with the hope that romance will bloom. In fact, as women usually discover, when they do ask men out, the men often love it, may even accept the date, *but* courtship does not follow. And in most cases, neither does marriage.

Consider this comment from a 1991 participant in one of

18

the Athena Institute's Searching for Courtship workshops. She is thirty-two years old, very attractive, never married.

> As a graduate of Bryn Mawr College, I entered the world of work believing that men and women were equal. That I had as much right as a man to initiate dates. And I did pursue a man. We dated for over a year and became great friends. In fact, I fell in love with him. Just recently he told me that he has proposed marriage to someone else. I was devastated. Women taking the kind of lead I did, learn . . . one way or the other . . . although we were told we had the right, it doesn't work.

I agree with her assessment, but I don't think this leaves you powerless. Your power lies in your ability to attract, to lure, and then to use *your* values in timing the expression of the intimacy that follows. When a man pursues a woman, the potential for marriage and successful sexual response is magnified. For a committed relationship leading to the kind of romantic attachment that can lead to a proposal of marriage, men must initiate the dates. Science shows it: A man needs to generate the energy for a specific woman in order to enhance the passion between them.[4] Take this initiative from him and you risk either his virility or his serious pursuit of courtship. Somehow it is in the process of pursuing and courting that he comes to decide that you are the woman for him.

A woman seeking courtship needs a clearheaded man who is specifically pursuing her. And she needs the power of restraint to put into action her most effective role. Biology

---

[4] In May of 1989, the first scientific study to test this assertion found it to be so. The duration of relationship depended not on the intention of the woman but of the man.

teaches the lesson. Throughout the animal kingdom the role of the female is to lure and make selections from those who court. Luring works. It creates a kind of magnetic force that draws men to you. If the male is the pursuer, the woman is the gatekeeper—she guards her biological riches and decides who has access to them.

The gatekeeper must be vigilant and discriminating. When a man does exhibit courtship behavior, does he have "honorable intentions" or is he engaged in a deliberate act of deception? Some men will lie to you to get a sexual connection. You need to be alert. You simply cannot afford a naïve attitude when you are ready to search for courtship. Here again, science can help women. With the issue of deceit, psychological research provides some answers. And the bottom line is—when a man wants to deceive you, it won't matter how smart you are. Until you have had enough time to know his character, you won't be able to tell whether he is telling the truth.

DECEPTION AND LIES— THE SCIENTIFIC PERSPECTIVE

In 1981 three social psychologists[5] published a classic review article on the nature of deception. They systematically studied over two hundred published research reports. Their work is valuable in the context of dating dynamics.

First, they defined *deception*.

---

[5] Drs. Myron Zuckerman from the University of Rochester, Bella DePaulo from the University of Virginia, and Robert Rosenthal from Harvard.

An act intended to foster in another person a belief that the deceiver considers false; the deceiver transmits a false message, while hiding true information and also attempts to convince the perceiver of his or her sincerity. It is an intentional and conscious act that is directed at another person.

"Sure I'll respect you in the morning."

"I don't sleep with my wife."

"Lie down. I think I love you."

"I'm confused about what I want; but I know I want to be close with you now."

Their analysis shows that certain behaviors occur much more often when a man is telling lies than when he is telling the truth. When you (as a potential victim of a deceiver) are alert, you should be able to minimize the deception against you. What are visual cues that deceivers (of both sexes) transmit in the act of lying?

· Their pupils dilate.
· They start shrugging as they talk.
· Their body language seems irrelevant to the content of the message; they touch themselves, fidget, and scratch.

The verbal cues are even more revealing:

· They make speech errors.
· They hesitate while speaking.
· Their vocal pitch rises.
· The quantity of negative statements increases.
· Irrelevant information is provided.

Who Best Detects Lies?

Having identified characteristics of lying, the social psychologists next evaluated how accurate people are at detecting deception. Their results may be surprising. First, they found that the would-be detector's self-confidence is irrelevant. How certain a person was of her ability to detect lies was unrelated to her tested accuracy. Second, as people age, they get better at detecting lies. Third, women are significantly more likely to interpret the deceiver's message as the deceiver wants the message interpreted than as the lie that it is. *In other words, women are more susceptible than men to deception.*

Although the experiments were done in laboratories and may not reflect real-life situations, these highlights may prove useful in your own life. Intimacy is seriously impaired when deception exists between two people.

When Deception Is Self-deception

Deception is destructive. Self-deception is equally so. It wastes your time and energy. It distances you from the possibility of a joyous courtship. *Any woman who is searching for courtship should make it a cardinal rule to avoid a sexual or romantic relationship with a man who is not currently a candidate for courtship.*

Any woman who is searching for courtship should take a clear look at her current relationships. Sometimes reflection will reveal that the deception is actually self-deception. (He said he couldn't make a commitment; she didn't want to believe it.) It is all too easy to maintain a dead-end relationship just for the sake of having someone. It may be hard for you to think of ending such a relationship, but dead ends detain you from your crystal-clear goal. Once you decide that you are ready for courtship and marriage, you need to focus your energy on men with honorable intentions. You need wholesome intimate relationships with men. And just as women need and should expect honorable intentions from men, they must transmit them.

WHO IS A CANDIDATE FOR COURTSHIP?

You are, if you have decided you are ready for courtship. This plan is for emotionally stable people who want to learn some new ways of conducting themselves, who are willing to try them, and who can keep trying when things go wrong. My road map can be used in conjunction with good psychotherapy for those who are uncertain about taking charge of their own lives, but it is not a substitute. If you cannot muster the kind of maturity and courage the directions call for, consider giving yourself the gift of individual therapy with a counselor or psychotherapist in conjunction with your use of this courtship map.

With or without therapy, these eleven principles (the Code) are designed to serve as guideposts for your journey. Even if you find one—or more—hard to do, the actions you take will bring you the pleasure that comes from doing things that build your sense of self-worth. If you can marshal the courage it will require to rise to their challenge, you are likely to discover the joy that is available to those who use courtship principles to search for a man to love and marry.

YES, GOOD MEN ARE AVAILABLE!

It is reassuring to know that there are many good single men out there . . . even now. All the good ones are not taken, although it may sometimes seem that way. Why does it sometimes seem that the married men you know are more desirable than the single men you know? It's basic psychology. A committed man is attractive precisely due to that fact —that he is in a relationship. Love, trust, and intimacy transform people, bring out the best in people. During courtship, and later in a committed relationship, men and women discover how to nurture each other and make each other better. Someday soon you will be nurturing a good man, and he you. In searching for courtship, your activities should increase the number of friendships in your life and enhance the lives you touch. Courtship involves both giving and taking.

If you think of your search as a journey, moving you forward on a beautiful path laced with varied scenery, you will open yourself to the magic of single life. You will encounter many other people who are moving along on their own journeys. Some will disappear after a brief introduction, others may bloom into friendships. When you are searching elegantly, those who have been fortunate to meet you should come away with the sense of having been graced by your presence. And you will come away from each encounter feeling richer than when you began it. You can become a good woman, one who radiates a joy of life that men find compelling. And you can meet your match in a good man.

To begin your search, your first investment will be your time. You need to learn to use it strategically.

24

TIME AND ENERGY,
THE COURTSHIP FUNDAMENTALS

If you want to be married successfully, you will have to
spend time with your spouse. (Obvious, isn't it?) If you want
to search for courtship successfully, you will be smart to
devote time, energy, and self-discipline to the process. *The
time you commit to your search for courtship is the same time
you will later divert to the courtship itself and then even later
to your new husband.* That is why I suggest that you schedule
three separate two-hour segments each week for your
search. As in any course, you make a commitment to be
there when course work is scheduled. But since this is your
own personal course, you choose your own preferred hours,
and you can change them from week to week.

Are you ready to begin your search? Had enough theory?
Good. Then I'll begin with the first action you need to take:
to take charge of your calendar and become the boss of your
own social life.

TAKING COMMAND OF YOUR
SOCIAL CALENDAR

It's time to establish the way you schedule your dates. Tuesday night by 9:00 P.M. (four days in advance of the weekend)
close your calendar to invitations for Saturday and Sunday.
Now, having closed the calendar to dates, take out your
calendar and look at next week. Select three separate two-
hour segments for "courtship searching." Mark them clearly
in ink. Think of them as important appointments, as vital to

your health as any doctor. (If you have already accepted two dates for next week, fill in the appropriate days, but be sure to make the one "appointment" remaining for courtship searching.) Don't worry if you have three blank blocks at first. Later, in Chapter 4, you will develop a resource directory from which you will select the specific activities to fill into these three segments. As the weeks pass, the three two-hour segments will vary with your own resource list and the dates you accept. Make your plans, one week at a time, each Tuesday night or Wednesday morning.

Starting now, the search for courtship becomes the focus of your romantic time and energy. This may require taking a clearheaded look at how and with whom you're spending your time. You may need to clear the decks of unsuitable candidates and/or activities that consume your energy but divert you from your goal (Chapters 2 and 3 show how). For now, the simple action of setting aside three two-hour segments per week starts unfolding the road map to chart your new direction. In the first week or two this searching time will be absorbed by the reading you are doing. Take your time reading through the first four chapters. When you get to Chapter 5, you will be on your way, going out to play three times a week.

YOUR COURTSHIP MAP

The diagram on page 27 shows the big picture: the map of how you get from here to there. We will go into the details of each stage later; but for now it may help to see an overview. Notice how the arrows show the one-way direction of a searcher's path. You begin by going out alone three times a week and continue to do this until you progress to the stage of a formal date. Formal dates can move into the forging-a-friendship stage or they can end without friendship, leading you back to stage one, going out alone. A friendship can become more elevated, leading you into courtship activities; it can end, sending you back to the start.

The progression of the five stages symbolizes the level of loss when a relationship ends and the inevitable distance you will need to go before you are ready to go out alone again. This is why it makes sense to restrain your natural impulses and go slowly with a new man.

This map cannot show the other truth about any courtship search: that you get faster at moving forward once you know how to do it gracefully. You move out of the starting gate with greater acceleration and confidence. You've been on this path before.

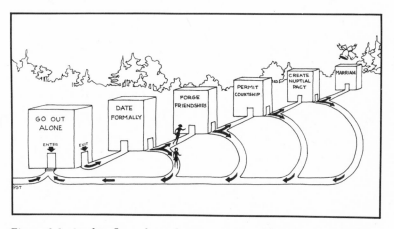

Figure 1.1. As this flow chart shows, your courtship journey advances along a continuum of five stages. At any point, should the relationship end, you return to stage one to begin the courtship-searching cycle again.

CALLING THE SHOTS

Meanwhile, what if a man who doesn't know your new approach should call you for a date after you have closed your calendar for the weekend? If you would like to go out with him, say:

> "I'd love to go out with you. I have already made plans for this weekend. How about next weekend?"

Although, as you will come to see, courtship requires that women permit men to make the dating invitation (*in the early stages of the relationship only*), women play an active role, too. The first feminine courtship province comes from being boss of yourself, from keeping your own calendar, planning events that *you* select. You are in charge! Your plan for an evening—whether it be sorting your socks, polishing your nails, or going out to a singles dance—is not relevant when you tell Fred:

> "This weekend's calendar is full. How about next weekend?"

Fred does not have "the standing" to know what activities you will be doing without him. If he asks what they might be, you must not tell him. That is your private business. It increases your dignity to limit your answer. Only say:

> "I already have plans."

Should he insist on knowing what your plans are or attempt to convince you to change them to suit his last-minute

28

invitation, your answer should be firmly noninformative. A lighthearted reply, "Just my own plans," is sufficient. Would you be so rude to ask a single man you hoped to date who else he was seeing and what he was doing on the Saturday night he was "busy"? Probably not.

But what if he insists? Or is so jealous that he demands to know? Isn't this a sign of his interest in you? From what I have learned, you are looking at a man who has not learned to be respectful toward women. (Only his needs count.) A man who will not treat your requests respectfully does not qualify for your time when courtship and a good marriage is the goal.

Likewise, the sweetness or thoughtfulness of the last-minute invitation is irrelevant. Neither a small nor an enticing lure (expensive theater tickets, for example) should alter your course. The QE2 is a stately ship that moves majestically and does not change its course in fits and starts. Think of this image as you politely decline Fred's invitation. Becoming a queen will attract a king. The man who learns to treat *your time* with respect will be treating *you* with respect. Gently clue him in through your own subtle action of suggesting a later date.

Gaining control of your own calendar is fundamental to gaining command of yourself. Scheduling your time puts new value on it. Your time is a commodity, to be spent but not squandered. Your new time attitude will also generate the self-respect you will need to present yourself as an adult and a courtship partner. And as you do it, you become it. Communicating your stature to the men who pursue you will build your strength of character and your dignity.

The man who invites you at the last minute can be forgiven that discourtesy if he responds to your polite counter by setting up a date with you. Instead of inviting him to call next week to set the alternative date, take action and schedule the date now. Say something like:

"Let's reserve the time now. Is Friday or Saturday better?"

The man who is unwilling to plan ahead is probably not a candidate for courtship at this time. Of course, given time to reflect, he may see the error of his ways!

Once you decide to journey to courtship, *your time is too valuable to waste on a man who won't behave like a candidate with you.* As a woman who has accepted the courtship challenge, your energy must now be devoted to the search for true, available, current candidates.

MAN, WOMAN—POWER AND RIGHTS

When romance is pending both the man *and* woman are in charge. As I have mentioned, I see the romantic heterosexual relationship as a dance. One with reciprocal power and reciprocal rights. One in which a genteel negotiation, rather than a power play, forms the basis for agreements.

Have you ever seen the carnival game in which a beanbag is thrown to knock over a hinged doll? The prize is won if the doll stays down after it is hit. In the case of the last-minute invitation, you are like that hinged doll. You must not permit a man to bowl you over. If you have already planned your weekend and he wants to see you at his convenience, he is not respecting your time. If you agree to see him, your acquiescence communicates your agreement that his time is more valuable than yours. Whether you realize it or not, you are agreeing that the two of you are unequal and that only his time is worthy of respect.

On the subject of women, men are often remarkably simple. Is *she* "the one"? Or is she a potential "sex object"? The way you get started has a powerful influence on the direction in which you head. When you convey that you have standards, a man may fight—but he will know—that you are to be treated respectfully.

In other words, your response to his last-minute invitation that you get together the following week provides the good manners of reciprocity while allowing him an opportunity to see you. By suggesting an alternative date for the following weekend, you are graciously preserving his dignity and your own—*if* you want to see him. Meanwhile, you stand tall and refuse to be knocked over by his last-minute scheduling attempt.

When you set standards that show a man how to treat you respectfully, you are taking charge of what happens to you. If he shows you by his *behavior* that he is capable of rising to the high standards you have set, you are acting to establish the necessary conditions for a wholesome, fun-filled courtship. Civility. Mutual respect.

THE DANCE OF COURTSHIP

Women set the pace, defining the role men shall play in the dynamic experience of loving. As a woman in the courtship dance, you can slow the pace, but you will find yourself at a dead stop if you attempt to accelerate it. Why? I believe the reason lies in his reproductive biology. It is the man who must summon the energy for pursuit. After all, his reproductive physiology is designed to play the anatomically prominent role. As it is with the anatomy, so it appears to be with the physiology and the behavior. Women need to honor the biology of men. And men need to honor the biology of women.

As a plug fits into a socket, males and females are designed to fit together. Considered separately, we are clearly different. A 1989 scientific report provides a typical example of the biological and behavioral differences that distinguish men and women.

WHO WOULD HAVE SEX WITH A STRANGER?

Drs. Russel Clark and Elaine Hatfield enlisted college students as decoys to carry out their experiment. Some were women; some were men; and all ranged from mildly unattractive to mildly attractive, although the range of attractiveness turns out not to have mattered. In their roles as decoys, the students stationed themselves on a college campus quadrangle and repeatedly approached a stranger of the opposite sex, another college student, to test their willingness to explore intimacies with a stranger. The decoy told the student that she or he had been noticing the student around campus, found the student attractive, and wanted to ask a question. Then one of the three questions was randomly asked:

1. "Would you go to bed with me tonight?"
2. "Would you come to my apartment tonight?"
3. "Would you go out with me tonight?"

Men and women turned out to be very different in the kinds of responses they gave to these intimate invitations. Not one of the ninety-six women agreed to go to bed that night with a strange man. More than 70 percent of the ninety-six men said yes, they would have sex with a strange young woman, unless they were previously committed for the evening, in which case they asked: "How about right now?" They said yes to sex regardless of whether the woman was attractive.

The opposite result showed up on the question "Would you go out with me tonight?" Men were unlikely to say yes to an invitation to go to a woman's apartment, and more unlikely to say yes, they would accept a date for that evening. Here again, women were opposite from men. Although none agreed to go to bed with a strange man, and less than 6 percent agreed to go to his apartment that night, half of them said they would go out with a strange young man (who did, however, appear to be a fellow student) that night.

MEN AND WOMEN ARE DIFFERENT

This and other studies show that many men are willing to agree to sex on a one-night-stand basis, provided they don't have to go out on a date or get to know the women better. Experiments show women are the opposite. Women tend to be willing to explore relationships but unwilling to agree to quick and easy sex. These differences emphasize the power of courtship. You, as a female, have something a man wants. He may have something (a capacity for courtship) that you want. You must use your powers of allure, negotiation, and restraint to test his intentions.

Women also need to protect their safety, because men are stronger, heavier, bigger, and much more willing to have quick and easy sex than women are. The studies on college campuses show that men often misinterpret the willingness of women. "Date rape" is commonly reported and, sadly, growing more frequent on college campuses. The man often contends that the woman was willing when the woman says she was not. As a single woman searching for courtship, you need to be cautious whatever your age. You need to protect yourself. One way to do this is to avoid the possibility that a man can have access to you before you are ready. *Avoid being alone with a man until you have had a chance to sound out his background and his character.* (Chapter 7 provides the vital insights into this topic.)

In order to take charge of your own search for courtship, it helps to recognize that men and women are different. In the sexual dance between a man and a woman, it is the celebration of these differences, the act of fitting them together that makes for the elegance of a courtship experience. As a woman, you should magnify and enjoy your femininity as it complements the masculinity you encourage in men. (I define femininity as that aspect of being female that lures the male to pursue her.) It is this mutual self-respect and appreciation of the other that draws us into a loving connection.

The courtship relationship is based on consideration, kindness, love, and caring about each other. Courtship is based on civility, not on the barbarity of date rape. In the dynamic intimacy between a man and a woman, what's good for one is good for the other. By following the suggestions in this book, you will be ready to begin an effective search for a committed, enduring, and joyous relationship.

Let's step back for a moment to get an overview as you get ready to set out on your search.

WHY COURTSHIP WILL CHANGE YOUR LIFE

The search for courtship is a *definite, positive act.* Courtship is not a random activity that just happens. Once you decide that you are going to take action to reach for what you want, you first need to prepare yourself. Then you set out on the journey. Like all journeys, the search for courtship will take you to new places, places you may never have been before.

It is important to recognize that people can and, in certain circumstances, do change. I think a leopard *can* change its spots. A man who learns what you require may be able to rise to your challenge. Consider men you have known who treated some women badly and others well.

Don't buy into the idea that "what you see is what you get." Think of the homely seed that can bloom into a lovely plant with proper tending and nurturing. What you see in a courtship candidate is *not* what you get. Love changes people. What you see is the raw material before love has been added—if the candidate before you is available. How does knowing this change the way you look at men? Your critical questions will be:

"What would he be like in the garden I design—where I nourish him and he nourishes me? How would he change? How would I change? What would the relationship that derives from those changes be like?"

35

You can change also, and you will surely need to *if* you want courtship and if you have not had it before in your experiences with intimacy. You may have to change your attitude, your way of seeing, your way of perceiving.

SUMMING UP

If you have had enough experimentation in your life and are ready for courtship and commitment, you can get them with an organized plan of action. The rules in the sexual dance of power and love between the male and the female of many species are remarkably simple. These eleven principles of the Code of Courtship will guide you to your goal of courtship by a prince.

1. *You acknowledge biology's rules and use his sexual attraction for you to negotiate for courtship.* Although constrained by societal customs and mores, biology provides the rules of the dance between male and female. The romantic dance between women and men is a sexual one. All life on earth is designed to reproduce itself. The hormonal systems that are encoded in the male and female define the basis for male and female sexuality. Hormones and sexuality are described in Chapter 8. You will learn to use sexual attraction to negotiate for courtship when you like the man. If he is unable to accept courtship as the basis for developing a relationship, you will be unable to accept his offers of relationship, as Chapter 3 details.
2. *You accept the legitimacy of your own needs.* You own yourself and accept your own needs. As you are an adult, these needs include having a *stable,* monogamous sexual relationship,

laced with love, affection, commitment, and mutual support. You need intimacy. If you are going to have sex with a man, you should experience the riches of intimacy that surround the physical sexual connection. A man unwilling to court you is unable to give what you need. A man who does not rise to the pursuit when you have set lures is not a candidate at this time.

If you are going to have sexual intercourse with a man, a minimum of once a week (except during bleeding days of menstruation when abstention may protect your health, particularly of the endometrium [the lining of the uterus]) is basic to healthy hormonal patterns. Although more sex is fine, sporadic on-again off-again sex is dangerous to a woman's health. (See Chapter 8.)

3. *You recognize the value of balance: on the one hand, the merit of positive solitude and reflection; on the other, the importance of maintaining an active social life.* You recognize the value of loneliness and the importance of positive solitude and self-reflection as you prepare to enter a relationship with another person. You realize that if you have just ended a relationship, you may need a period of quiet mourning before you will be ready to search actively. You allow yourself some breathing room, some solitude to regain your composure and command of yourself. (See Chapter 2.) Likewise, you recognize the need for an active social life and make plans to go out to play regularly.

4. *You communicate what you want.* You feel free to communicate what you want—and to ask what he wants because the knowledge is fundamental to your well-being. You realize that by communicating you maximize your chances of getting what you want. (See Chapter 5: "Going out Alone.")

5. *You strengthen your capacity for self-control and your dignity by taking command of your calendar.* You are ready to exercise

the capacity for self-discipline and self-control. As in any goal, you understand that you must work for what you want to achieve. You have the self-discipline to postpone immediate gratification in order to reach for a larger and more elevated goal. Taking command of your social calendar is fundamental to this process. (See Chapter 2: "Readying Yourself" and Chapter 6: "Formal Dating: Rules and Roles.")

6. *You develop your capacity for honesty and your ability to detect deception.* You have the capacity for honesty. You know or are willing to learn how to discern truth from deception in the men who pursue you. This means you give yourself time to examine the character of a man before you decide whether he is a candidate for courtship. Before he is a candidate, sexual intimacy is premature. Sex before candidacy will detain you from your goal. In the same way, you will examine your own conduct and attitudes to avoid self-deception. (See Chapter 2.)

   Likewise, you are willing to exercise dignity always and to speak only the truth. It is okay to be silent or to refuse to answer a question; it is not okay to lie. You become what you do. Short of tyranny, there is no survival value in lying. Lies tend to haunt, not help, your relationship's future. To be worthy of courtship, you must develop an honest character. This takes courage.

7. *You acquire basic hormonal and sexual facts.* You know or are willing to learn how your own and a man's sensuality work. (Chapter 8 reviews these sexual basics.)

8. *You understand and live the dignity of good manners.* Civility is the lubricant of social intercourse. Sometimes it will be necessary to decline an invitation. Do it kindly and clearly—maintain your self-respect as you say, "No thank you." (Chapters 2 and 6 provide many examples.)

9. *You recognize that a positive attitude engenders personal mag-*

netism for attracting legitimate courtship candidates. You understand how a positive attitude attracts healthy relationships and how a negative attitude repels them. Much like a mirror, your personal magnetism attracts what is reflected in your emanations. You are willing to exercise self-discipline and honesty in order to draw goodness to you as you journey toward a new life experience. (See Chapter 7: "Forging a Friendship During Formal Dating.")

10. *You understand the importance of projecting a good impression, but nevertheless are slow to judge others.* You understand the importance of good impressions, yet you know that they can often be misleading. You will strive to provide a good impression—of dignity, self-worth, and kindness to others. And you will be slow to judge others, tolerant, and forgiving.

11. *You realize that there are many good men searching and muster the courage to end all romantic relationships that are not leading to courtship.* You are willing to accept that there are many good single men—bewildered, confused, and searching just like you. Your chief tasks will be to:
    a. Get yourself in hand, put your past in *perspective* and learn from it. (See Chapters 2 and 3.)
    b. Find good candidates. (See Chapters 4, 5, and 6.)
    c. Teach them how to court you. (See Chapters 7, 8, and 9.)

You recognize that you may need to end a relationship that is currently consuming your time but not leading toward courtship in order to free your time and your emotional energies to search for courtship. (See Chapters 2 and 3.)

Let the search for courtship begin!

TWO

Readying Yourself

In spring, male robins establish their territory by patrolling its borders while warbling and singing assertive calls. Meanwhile, each is building a nest for a prospective mate. The female robin has the luxury of choice, judging a male's appropriateness by his size and the quality of his territory. Does it include some blueberry bushes? Is it large enough? Safe enough? Who could blame the female for selecting the best home she can find?

You can select goals and achieve them.
You will then become what you do. Choose wisely.

Put on a pair of rose-colored lenses and the world takes on a rosy tinge, but look out through a tinted gray glass and the filter will cast a shadow of gloom. Untinted lenses are often the clearest, but they can absorb the glare and blind us. The color of the lens affects what we see; and what we see influences how we feel. Attitudes are similar.

If you focus on the bad experiences you have had with men and conclude that most men are bad, you will limit your opportunities. Even bad experience can offer a kernel of goodness. You can make something good out of past troubles by recognizing the lessons they can teach.

When you decide that committed love is a gift that you want, and you know you are willing to give and receive it, your attitude can help you get ready. You need the rose-colored lenses of optimism in order to find good men. *And you need a clear vision of what you want, a steely sense of purpose that helps you recognize your greatest power: that because you become what you do, you can select goals and then achieve them.*

Soft and hard—optimism and steel—combine to build an attitude that can get you to courtship. In large measure, you can choose the color of your "lens" when you decide to take charge of your own well-being. To search for courtship and win, it helps to have an optimistic perspective tinged with reality.

Getting ready to search for courtship takes thoughtful effort. Before going out to meet men, you should encounter yourself and prepare. Then when you do connect with a good man, you will know what to do to get what you need. In getting ready, you may need to focus on three areas: adjusting your attitudes, defining new actions, and making plans. This chapter outlines what I have learned from many women who succeeded at courtship and went on to establish loving, respectful, joyous marriages.

Certain attitudes, actions, and plans will launch you most gracefully.

The attitudes are:

- Deciding to be in charge of your own life using truthfulness and optimism
- Counting your blessings
- Acknowledging and confronting your pain
- Recognizing that you will make mistakes and can learn from them

41

The actions include:
- Claiming adult status
- Building your nest
- Ending unproductive relationships
- Taking journeys into "dark tunnels" whenever they loom before you
- Building attractiveness and vigorous health

The plans include:
- Taking inventory of your responsibilities
- Recognizing and organizing the way you spend time as you set a new pace for your life
- Keeping a journal to monitor your progress

Let's start with the attitudes—the filters through which you perceive your world.

THE ATTITUDES

Depending upon your age and the way in which you were raised, the decision to take charge of your life can be relatively simple or remarkably complex. The feminist movement has so altered the expectations of women that the very definition of femininity and good manners has been dramatically changing over the last twenty-five years.

Take some time now to examine your assumptions, to see what filters you are wearing, as you begin to plan your search for a man to love. Consider how Bianca reacted to her situation.

BIANCA'S STORY

Bianca's story is sad but not uncommon. When she married Bill eighteen years earlier, he was struggling to launch his construction business. But later Bianca enjoyed the pleasures of Bill's success: their large, lovely home, a grand swimming pool, and no-holds-barred charge accounts. Perhaps because the financial freedom was so new to her, she seemed to discuss it all the time. She was frequently bragging about her newest purchases and Bill's lucrative business—especially to her best friend, Sharon.

Then the bubble broke. Bianca and her daughter, Penny, returned home after a visit to Penny's sick grandmom to find Bill gone. Shock followed. Bill had left her for Sharon, Bianca's "best friend."

Bianca's bitterness was so great that her verbal invectives created a constant trial for those around her. She fumed and she ranted. She had concluded that all men are louses, that friends could not be trusted, that she would never trust again.

As the years went by, her world became smaller and smaller, her personality so distorted that only her children would tolerate her. She dated occasionally but never for long because her angry attitude drove her friends away. She's old and lonely now. Pathetic but not uncommon.

This true story is just one variation on a theme of acrimonious divorce. But Bianca is a classic example of a bad attitude. Unproductive attitudes are terribly self-defeating and self-limiting. Bianca needed to seek help to confront her difficult situation and to overcome it. Instead of blaming Sharon and Bill, she would have been better off to join a gym and pound out her anger on a squash court. Or dig gardens. Or tear up an old floor and rebuild it. By diverting her anger into a sport or productive project, she might have built her muscle tone and improved her attitude. She should have focused on the positive—her health, her capacity to contribute service to others, the marvel of her children's presence in her life. She needed to face the future, to look at the new life she now needed to build.

Mary, another woman I met, faced a similar problem. Consider the way she handled it.

MARY: THE CHALLENGE AND THE COURAGE TO CHANGE

Unlike Bianca, Mary had courage. When her husband, Vernon, began to stay out late "on business" and came home sullen, she was sad. She tried to discuss it with him, but he would turn away. She felt deeply hurt, but she had a strong character. Mary began thinking about what she could and couldn't do to improve her life. She decided that she needed to establish a life with some separate elements—a life that would satisfy her need for warmth but avoid creating a bigger problem than she already had. She was committed to monogamy and she didn't want to leave Vernon.

She began to focus on new activities—taking up her old career as a photographer and turning her talent into a part-time job with an advertising agency. The time she used to spend with Vernon in the evenings she now spent in the library catching up on new photographic techniques.

The day that Vernon told her he wanted to end the marriage was both a low point and the beginning of a climb out of the depths. She found a sensitive woman therapist to help her. She went to see a lawyer to learn what her rights were. And she got on with her own life, refining a new attitude.

The inspiring thing about Mary was her positive attitude.

She acknowledged that she had suffered, but she expressed relief that now she could get on with a new life. And she did. She came to an Athena workshop on courtship to learn the ideas that unfold in the following chapters. A year later she was married and enjoying a deep pleasure and a sense of wonder in the journey she had taken.

Consider another unproductive attitude: "waiting behavior." If you believe in fairy tales (the ones where the princess waits until her knight in shining armor rides up to save her), you may have unwittingly accepted the idea that in order to have a masculine erotic power in your life, you need to be passive. That is not true. If you believe that women are in charge of their lives, you may have decided that they should never permit a man to "sweep them off their feet." With that attitude, you will miss a lot of fun. If you can combine the tough and the tender, high standards and compassion, your prize can be a more dynamic relationship than if you insist on keeping an attitude that is either too rigid or too passive.

Taking turns at being in charge is a nice way to do things. It brings peace to the soul to be able to surrender and follow sometimes. On the other hand, taking command of your life gives you a sense of power and the glow of excitement when you set your goals and then achieve them. Passive attitudes (never setting important goals, for example) can lead to a sense of helplessness and depression, feelings women have suffered in disproportionate numbers for generations. To get ready to search for courtship, it helps to become both tough and tender.

Bianca became tough. She wasn't going to let another man take advantage of her. And she wasn't going to fall in love again. But she missed the tender part, being open to love. Let's look at each aspect separately.

Your first question involves the "tough" part: "Who's in charge here?" Hopefully, the answer already is "I am!"

DECIDING TO BE IN CHARGE

For many women, the idea that it is okay to be in charge of their own lives has radical overtones. Many of us were taught that we are not in charge; and for some the message was so subtle that it has been accepted on a subconscious level.

Were you raised to believe that you are in charge of your life? Or were you trained to be quiet and act "feminine," letting men feel "masculine" at the expense of your own development? Did you grow up believing that you could get anything you wanted, provided you went after it assertively and with clear purpose? Such early teachings dramatically affect our adult assumptions.

A jailer's key has no value for one who does not acknowledge that bars surround her. Consider the following instructions such a key. They show what locks need to be opened, but only you can do the opening. And only you can walk out to freedom when the doors are unlocked. Most of us create our first prison by inappropriately relegating the control of our lives to others—others who may not even want that much responsibility over us.

To journey to courtship, live the attitude that you will take charge of what happens to you. If your past relationships have led to pain, examine them. A close and careful look will usually show what you need to know. Your goal is to avoid repeating that kind of distress.

One way to quickly assess how in charge you are is to take a good look at your attitudes about blame.

Who Is to Blame?

Although it is natural to blame someone else when you are treated badly, this focus delays the solution. One way or another, wherever you are now has something to do with choices you made in the past. Blame implies that you have accepted the idea that you are not in charge. In the twenty-seven years I have known her, Bianca never experienced another loving relationship with a man. She projected a negative attitude and rarely even went on a date. Always blaming Sharon for "stealing her husband," she lived inside her angry shell. When a woman blames her difficulties on others, she stays locked in her jail. Even if you have been treated badly in the past, you can dramatically change your future. Like Mary, who was discarded by her husband but went on to build a better life, you can focus on the future and build a good one.

Embrace the Code of Courtship and you will put an end to being treated badly. Taking charge means that you accept responsibility for heading in a new direction of your choosing. When you want to move into a new place, you need to make new kinds of choices. Those who fail to accept responsibility for where they are now are doomed to continue in the same way and perhaps to repeat the same mistakes that led to their current problems. When you take responsibility for where you are now, you create the opportunity to move yourself into a better place.

Take a close look at your history in order to learn from it and mold a better future (more on this in the next chapter).

And use *truthfulness and optimism* to move into the future. By combining a tough honesty with a gentle optimism, you can develop a savvy perspective.

COUNT YOUR BLESSINGS

We know from the deception experiments described in the last chapter how easily women can be deceived either by men or by themselves. As you put on the rose-colored lenses to develop a good attitude that projects cheerfulness, you also want to avoid self-deception. How? Consider this truthful method for building optimism. Focus on the good things in your life first.

Something magical happens when you list your blessings at the start of your journey. You give yourself momentum, provisions for the trip. Table 2.1 provides an exercise to help you focus a positive attitude. Take a few moments to review it, then get out a piece of paper and perform the exercise. Its purpose is to allow you to "put on rose-colored glasses" truthfully.

If you begin and end each day with five minutes' reflection on blessings, both global and unique to the day, you will give yourself the gift of rose-colored glasses. You will have focused your vision on good feelings and will have redirected your own reality. In large measure, we each can choose where to focus our attention. Start focusing more of your energy on the positive aspects of your life and you will be rewarded with happier feelings. As you become cheerful, you will attract an ever-widening circle of good relationships that will enrich your life. Positive people emanate a magnet-

TABLE 2.1. COUNTING BLESSINGS

List the people you love.
   my best friend, Caroline
   my brother, Anthony

_____

_____

_____

List the blessings the gift of life bestows in disproportionate abundance to women.
   warmth
   compassion
   lightness, humor
   empathy

_____

_____

_____

With what specific physical blessings have you been endowed?
   clear skin
   bright eyes

_____

_____

_____

What spiritual blessings have you received?
   a confidence in a benevolent higher power

_____

_____

_____

What intellectual gifts do you have?
   curiosity
   good verbal skills

_____

_____

_____

What blessings of family life do you enjoy?
   a close supportive relationship with my brother

   _____

   _____

   _____

What blessings of friendship do you enjoy?
   loyalty from Caroline, Sue, Kate, Jen

   _____

   _____

   _____

ically attractive force. Still, we need to acknowledge that life contains both joy and pain. A positive attitude should be based on truth.

ACKNOWLEDGE AND CONFRONT YOUR PAIN

Life contains suffering. Inescapably. In those plummeting moments of isolation that sometimes hit, the single person can feel despair. In my twenty years of studying women's health issues, I have heard many similar comments about such pain. Waking in the night with a feeling of panic and recognizing that no one is there to offer comfort, which magnifies the panic. Feeling devastated. Crying. The sense of isolation resonates. And it can feel as though it will never end. Loneliness is real. Being single is the very state of being alone. It has to hurt sometimes. Although a bad marriage is probably worse than the occasions of loneliness single people feel, a good marriage can be much better. It can offer a life partner, an end to loneliness.

Until you find your courting partner, there are healthy
things you can do to manage these moments of isolation.
There are ways of being alone that feel positive.

To find a good relationship, it helps to recognize when
and how you are most vulnerable. Knowing where you are
will help get you where you want to go. Take a look at Table
2.2 and complete the answers.

TABLE 2.2. ACKNOWLEDGING PAIN

The times when I feel the most pain are usually:

_____
_____
_____

The reason for the pain is:

_____
_____
_____

My two biggest fears about being single are:

_____
_____
_____

The percentage of my time that I feel pain is about:
_____ % During the workday
_____ % After work till the next workday begins
_____ % On weekends
The times that I am most likely to feel lonely are

_____
_____
_____

Loneliness comes in (check one or the other):
   Regular repeating cycles _____
   Random unpredictable times _____

What can you do about this pain, those moments when you feel lonely and isolated? Some things can be done to soothe the pain now, others through the actions you take in searching for courtship. First, in the short run, there is an immediate antidote to isolated stabbing moments of loneliness that any person can employ. I call it my exercise in positive solitude to "pluck the weeds."

Pluck the Weeds

If you think of your attitudes as if they were a garden containing flowers and weeds, you would know that you must be vigilant in plucking away the weeds—the bad attitudes —in order to enhance the growth of the good ones—the flowers.

Positive solitude is an attitude. It means enjoying a sense of peace and quiet within one's soul. Loneliness is also an attitude. It reflects fear of one's isolation from others. Think of loneliness as you think of weeds, something your mental gardener must regularly address to keep the garden blooming. Once you take action to engage in the three social events per week (introduced in Chapter 1 and developed in Chapter 5), your experience of isolation should become more manageable.

The first weed-plucking task is this: In the midst of loneliness, focus on shifting from the idea of "loneliness" to the idea of "positive solitude." Close your eyes and pretend for a moment. Lie down, become quiet, and imagine you are so surrounded by your loving family or friends that you need some time off to get some peace. Think of this need to get off alone when you feel lonely. Imagine the feeling of loneliness shifting into the relief of time off, time to engage in positive solitude before going out to play again.

Once you are socially active (Chapters 4 and 5), the way you embrace your time alone largely determines whether it is painful or pleasurable. *Usually you can take action and claim the power to change loneliness into positive solitude.* The solution is not intuitively obvious. When we feel lonely, it is common to try to fill up the space with various noises to dampen the pain. Making phone calls, turning on the television, seeking diversions. Instead, to eliminate the feeling of loneliness, I suggest the opposite. Do not fill space with diversion. Rather, close your eyes, do the "time off" exercise, and deliberately choose to be alone some of the time when you feel lonely.

A subtle but powerful shift should occur. If you embrace positive solitude by engaging this exercise and *staying* alone some of the time, you will help prepare your spirit for a positive search for courtship.

The reason speaks to some basic human needs. You need time to be still, to collect your sense of your own being, to mourn the loss of a relationship if that is your current experience, and to refocus in order to enhance your joy in life.

SPIRITUAL LIFE

Positive solitude also embraces the spiritual life. The solace of religion is available to some. If you are fortunate enough to have a spiritual life that you can share as part of a religious community, make use of it. If you are a Christian, a Jew, or a Muslim, go to church, synagogue, or mosque regularly and participate in the spiritual life of the group. These worship activities can help connect you to the rest of the faithful and lessen your lonely feelings. They can add balance to the rest of the week.

If you do not embrace a spiritual life through organized religion, find another way to connect your being to the pulse beat of all of life's being. Do it in the physical presence of others. Different people use different ways to do this. What matters is finding your own way. Spiritual life in groups is profoundly important to well-being. There are many books that can guide you into nonreligious forms of spiritual life, such as *The Course in Miracles,* published by The Foundation for Inner Peace, Tiburon, California 94920 (1975, 1985). *The Twelve Step Program* has various published versions. Meditation groups that get together on a regular schedule can also serve this purpose, even without a written guide.

In all of the successful programs there is a common thread. People gather together based on a common interest. When you meet someone you like through a spiritual, political, charitable, or educational association, you have a major interest in common and a built-in basis for getting to know more about each other.

Yet you are free of the pressure of communicating should you prefer to be quiet. Being in a community without having to do any work of communication, social exchange, or performing is comforting, restorative. Without words, you can share a spiritual life with the group as you sit quietly surrounded by others, connecting to the depth and richness of all life. I suspect that emanations from other beings— whether electrical or chemical—add something to our human experience that science has not yet begun to measure. But those who experience it know about it. Perhaps publicly listening to a poetry reading or a symphony or an opera can open you to this feeling.

Perhaps by emptying your mind and taking in the beauty of a flower or landscape in a public park, you will feel the powerful peace spiritual experiences can offer you. To experience spirituality is to focus on the beauty of life outside yourself as you connect to a more elevated level of being. You might go to a library and spend several hours there on a regular schedule. Open windows of your awareness in the library, in your house of worship, in museums. Scan the books, magazines, and works of art and select visions that will expand your mind.

Certain solitary actions conducted in the presence of others can fill spiritual needs. Try reading the Bible, particularly the poetic passages that speak of the pain of the soul and its resolution through spiritual connection. You might try Ecclesiastes, the Psalms, the Proverbs, the Song of Solomon, and the Gospels of Matthew, Mark, Luke, and John.

Perhaps your spiritual connection will be through a nondenominational group. Or try exploring music. The object of all these activities is to experience the magical art of being: to be still and recognize what surrounds you while in the physical presence of others. Life on earth has a social aspect. Living beings need physical connection to the emanations of other beings. They especially need to relax in the presence of others without conversation. Search and explore different ways to find this spiritual life and you will be well on your way to eliminating the sense of isolation and despair that haunts so many people.

OWNING A PET:
THE SCIENTIFIC EXPERIMENTS

You might consider getting a pet. When you share your home with other living creatures, your sense of isolation dramatically diminishes. Again, science provides the proof.

In the early 1980s a series of experiments were published by a team of research scientists at the University of Pennsylvania.[1] In the ten years that followed, their experiments continued to expand and reinforce their conclusion. They showed that owning a pet reduces stress, increases well-being, and lowers cholesterol levels and heart rate when a person is under duress.

While science is helpful, common sense will tell you the same thing. Imagine coming home from work to a dog, a joy-filled bundle of fur wagging its tail and jumping for joy just to see you. *You.* A pet that wants only to hug and lick you. A pet that asks nothing more than competent training, food, water, and companionship. Dogs are remarkably loyal, loving, and forgiving creatures. They come in many sizes and a variety of temperaments. Some can live in an apartment and be paper trained. Others need large grounds on which to bound forth every day. They can be costly, or you can get them almost free at the various shelters. A mongrel can give the same unconditional love as a show dog.

Dogs are ideal companions because they follow you wherever you go, sit close to you whenever you let them, will usually hug you when you ask, and will love you no matter

---

[1] Drs. Erika Friedmann, Aaron Katcher, and colleagues initiated this work at the University of Pennsylvania. Today Dr. Friedmann is a professor and chairman of Health and Nutrition Sciences at Brooklyn College.

how you look or feel. And you'll never have to sleep alone if you own a dog.

Or you might prefer another type of pet. Cats, birds, even fish swimming in a tank and houseplants help connect a single woman to life beyond herself. The scientific studies are clear. Other living creatures help reduce stress and loneliness. Why? Perhaps because they get us *out* of our "poor little me" mind-set and make us care about another. Perhaps because they connect us to love.

The other kind of loneliness is the pervasive attitude, as opposed to isolated stabbing moments. Pervasive loneliness often reflects an underlying fear, a fear that being alone is permanent, a fear that you will never find a good mate. When you acknowledge this loneliness and find the courage you need to recognize and confront it head-on, you will be able to overcome it. Rather than using painkillers, such as sweets or alcohol, or clinging to the phone or TV to avoid being alone, for this deeper sense of pain a more powerful antidote is available. The journey starts with a series of small, measured steps.

RECOGNIZE DARK TUNNELS

After you have found a way to connect your spiritual being to the world outside yourself, the next step in dissolving pain is through your mind. If you consciously enter what I call "dark tunnels," you will overcome loneliness in a healthy way.

Imagine a long, black tunnel winding its way through a mountain. You, the single woman, have just ended a relationship with a man. It wasn't very good. It offered more pain than pleasure. And as you (or he) ended the relationship, some part of you accepted that the parting was probably for the best. What did you do next?

One way or another, you entered into a "dark tunnel." The sense of being alone, the loss of a physical and maybe even a spiritual connection, seems something like darkness. You enter into that tunnel with a groping sense of the darkness in front of you. The deeper you step into the tunnel, the darker it gets in front of you. If you happen to look back over your shoulder, you can see some light cast from where you came. If you go forward, it gets darker. I think the scariest part of searching for courtship is the need to consciously enter into dark tunnels in order to reach the other side and find light again. Sometimes it can feel as if you will get lost in the tunnel and never come out. Whatever it was that caused the need to search for something new—a romantic breakup or finally getting a lonely life in hand—the journey to courtship takes you into new places. When you first go into the new place of the tunnel, it can seem to be very dark and scary.

There is another problem with the tunnel. As you first walk into it, you move into the darkness. The farther you go, the darker it gets. And as you start to walk into the darkness and look back behind you, the light grows dimmer as you travel deeper into the tunnel. Here lies the problem. When a person feels fear, the temptation is enormous to turn around and run back to the light. From a position of darkness, the light seems attractive. It is easy to forget why you left the light to enter the tunnel. When you are in the tunnel facing pitch blackness, even a poor-quality light can seem worthwhile.

The lure is powerful, and if you let it, it can pull you back to the light from which you came. Don't do it. Just keep going forward—plunging into the darkness of the tunnel in front of you. In order to search effectively for courtship, you need to realize the importance of the tunnel. It is only *after* you plunge fully into the darkness that your eyes adjust. After some time you can grope in the darkness with less confusion. After a while you get used to the dark. A little while later a dim light starts to emerge from the darkness ahead, and slowly you can discern where you are going. Ultimately, as you forge ahead, you come out at the other side into the full light again.

To successfully search for courtship, you must plunge into the darkness so that you can adjust to it, respond to it, and get on with your new life. Shortly after doing so the fun can begin. Meanwhile, the *price* is courage. You must consciously enter the tunnel—not pick up the phone, run out to a friend's, drink away the pain, or otherwise hide from the reality of your single state of being. The results are marvelous. As you enter the tunnel, your courage will grow. You will become stronger. And if you are wise, you will develop a heightened sense of humor.

To search for courtship, you must enter these dark tunnels all by yourself as a grown-up. You must claim adult status and be able to stand by yourself. The *power* of a woman is developed and exercised in her bravery, her ability to face her fears and stand alone. She does not need to scream or shout. She does not need to exercise control over another person. In fact, as a woman spends her energy trying to gain control over someone else, she depletes the energy to build her own power. She must overpower her fear.

In later chapters I will expand on this theme when I suggest that you go to social events all by yourself and I will show you how to do it. In this chapter my purpose is to plant the seed of the idea so it will have time to sprout before we get to the chapter on finding and circulating solo among eligible men.

Happily, *it is in the doing that one builds the strength.* Don't worry if you are scared. So is every mentally competent soldier who enters into battle. The bravery comes when he accepts his condition and still moves forward. Overcoming fear, rather than giving into it, develops bravery much as exercising muscles develops physical strength. Action precedes emotional reward. The price for courtship includes overcoming your fear of the metaphorical dark.

If you have your *attitudes* in shape—you have agreed to be in charge of your life, you have counted your blessings, acknowledged your pain, made a habit of spiritual connection, embraced positive solitude but considered getting a pet, and accepted the inevitability of dark tunnels along your journey—you are ready for *actions*. Attitudes are fundamental, but actions are necessary.

ACTIONS

CLAIMING ADULT STATUS

Try this statement, saying it aloud or to yourself:

"I am responsible for what happens to me."

When a woman can say that, she is either an adult or well on her way toward this goal. Courtship is for adults, and contrary to the myths of fairy tales, not for grown-up little girls who await Prince Charming to rescue them from their own emptiness. You might already be an adult. If not, growing up and claiming responsibility for what happens to you can be one of the most exciting passages of your life.

Money Matters

Imagine having a job that pays well enough so that you can afford regular vacations, plus domestic help and baby-sitters so that you can go out socially whenever you want. If you have these things, it will be much easier to search for courtship. Even if you don't, you can still search if you use some ingenuity. For many women, *adult status begins with economic independence,* gaining control of money.

The American culture pays women substantially less (seventy cents for every dollar a man earns) than it pays men for similar work. In other words, men earn 42 percent more than women for equivalent work. To make matters worse, women usually have the responsibility for child care. But, despite these obstacles, it is important for women to try to achieve economic independence as they travel toward courtship. It is unwise for women to abdicate developing their own ability to earn money in the hopes that someday a man will come along and allow them to stay home and raise children while he takes care of all of their economic needs. Although such a possibility might seem wonderful, it is dangerous to count on it. Hoping for dependency will limit your freedom much as the bars of a jail limit a convict's. Growing up and taking charge of one's own economic situation is hard work, but the rewards are great.

If establishing your professional or career status is one of your goals, you must present yourself as a competent adult in the workplace. Professional growth requires discipline, imposing order upon chaos. You will thrive when you set goals and go for them, but it is important to separate the place of work from the place of romance.

Avoid Romance Where You Work

If your goal is economic independence, professional development, and promotion, your work behavior should not be focused on the erotic dance. Although we hear romantic tales about love blooming at work, these stories can be misleading. They're probably the exception rather than the rule. Women tend to marry up and men down. That means a woman's workplace romance will generally be with a professional superior.[2] Although there are exceptions,[3] the usual practice is for men to court women who allow them to feel powerful, bigger, and more dominant. The erotic dance thrives on this difference of power and softness. The workplace does not. Combining them takes two very different qualities of being—professional and romantic—and inappropriately puts them into the same place, diminishing both.

Worse, job-site romance creates unnecessary risks to your economic situation. It is the woman who usually loses

[2] The reason for the marrying up in women and down in men involves a lot of complex biology that has to do with sexual dominance and power. But the fact remains. Studies of medical students and other groups have consistently shown the tendency for men to choose candidates who are not quite their professional equals.

[3] When a woman does allow a man who is a professional or economic inferior to court her, she runs the risk of other serious problems. A claim of sexual harassment if and when the relationship ends can be a potential land mine.

professionally when workplace romance goes sour. After a relationship has bloomed, flourished, and died, often the former lovers are no longer able to work in the same setting. One must go. Ask around and see for yourself. The less powerful job, usually belonging to the woman, is most expendable. Most often, the *woman* leaves. Rather than risk that kind of vulnerability, consider the work site off-limits for romance. The work site should be where you go to work, invest your energy in developing your capacities and career goals, and earn the living that establishes your adult status. (However, if that attractive manager has some attractive friends, you may want to do a little networking.)

There is one more reason to avoid workplace romances. Once you get yourself going out three times a week and dating heavily (Chapters 4, 5, and 6), you might find it healthier to separate your work and social life. Your social life can be kept more private if it isn't conducted in full view of your co-workers. Once you get going, the searching for courtship plan will have you dating many men. It takes time to pick the one best suited to you. Many of the early explorations are destined to be short-lived. When these end, you will not have to face day-to-day encounters with a former candidate. A nonromantic professional life will let you do your work more effectively. Since you won't be dealing with emotional trauma where you are trying to work, you will gain independence faster.

Have faith, and soon you will find there are many other places to go to find good single men. (Chapter 4 outlines about thirty to get you started.)

Handling the Ardent Pursuit of a Male Superior

If a co-worker keeps pursuing you against your wishes, you may be dealing with sexual harassment. Harassment occurs when a man pursues, makes a pass at or suggestive remarks to a female co-worker who clearly does not want these attentions. Thanks to the public charges brought by Anita Hill, things are changing. Women do not need to keep sexual harassment a secret. This is probably the best time there ever was to let your pursuer know, very clearly and with great dignity, that you are not interested in his pursuit and would appreciate his respecting your wishes and not communicating his interest in you anymore. In this situation, high seriousness, a straight comment, and *no* smiles will help convey your dignity and sincerity.

If, on the other hand, despite the above warnings, you are so tempted by the pursuit of an attractive male superior that you are inclined to risk dating him, there are things you can do to protect your job. But remember: You're dealing with professional dynamite. For the sake of your economic security, you must treat this suitor with the utmost diplomacy. Keep a light tone and use tactful humor wherever possible. You might say something like:

"I find you attractive and would agree to go out with you in a minute if we didn't work together. But you know the problem of mixing business with pleasure. It wouldn't be a level playing field unless we agreed to some serious basics in advance—such as, no familiarity or favoritism at the office. And parking our social life with our cars in the company parking lot in the morning. Could you handle that? It probably is doable, but it wouldn't be a piece of cake.

"And then there's the office grapevine. What happens to my career advancement if management says I'm only getting good reviews because I'm dating you? What do you think?"

The words you use are not as important as taking the action of discussing the emotional and economic risks. If you discuss these before consenting to dating him, you will at least get some idea of his sense of fairness and sensitivity to your situation. Before you decide to go ahead, the two of you should agree on how you should proceed to avoid risk to your job, your advancement—and a possible explosion on the job.

Defusing the Dynamite

Once he has understood what he is asking of you, it should be relatively simple to enlist his help in preventing a problem if you still want to go out with him. Ask him to help figure out a way the two of you can separate your work lives if you are going to start dating.

Perhaps he can get you *promoted* or shifted into another department. Perhaps he can shift himself. Perhaps he can find another solution that removes the two of you from day-to-day contact at work while it elevates your professional stature through a promotion, job transfer, or lateral shift. If he is seriously interested in you, your request for protection should seem reasonable to him. And if it does not, you have important information about his character. He wants what he wants for himself. He doesn't care enough about what the consequences might be for you.

As chapters to come will explain in detail, courtship requires his ardent, sustained pursuit. Men know in the first ten minutes whether a particular woman excites them enough to make that effort. If you do request his help and he is honorable, he'll be glad to protect your situation by securing your downside. If you don't excite him that much, you have gained that valuable information. He's not worth your risk. Why bother when the searching methods of Chapters 4 and 5 will get you out three times a week anyway. Soon you will be meeting lots of good single men who are looking for a woman to court!

If the man pursuing you is your equal, the rules of safety shift slightly but not very much. Consider all sides when deciding whether to accept a man's pursuit. Before accepting such a date, think through the downside and what you would do if the relationship soured. You will be protecting your economic life. If you are the superior, think carefully here, too. Will your actions be viewed as harassment? Consider protecting yourself from the risks by using your power to arrange a transfer—if you really want to get started.

Meanwhile, you will have to come home at the end of the day. Home is where your nest is. In getting ready for courtship, the next action is to build and decorate your nest.

BUILD YOUR NEST

As a single woman, you have an opportunity that bonded couples don't have. You can create a home environment that appeals to your own taste. You are the boss. Make use of this opportunity and create the most beautiful nest your circumstances allow.

An aesthetically pleasing environment does not require an enormous financial outlay. In fact, in these cautious economic times, many interior designers will rearrange the furniture you already own to give your place a "face-lift." The thoughtful rearrangement of furniture, color accents in well-chosen accessories, flowering plants, paintings or prints on the walls, all contribute to a home's beauty.

The nest you create will communicate powerful messages to your dates. Your capacity to create a lovely environment says something about who you are and what you can offer in marriage. Make it wonderful. Design your nest to inspire good feelings in you and someday in your future husband. Flamboyant or subtly understated, it is your song.

Creating a new or enhanced home environment is time-consuming, but it can be great fun. Go to the library and study magazines and books on decorating and architecture. Go to museums and posh furniture stores. Consider it an aesthetically pleasing journey that will enhance your creative abilities and give you a greater appreciation of beauty. Put what you learn to use in your own home. Your refurbished living quarters will proclaim that you are worthy of a lovely environment.

SCHEDULE YOUR TIME— DO NOT SQUANDER IT

If you have already started reserving three two-hour sessions each week for your search for courtship, you probably have already discovered a heightened sense of confidence. Reading these chapters is a good way to begin filling your courtship time. The very act of taking command of your time gives you a sense of power. Now let's look at the other elements of a well-balanced life. These, too, deserve your thoughtful analysis, conclusions, and control.

Take a look at Table 2.3 and try doing its exercise on a separate piece of paper. As you use it regularly to review your progress, you will see how well it can serve to put you in charge of your own life drama.

By taking this exercise, adapting it to your individual needs, and thoughtfully studying your own inventory, you may see areas where change makes sense. When you make a conscious decision about how you will use time, you claim power over your life.

The questions to ask yourself are:

- What do you want to do with your time?
- How do you spend it now?
- What must change?
- What are your new priorities?

The priorities you have chosen define the quality of your life. Whether we take inventory or abdicate power and fail to claim command of our lives, the days of our lives will pass. The average American spends more than fifteen hours a week in front of a television set. By reducing their TV time, most women can release many hours for new priorities. When you spend time thoughtfully, you can achieve your goals sooner.

The reward that comes from successfully balancing your use of time and energy includes a joie de vivre that you will transmit as you go out searching. For many women, taking

TABLE 2.3. TAKE AN INVENTORY OF YOUR TIME

	HOURS PER WEEKDAY	HOURS PER WEEKEND	NOW (%)	IDEALLY (%)	CHANGE PLANNED
Work 1: Job and travel					
Work 2: Family responsibility					
Work 3: Job development, exploring ways to enhance work (new job search, improving skills)					
Relations with family					
Relations with friends					
Relations with men not leading to courtship					
Solitude					
Spiritual fitness					
Physical fitness					
Building attractiveness: nest building, fashion					
Rest/sleep					
Searching for courtship					
Reading and study					
TV					
Other					
Other					
Other					

command of their calendar is as difficult as taking charge of their muscle tone or their nutritional life. Each of these efforts enhances one's life.

Time Constraints

Busy women with small children at home may find three evenings a week hard to schedule for courtship searching. Lunchtime can be used effectively. Meet candidates for courtship at lunch or during a walk in a park. You will find men in most public places where people go to eat lunch. Chapter 4 gets you started on discovering where to go.

When you have completed the inventory of how you are using time (Table 2.3), you may be able to liberate more time on weekends and evenings to go searching for courtship by identifying less important activities that you can eliminate.

Some women conclude that their schedule does not allow enough time to devote to courtship searching. For example, a single mom with a full-time job and a commitment to aerobics asked whether she should realize that this is not the time for her to meet someone and just accept her single status. Only you can determine the relative priority of a man to love in your life. When you have finished taking inventory, you will be able to judge your own value system. Perhaps you can find ways to combine elements. For example, take new courses in aerobics at a coed gym. See Chapters 4 and 5.

Time Excesses

Some women have unlimited time to devote to searching for courtship, particularly those who do not work and are new

to an area. If you have unlimited time to search for courtship, something is missing from your life. Taking the inventory exercise will show you where the gaps are. There can
be an impulse to go searching a great deal more than three
times a week. If this is your situation, I suggest you develop
your schedule so that you have meaningful *work* to do every
day. It does not matter if it is for pay (if you are economically independent), but it does matter that an adult make a
contribution to the culture through work in order to have a
sense of well-being. Your life should be so richly filled with
balanced activities that you no longer have unlimited time
to donate to the search. By making work a part of your life,
you will emit a more substantial image and become more
attractive. To learn where to meet men, see Chapters 4
and 5.

ENDING AN UNPRODUCTIVE RELATIONSHIP

An unproductive relationship can take many forms. It is
unproductive either when the candidate is unsuitable or
when he is not able or willing to court you *now*. If you could
not possibly accept his proposal of marriage, the best thing
you can do for each of you is to bring the relationship to a
graceful close.

Break up with a kind, loving, wonderful man you're not
in love with just as quickly as you recognize your feelings.
The last thing you want to do with a kind, loving man is
lead him down a path that is going to end in his rejection
anyway.

Be gracious when you break up. Say something like:

"You are a kind, loving, wonderful man. The woman who falls in love with you is going to be very fortunate. But for me the chemistry isn't there, though I wish it were."

Later you might introduce him to others who might appreciate him.

Ending an unproductive relationship with a kind man demands your careful consideration to limit his pain of rejection and loss. Since it would be cruel to continue a relationship with someone you know is unsuitable, kindness demands that you tell him if it is not working for you. Sooner is less painful than later.

But what about the man who has been stringing you along? What about when the man you are dating doesn't offer a feeling of security and doesn't show a strong interest in building a future with you? You need to take action to make your life better. Reject the man who is willing to provide only a little bit of what you earlier told him you needed.

In courtship, as in any equitable relationship, people consider each other's feelings as valid realities, worthy of immediate consideration. Once you decide to search for courtship, you need to weed the inequitable relationships out of your life. In a healthy and wholesome relationship, the very knowledge that you have a need should be sufficient for your friend to listen carefully, discuss it with you, and see what he can do to be helpful. The words he says are much less important than the attitude and actions that follow. If your feelings are not valued, the man is not a candidate for courtship. He is someone to reject. Firmly. Immediately. You can't "change him" to be considerate. It takes too long for an adult to develop this quality of character. He will have to suffer many rejections before he can possibly conclude that he needs to alter his personality. Your task is to search for courtship, not "raise" a grown man or "finish" an incomplete one.

Tell him you have decided you will not be able to continue seeing him. Tell him why. And then say good-bye. Head for your new frontier—the suitor you will find as you get ready to take charge of your new direction. Don't look back.

Often men who have not learned to value the feelings of women have difficulty believing a rejection is real. They don't believe it because it hasn't worked that way for them in the past. *Once you have decided that a particular man is not able to court you at this time, your well-being depends on rejecting his further use of your time.*

If he is unwilling to treat your expressed wishes with respect and continues to pursue you, you will need to do two things:

- First tell him that you would like him to stop calling and pursuing.
- Then take action.

Get an answering machine and do not under any circumstances return his call, no matter how effective his coaxing may be.

When you decide to reject a relationship, you have to stop spending time on it. Your time should be devoted positively to the search for courtship.

When you decide to reject a man, be specific, clear, and as gentle as possible. Telling him should take only a short time. Your choice of words is less important than your decision—to shift gears, change your direction, and spend your energies elsewhere. Do not be cruel—just firm and clear.

So often in the workshops I give, women describe the weeks, months, and sometimes even years they remained embroiled in relationships with men who ardently pursued them only when rejected, men who invested time, energy, courtesy, or anything else she said she wanted, only to win her back. Your time is precious. If you are spending your time and emotional energy dealing with a man who is not considerate of you, you are dissipating your energy and diverting yourself from your goal. Your use of time is critically important to your success in searching effectively for courtship, love, and marriage.

If you find yourself addicted to a man, if you discover you are unable to break up with him although you have concluded that he is not a candidate for courtship, you might consider working with a therapist to help you figure out the nature of your addiction. Searching for courtship is not for addicts nor for the incapacitated. But before you spend the time and money on therapy, I suggest you give my plan a try.

Just do it. Don't spend time answering his pleas. Get on with your life. Recognize that your energies are precious. Do not respond to his requests to discuss the relationship, to reconsider, or to just "talk." When you stop permitting an inconsiderate partner to knock you down as though you were a hinged doll and he the beanbag, you *will* feel better, stronger, ready to search for courtship. Imagine harassing a former boss who fired you, asking him to reconsider. You

wouldn't do that, would you? When you reject a relationship, you become the boss. You shift your energies to activities that will provide what you deserve. You recognize that
you don't have any time to squander. Go back to Table 2.3
and take a new inventory to help you get focused on where
you are going to use your time. There is power in taking
command. You will need this power to search for courtship
and win.

BUILD ATTRACTIVENESS AND VIGOROUS HEALTH

Consider this metaphor:

> When a traveler finds herself at a river's edge in the middle
> of flood season and unable to cross the water, there is some-
> thing she should do as she waits. *Build a raft.*

By eliminating unproductive relationships, you will gain
some time to get yourself ready for searching. Use some of
that time to make yourself more attractive. Become vigor-
ously healthy by improving your awareness of good nutrition, taking regular exercise, and doing other activities that
focus on you. You might consider regular aerobic exercise
or another activity to tone the muscles. A healthier diet will
also enhance your figure and make you feel better. Evaluate
your wardrobe and find ways to use clothes to enhance your
appearance. All these activities will make you more attractive as you set out on your search. Table 2.4 will help you
plan your self-improvement program.

TABLE 2.4. BUILDING ATTRACTIVENESS

	CURRENTLY (DESCRIBE)	DESIRABLE CHANGES	GOALS
Posture			
Grooming			
Eating Habits			
Wardrobe			
Spiritual Attitude			
Physical Gestures			
Verbal Expressions			

To help you with eating habits, a questionnaire we regularly use at the Athena Institute can be found in Table 2.5. When you respond to the questions, the kinds of shifts that make sense to consider will become obvious. If you do make them, you will feel better, have more energy and greater well-being.

TABLE 2.5. EVALUATING YOUR NUTRITION

Answer yes or no.

1. *Variety*

   Do you tend to eat the same thing for lunch every day?

2. *Fat*

   Do you eat french fries, fast-food burgers, and potato chips more often than a fresh chicken dinner or broiled fish?

3. *Fiber*

   When you select breads and cereals, are they made with refined white flour instead of rye or whole wheat, and are cereals made with sugar, as opposed to natural cooked cereals like oatmeal?

4. *Sugar*

   Do you eat more than three or four high-sugar desserts or sweets each week?

5. *Salt and Nitrites*

   Do you often eat processed meats like hot dogs, bologna, or smoked meats?

6. *Alcohol*

   Do you have more than one or two alcoholic drinks a day? (One beer, a six-ounce glass of wine, or one shot of whiskey counts as one drink.)

7. *Exchanging Meals for Nonnutritive Consumption*

   Do you often have alcohol with a salty snack rather than a meal?

8. *Weight Control*

   Can you pinch more than an inch at either your waist or your thigh?

9. *Fruit*

   Do you eat at least two servings of fresh fruit (juice doesn't count) each day?

10. *Exercise*

    Do you exercise at least three times a week? Do you feel better or worse when you finish?

11. *Life Stresses*

    Do your days seem to provide so much stress that they feel unmanageable?

12. *Lifestyle and Eating*

    Does your particular work or social lifestyle make it hard to eat well because you eat out, travel, or are single?

13. *Vegetables*

    Do you eat either fresh or steamed frozen green or red vegetables every day? (Canned vegetables do not count.)

14. *Calcium*

    Do you drink at least two large (ten-ounce) glasses of milk or their calcium equivalent each day?

To score this test, add up the number of points as follows: #1—No = 1; #2 —No = 3; #3—Mixed = 1, No = 2; #4—No = 1; #5—No = 2; #6— No = 2; #7—No = 3; #8—No = 2; #9—Yes = 3; #10—Yes = 3; #11 —No = 1; #12—No = 1; #13—Yes = 3; #14—Yes = 3.
The higher your score, the better your nutritional habits. The maximum score is twenty-five.

Having taken hold of your *attitudes* and decided on the *actions* that are relevant to your preparation for courtship: claiming adult status, building your nest, scheduling your time, ending unproductive relationships, building attractiveness and vigorous health, it's time to make your plans. With these exercises completed, you have the information you need to effectively plan for courtship.

PLANS

The five inventories you have taken should help you in your own assessment. If you are like most of us, you will find that there is a great deal you can be doing as you are getting ready to search for a courtship partner. Since you become what you do, you can select goals and achieve them. Specific plans will engage your energy, your focus, and your spirit as you prepare to be available for a true candidate for courtship. Here we have reviewed what you need to do to get yourself ready. In the chapters to come, the focus will shift to the dynamics of the man-woman relationship. Soon you will be on your way to finding men who are worthy candidates for courtship.

As you learn how to set the pace of the journey, you will discover that the journey is joyous. Deciding that you are in charge of your own life can promote a cheerful optimism.

Consider retaking each of these exercises with some regularity. Using the cycle of the moon each month to schedule pause and reflection is one way to chart your growth. Or maybe you prefer some other regular time frame to revisit the five exercises of this chapter. As you do them, you will be changing. The changes you make will be the ones you have selected.

Summing Up

With a focus on your own *attitude,* the *actions* you need to get ready, and the *plans* you need to activate these actions, you should be well on your way to a productive search for courtship. Let's look next at your own "herstory." The goal is to use your past to mold a future that will lead to courtship and marriage.

THREE

Use Your History to Mold Your Future

After spending years at sea, where it eats ravenously to put on weight, the salmon returns to the original stream of its birth. With this goal, the salmon migrates enormous distances, pushing upstream in order to ensure the new life of the next generation. In ways unknowable to it, the salmon replays its history, for the birthplace is the spawning ground of its parents and countless previous generations.

By her thoughtful reflection on history
A woman can build a different future.

The history you bring to your search for courtship—relationships, love affairs, dates, male friends, crushes—is a valuable asset. Far from being something you discard or hide, you can change your course and choose a different path by confronting your past, understanding it, and integrating its lessons. Your new course will put you on the high road to courtship.

A past littered with painful relationships is sad, but it can be turned into an asset. In 400 B.C. a wise Greek named Aeschylus was convinced that wisdom was possible only through suffering. Perhaps he was right. Your history can provide a serviceable route to a good future relationship. Since you can learn from experience, studying your history makes sense. You are what you have done and you become what you do.

Sometimes you are ready at last to search for courtship and to marry *because* of your history. You have had the sizzle. You know about the highs and the lows that come from nonmonogamous and nonpermanent love affairs. You want better for yourself. You know that you deserve more. What you may not know is that history often repeats itself until you gain insight into and change your behavior.

YOUR HISTORY LESSONS

Think back on your past loves and relationships. Before going out to search for courtship, it helps to take the time to evaluate what worked in the past and what didn't. As this chapter unfolds, written exercises help you focus on some key questions:

- Do you feel you have no control over your relationships?
- Are your relationships random fumblings?
- Do your relationships fall into a pattern?
- Do you feel you are unlucky at love?

As you remember your past, the exercises will help you focus on the similarities in your history. Do you seem to be drawn to a certain type of man? Perhaps you have been repeatedly involved with one who won't give you commit-

ment or caring. Is there a pattern to the way you have entered into intimacy? You might discover there is a difference
between what you thought you must have in a man and
what you actually need or want. Even if you have had only
one or two relationships, you have amassed information
about how you relate to a man. If you're currently in a
relationship and curious about your future, remember that
with every passing day you are generating history. History
doesn't have to be antique to be valuable. If you're not in a
relationship now and want to be, read this chapter from a
preventive point of view, to heighten your awareness of
common pitfalls.

Most of us tend to keep repeating the same history. But
we don't *have* to accept our previous classification as "bookworm," "party girl," "wallflower," or "cheerleader." The exercises in this chapter will raise your consciousness and get
you ready to change your future. Use them to decide on
specific changes to get you to courtship.

Another way to help pinpoint your pattern is to review
your relationships in terms of the eleven principles of the
Code of Courtship. The fewer principles honored, the more
chance for the relationship to derail. Do you see a repeating
pattern? Do some principles seem natural, others harder to
achieve? Now you know where to focus your efforts. Can
you use your past to design a better future? Absolutely! You
can do it.

How to Read Your History

The stories of three women who attended a workshop, explored their histories, and built a better future may get you
started.

Leslie, at twenty-five, told me she had a bad history. She went through a pretty wild period. At the time she thought it was a "liberated" thing to be sexual with a lot of men. Now she felt terribly embarrassed. She would see these men and feel shame. She asked what she could do about these feelings. And how to avoid having her history known. So many people knew about her that she kept fearing that someone would tell any new man she might date.

I suggested she recognize that she had no more reason to be ashamed of her former behavior than each of these men had. Her rules about sex are new and clear. Now she is searching for courtship. She has changed her goals and her standards. Sex is reserved for her courtship partner, and until she finds him and tests his intentions, her choice is celibacy. Those old wild oats are ancient history. The focus has shifted. She agreed to try the activities described in the Code, and shortly afterward she met a new man. Within six months she had accepted his proposal of marriage.

Stacy's story also illustrates how combining a look at history with the Code of Courtship can be used to guide a woman to marriage.

At forty-three, Stacy had been a single mother for the last fifteen years. She had many relationships, some of which had started off wonderfully. But somehow each of them had ended without the commitment she so dearly wanted. Once she came to the Searching for Courtship workshop, she studied the Code. As she studied it, she expressed a growing awareness of her own role in the history she had been experiencing.

Stacy told me that the first principle showed clearly what she had failed to do in the relationship she had just ended.

Four years earlier, when she was an investment broker at one of the major brokerage houses, Stacy had met George, a physician. He pursued her with a fury, and she set aside her usual pattern of reasoned thinking in the heady rush of the early romance. She went to bed with him before she knew if marriage was something he was seeking. Four years later, after many weekends together, she realized he would never propose. After attending a workshop, she recognized the truth of principle eleven, that there were many good men searching, and she mustered the courage to break off the relationship with George. She started to go out to search for men on a regular basis, and the last time I spoke with her, discussions of marriage were looming with her new man, Evan.

With the first principle in mind, she had gone out to play knowing she would use sexual attraction as a starting point for courtship instead of for passionate impulse. When she began her love life with Evan, she took it slowly. She first confirmed that Evan wanted a permanent bond. More important, Evan discovered that she was a woman who required courtship, and he gave it to her.

Frieda also had a problem that she solved.

Frieda was thirty-eight when she attended a workshop and explored her history with men. As she did, she recognized that her problem centered on principles four and five. When men began to show interest in her, she would typically respond with pretty much whatever they wanted. Her usual experience was to receive a phone call on a Friday afternoon from a new or not so new man who would ask her what she was doing this weekend. And usually the truth was she had no plans. Then when the man would suggest that they get together, although she felt uneasy about it, she would agree to see him at the last minute. She didn't like this, but didn't know how to change it. Through the exercises that follow, she learned how to communicate what she wanted. More important, she strengthened her capacity for self-control and her dignity by taking command of her calendar. Her life changed dramatically.

Looking at your past has probably revealed some evolution in your relationships, but the lesson doesn't stop here. You will learn how to use your history to mold your future, you will figure out where the men are, and know what to do when you find them. It is time to break out of your past patterns. If you have been thinking of yourself as a hapless victim of fate, stop. You are in charge now. You are calling the shots, making the choices, directing the course of your love life. You are responsible—in the most positive sense of the word—for your own actions.

In this chapter you'll benefit from the experience of your own history as well as from more of the experiences of real women, participants in Searching for Courtship workshops. As they have described their difficulties in the workshops, we have developed positive solutions to them. The questions they raised and answers we found together can help focus your own solutions.

Most of the stumbling blocks women experience come down to the type of relationship they had with a man. If you don't have relationships right now or if you don't even know where to find dates, that's okay. In the next chapter we will focus on where to find the men. Meanwhile, the stories can target your awareness. Once you find the men, you will know how to avoid the most common mistakes that others have made.

In order to mine the past for valuable insights, it helps to break down intimate relationships into three basic periods: getting started, the middle ground, and the conclusion. The rest of this chapter is divided into these three stages, describing the most common obstacles of each.

STARTING BLOCKS

When it comes to getting started in a relationship, the main pitfalls are false starts—getting intimate too early, for example—or false starters, men who are unsuitable courtship candidates. The Love History chart (Table 3.1) focuses on the early stages of a relationship. You might find it useful to make several photocopies of this exercise and spend some time thoughtfully filling out your first one now. If you're just starting a relationship, the exercise can help you crystallize your thoughts about where you have been and what you may choose to do with this new man.

MAPPING OUT YOUR LOVE HISTORY

In Table 3.1, list the five men you most recently have had some type of intimate relationship with, regardless of how it turned out.

For *Initiator,* indicate who first suggested getting together (you or him).

For *Attractive force,* jot down the attractive feature that drew *him* toward you. Then, to the right of the divider, list what attracted *you* to him. Was it physical attraction? Status? Attitude? Money? Power? Tenderness?

For *Clarity of perception,* estimate how clearly you perceived his attraction for you. Use a scale of 1 to 10 for how much he wanted to get to know you better. (For example, if he showered you with poems and flowers or said you were the woman he had been searching for all his life, the score is a 10. If he called you "Girl" or by the wrong name, give it a 1).

For *Timing—Intimacy, duration,* tally how many dates passed before (and if) physical intimacy occurred. Then note the duration of the entire relationship.

For *Principles honored,* jot down the code number of the courtship principles you employed in that relationship. Refer to page 10 for the code numbers.

Once you're done filling out or thinking about the chart, spend some time analyzing the information. As you look over your completed chart, don't be surprised if the primary attractive feature seems to be physical or sexual. The mag-

TABLE 3.1. YOUR LOVE HISTORY

NAME	INITIATOR	ATTRACTIVE FORCE		CLARITY OF PERCEPTION	TIMING— INTIMACY, DURATION	PRINCIPLES HONORED (BY NUMBER)
		HIS	HER			
Peter	He	"you're beautiful"	mystery, foreigner	8	3 dates 1 year	2, 4, 9
Bart	Me	sensitive	humor	10	6 dates 8 months	2, 4

netic power of intimate relationships *is* sexual. Attraction is what draws a man to a woman, and usually he recognizes that the attraction is sexual. A man is drawn to a woman because he sees her as a potential candidate for physical intimacy. This is perfectly normal. The biology of the healthy male is designed for sexual connection. Translated into human behavior and feelings: He desires to connect himself physically to a particular woman. He is drawn to approach her.

Since men and women are different, the attraction that initially draws them to each other is likely to be different. While he may be thinking:

"Wow! I'd really like to get physical with this woman!"

she may be thinking:

"I'd really like to get to know this man, see what he is like, see whether he is 'the one' for me."

He may be thinking sex or trophy. She may be thinking trust, protection, or friendship.

It doesn't really matter whether the attracting force is the same or not. What matters is how you handle yourself when you want to be courted. When a man is eager to be with you, you have a special opportunity. You have the power to decide how to channel his attraction. You can use it to build the best possible future, or you can let it use you.

Many women at the workshops mentioned that after sleeping with a man they seemed to know him better. But having sex with a man to find out what kind of person he is doesn't work for courtship. Although the very act of intercourse requires stripping away the armor of clothing and public façades, a man may not reveal anything to you. Why? Anyone can lie with their passion—almost as easily as with other instruments of communication. First, judge his character. Find out if you respect him and trust him enough to bestow upon him the rich gift of your sexual intimacy.

The way Louella, a twenty-five-year-old never-married nurse, used her history is instructive.

Louella studied the Code and decided that she needed to work on developing her capacity for honesty and her ability to detect deception. When she reviewed her history, she discovered a pattern, one in which she would get started with men only to discover that she had been deceived. She decided to focus on this need for honesty and to be very sure to only and always speak the truth.

It was a major effort to change her habit, but the reward was a new kind of freedom in her dating relations. She felt more relaxed when she didn't have to remember what she had said. Her energy increased. She felt great and had a good time as a single woman out in the world.

She stopped telling white lies to please others and worked on speaking tactfully but truthfully. She told the truth, only the truth, but withheld facts that she did not want to share. When men would ask her personal questions that she did not want to answer, she told them so. But she didn't lie. Slowly, and then more quickly, her confidence began to increase. As her confidence grew, she found out that more men expressed interest in her.

The last time I spoke with Louella, she was dating two men and having a good time with each of them. She was not ready for intimacy with either and had told one of them so when he had suggested sex.

THUNDERBOLTS—DON'T GET BURNED!

Thunderbolts—those electric jolts of erotic energy, those out-of-the-blue attractions—are a tough challenge if you have decided you're ready for courtship. Thunderbolts require you to use your head at the very moment that your blood is rushing down from the head into the lower regions of the pelvis. Without a doubt, the physiological responses are delicious, seemingly irresistible. Nature designs us to want to reproduce, to continue the species, to survive. The sense of power and attractiveness these instincts create can mislead you. They can feel so good that they may tempt you away from your natural common sense. Study your history to remind yourself where instant attractions led when you followed them too readily. They probably did not lead you or your friends into courtship and marriage. Within a few weeks of the initial strike, somebody is usually left wanting and in a state of imbalance. When your partner is there, the highs are tremendous. When your partner is absent, the lows can be devastating. That's not to say you should avoid thunderbolts, but be smart and recognize them for what they are.

Thunderbolts provide you with an opportunity to establish respectful treatment, but you'll have to retain command of yourself. Instant attraction, "chemistry," is definitely not necessary for a good marriage. Romances that build slowly can build as beautifully or better than those that start off with a big bang. Wanting "love at first sight" reflects grandiose wishes more than it reflects the reality of long-term relationships. The exquisite complexity of an intelligent being can take a lifetime to truly know. Why demand it in the first moment? Channel the force of attraction as you take charge of your life.

The highest and best use of his powerful physical attraction is your delicate exercise of restraint. When you are doing it right, you will know it. This keeps the man coming toward you. The longer he does, the more time you have to evaluate whether he is a candidate worthy of your intimate energies.

Spotting negatives before you take a risk. Go slowly and hold off on sexual intimacy until you have had a chance to explore his character, attitudes, and values. Observe how he treats his family and friends. Look at how respectfully he responds to the wishes you express, to wait for intimacy until you have time to know him. Notice his drinking patterns. Take a look at whether he is willing to invite you to his family and work outings. Evaluate his attitude about telling the truth. See if his work life is well organized. If your answers are negative, or unknown, he is probably not a good candidate for courtship at this time.

Now ask yourself the same questions. How would you be judged? If your answers are negative, you probably have some growing to do before you will be ready for an enhanced courtship. Remember, elegant courtship is a mutual activity between consenting, considerate *adults*.

When you use your history to mold your future and have an understanding of sexual basics, you will know that *the smartest thing you can do with a powerful attraction is to restrain it as you explore the man's character, his ethics, his goals, and his values.* You won't be able to evaluate these qualities if you are spending your time together in passionate embrace. If you do go with the flow of passionate feelings first and later discover that his character is inadequate, the energy you diverted to passion will have been wasted. And if you have spent intimate time together, you may be left burned out, depleted, and exhausted. Alone.

It is important to exercise self-discipline in order to restrain the impulse for instant sexual fulfillment. If he won't give you the time to form your judgment—no matter how great his appeal—he is not currently desirable for courtship. He may be a short-term gratification to your ego, but long-term, he's not. Save yourself a larger grief. Take advantage of your knowledge of history and use sexual attraction to hold his interest as you check him out. Hold off on its fulfillment until he has met most of your candidacy criteria. Restrain yourself and you will be able to win time, energy, self-mastery, and an enduring love.

If you are already seeing someone with whom you became intimate too soon and now he seems less interested, you can assume that the relationship was doomed from the start. The best thing you can do is cut your losses and pull back. Consider the first fundamental rule of courtship—use sexual attraction to negotiate for courtship. If you were already sexual before you knew if courtship was a possibility, the message you have communicated is pretty well imprinted on the man. He will consider you a sexually available woman who doesn't require courtship. As the analysis of your past has probably revealed, things don't just happen. You have to *make* them happen. When women become intimate *after* courtship was agreed upon, they go a long way to avoid feeling diminished later. The fallacy of "love at first sight" is its suggestion that quick and easy intimacy leads to elegant relationships. It's usually just the opposite.

Kate's story has a slightly different twist. She found that Bill's courtship patterns changed when sex began. She had been slow to agree to sexual intimacy, but even so, once it began, he seemed to treat her differently, less like a treasure. A good way to assess courtship potentials is this: If it gets better as you move into deeper levels of intimacy, you are probably doing something right. But if it gets worse, you will need to ask, Why? What happened? Or the harder question—was he really "available"?

Eventually, most single women discover the truth—that not every man is available, not every man is honest, and not all honest men are that way all the time. Reality is dappled. Only some of the men who appear to offer commitment can actually provide it. Kate decided to break off the relationship because it was degenerating. Within three months she had begun to date several new men and was feeling cheerful because her goal of marriage was clearly in focus and she had learned how to command respect.

Viola described her history with Alfred, a Casanova:

Whenever he was with her, he paid close attention to her. He learned how to touch her. He looked closely at her when he was making love with her. He studied her in order to learn what she liked. And then he gave it to her. They would spend hours engaged in lovemaking (compared with the national average of seven to fourteen minutes). She loved his attentions but hated his frequent disappearances.

The relationship would go along steadily for six or eight or ten weeks, then he would abruptly disappear from her life without warning. Two or three weeks later he would call and ask if he could see her that night. He would apologize for abandoning her and tell her he was confused and had been lonely. He told her he was undergoing psychoanalysis. He described what a horrible childhood he had had. He would ask her to be patient and express his hope of being cured of his fear of commitment. So gentle were his apologies and so sensuous his lovemaking that her heart would melt and she would resume the quasi-relationship.

She realized that her love for him was taking her on an emotional roller coaster—high one week, miserable another, and she didn't know how to resolve the situation. Eventually, she entered therapy in order to break away from him. She did get over him as she built a healthy single Code of Courtship. Today she is happily married to a different man, one who is giving and cheerful.

PROTECT YOURSELF
FROM BEING A TROPHY NOTCH

Single women can protect themselves from potential heartbreak at the hands of a Casanova by understanding that it takes time to learn the subtleties of another person's character and by giving themselves all the time they need. Given time, a man reveals himself. By restraining herself until she can examine his character, a woman minimizes her risk of injury. If he won't wait till she's ready, he isn't available to court her. And one more thing: Although the extensive love-making characteristic of the unavailable man is biologically sound in a vacuum, most of the other, very valuable, elements of intimacy are usually missing. The sum total of what he offers will leave his partners feeling bad. Courtship feels good.

THE MAN WHO CHEATS

Men who are not available are taboo for the woman in search of courtship. It's a hard line, but one worth following. Whether he is committed to staying single or publicly committed to another woman, becoming intimate with such a man will erode your sense of well-being. Dallying with people who are willing to toy with you is self-destructive. If he is married, it means that you, too, are playing a pivotal role in an unhealthy triangle. This is not a part of searching for courtship. Dallying will eat at your dignity, diminish your joy, and deplete your honest approach to life. Playing any part in an adulterous triangle is self-destructive.

Men who cheat keep you from finding men who don't. Spending your time with such men will squander your resources. Consider Penelope's story.

Penelope is involved with a married man who has told her his is a loveless marriage. Prominent in his community, he won't leave his wife. She knows that nothing will ever come of this dalliance, but sees little harm in it. Penelope is on a self-destructive, delusional path. The energy and unmet needs that would otherwise drive her out to find a suitable candidate are being diverted. She is heading into a dead end. She is left alone on Saturday nights, Christmas Eve, and when the toilet backs up. She's doomed to loneliness and the further disintegration of her self-esteem if she continues this way. Logically, she agrees but claims she is basically content. Except on Saturday night and Christmas.

I directed her to a good psychotherapist, a woman who will understand and work with her and help her discover what her problem really is. The longer she stays in this relationship, the greater her problem will become and the more help she is going to need to build a healthy life. Penelope sent me a note about a year later to say she was moving to Tampa, where she had a new job. She was excited about building a new life as she broke up with her "friend."

To search for courtship a woman needs to avoid being part of an intimate triangle. If an already involved man says he wants to get started with you, tell him to come back again when he can offer you a clean start, out in public. If he can't make that offer, he is proposing a trap.

LOVE TRIANGLES

When a man or a woman has a spouse *and* a lover, a dangerous but neatly balanced triangle has usually formed. The spouse and the lover together serve to complete the love life of publicly bonded, nonmonogamous persons. Intact intimate triangles are highly stable, but when they do come apart, the entire structure dissolves. When the marriage breaks up, usually the love affair does too, according to a marital therapist who did an extensive study on the subject.[1] Everybody loses.

If such behavior is in your history, as it is in many single women's, you can make good use of past pain. Think about it. Look at where it led you. And resolve never to participate again. Meanwhile, use your time to search for courtship.

Another kind of triangle, which at first glance seems different from the adulterous triangle, sets up a similar trap for all three players. It involves intimate connections between two men and one woman or two women and one man. One of my staff experienced this type. It was a more subtle triangle, and it caused her discomfort until she examined it and eliminated it from her search for courtship.

> Ellen was twenty-four years old. As she described it, she had been best friends with Jim until recently. During the course of the friendship, Ellen found herself the pivotal point of a triangle. Her girlfriend Sue and Jim were in a romantic relationship. Both confided in her about it. Sue was intimate with Frank, while pretending to be monogamous with Jim. Sue had lied to both Ellen and Jim about what she was doing with Frank. When the truth came out, both Ellen and Jim were so angry about being lied to that they each rejected Sue.
>
> With Sue gone, Ellen and Jim grew closer and their friendship soon led to a romance. But problems developed within two months. Once their relationship changed from friendship to romance, Jim changed his behavior. He would be intensely interested in Ellen for a short period of time, ranging from one to several weeks. Then suddenly he would

[1] Frank Pittman, *Private Lies* (New York: W. W. Norton, 1989).

withdraw for seven, ten, or fourteen days and Ellen would hear nothing from him. She asked for help in figuring out how to conduct herself to get better treatment from Jim.

If Jim had been intimate with Sue while considering Ellen his best friend, then Sue, Ellen, and Jim had been engaged in a triangle even before Sue's infidelity was discovered. Jim's intimate connections were split between the two women: sex with one, emotions with the other. Subsequently Ellen "filled in" for the missing sexual relationship while Jim was getting over Sue. He never courted Ellen and was not likely to start once sex had already begun. Ellen did not use the ripening sexual attraction to negotiate on her own behalf. Jim had already established in his own mind "what kind of woman" Ellen was. Easy, friendly, available, but not a candidate for him to court.

I suggested that Ellen immediately call a halt to this relationship. By ending it herself, she could salvage her self-esteem and rebuild her dignity.

Of course, when Ellen rejected Jim, he suddenly found her much more interesting and valuable to him. He followed the typical script, appearing to court her now that he recognized he had most likely lost her. But if she were to resume seeing him, he would probably renew his old behavioral cycle of approach and avoid (avoiding each time he starts to feel too close to the possibility of commitment). Unfortunately, it was probably too late to change Jim's behavior to serve Ellen's best interest. He was not likely to believe she had suddenly become a person worthy of courtship even though she had now decided she was.

It would be much more productive for Ellen to use this experience as part of her history. She can learn from her experience of how men behave with women they do not value. She can resolve to start off on her new relationship as a woman of value, following the Code, backing away whenever she is not being treated in a worthy manner.

About four months later Ellen called to tell me how much her romantic life had improved. She had embraced the Code and discovered the power it gave her. Formerly unable to find good men, she now found herself pursued for dates, and life had become fun. She was excited at the respect she now commanded and loved the way she felt about men.

THE MAN WHO CAN'T OR WON'T COMMIT

The chronic bachelor can be just as damaging to a fledgling courtship if he has a problem with commitment to a woman. His is another kind of approach-and-avoid pattern. He consumes your energy but won't permit roots to develop.

When a man is obviously attracted to you but says he is unable to make a commitment to you now, believe him and recognize what this means he wants. He would like to be intimate with you, but he doesn't want you to think he owes you anything. He is not able to offer you courtship. Don't waste your time! This man will not provide you the kind of wholesome, wondrous, beautiful courtship you can have. If you spend time with him, you will be diverted from your goal of marriage and family. You will be moving in the opposite direction from where you want to go.

These are the more obvious ways a woman can squander her time. Now let's look at the more subtle issues.

WHEN DATING A MAN WHO IS DATING OTHERS MAKES SENSE

If your idea of dating involves going out together, spending time together, and getting to know each other without sexual intimacy, you can accept a date with a single man who dates others as well. And plan to have fun with him! But *only as long as he is able to take you out publicly.* Single people have the legitimate right to date more than one person at a time. Those who are searching for a love partner must make maximum use of their time and energy. It is appropriate to be getting to know several people simultaneously. However, don't consent to physical intimacy without a clear agreement for exclusivity.

When you are searching for courtship, intimacy should be postponed until you have both agreed to a mutually considerate honoring of its meaning. Be direct. When he asks for sexual intimacy, tell him you like him and would love to get to know him better. Then let him know that if he is ready to explore intimacy, you will need an exclusive relationship. Tell him that if he isn't ready for that, you are willing to delay intimacy and keep dating him anyway. Make it clear that if he wants to be intimate with you while he dates other women, you are headed in different directions.

If he agrees to be exclusive, go a step further and ask for his promise to stay exclusive until one of you gives the other notice to discontinue this agreement. In other words, make sure the two of you agree so that it is not necessary to keep checking. You will have made a commitment, and if his character is good, you can be sure of a monogamous relationship for the duration of the relationship.

100

The time to tell him your rules comes when he starts reaching for physical connection. When he wants to kiss deeply or have intercourse.

When Physical Intimacy Should Occur in a New Relationship

Couples vary enormously in the speed with which they begin to get physical with each other. From the first handshake to the first kiss to the first sexual intercourse, a dating couple is on the road to ever-increasing physical intimacy. The age of the man, the level of his libido, and his value system profoundly influence his need for physical connection. For a young man in his twenties or early thirties, it probably occurs around the third, fourth, or fifth date. By the fifth or sixth date, if he does not find you sufficiently sexually attractive to give up dating other women, he is not likely to become more attracted to you as you continue to date.

Usually a powerful sexual attraction hits men pretty hard and very fast. Probably within the first five minutes. The greater the power of his attraction to you, the more power you will have to achieve what you want. There are exceptions. Biological age plays a significant role. The libido of men declines with age; older men tend to be less driven by their biological urges and to be more sophisticated in their pursuit. Biologically older men may date longer and with greater patience before expressing their need for sexual connection.

For women, attraction and sexual interest also seem to

vary with age. In a very young woman (early to mid-twenties), sexual desire often comes more slowly than in a man. Since each woman has her own biological time clock ticking at its own pace, no hard-and-fast rules can define every woman's pattern. The man's role is to project his interest in intimacy and ask you for a physical relationship. Your role is to manage his approach.

If he is unable to agree to exclusivity and you like him very much, you still might have something to gain if you continue to see him without sexual intimacy. For your own emotional balance, though, consider setting limits on your dates with him and search for courtship with other men as well. Do *not* have sex with him without exclusivity, no matter how much you like him. Going to bed with your date is *not* the same thing as playing tennis with him. And going to bed before you have forged an exclusive relationship that is part of courtship will delay you from your search. Chapters 7 and 8 provide more detail.

A balanced life is crucial to assure your emotional stability as you wait for the slow bloomer to make his moves or restrain a fast mover. If you keep your options open, your active search for courtship will take you in new directions, and these will remind you of the rich diversity you can enjoy when you take action to build a full social life.

Taking control of your life, yet allowing a stronger force —a powerful man—into it can lead to high art in courtship, especially when his strength enhances and protects rather than overpowers yours. A stronger male can enhance a woman's erotic experience, but that also depends on what kind of sexual experience you want. Your history can teach you this lesson. Do you want a man whose sexual drive is greater than yours, so he continually expresses his need for you? Do you want a man with a low libido whose major interest is companionship? Until you have had both experiences, you may not know. If you are not experienced, you may not be sufficiently knowledgeable to be ready for courtship. You may need to have relationships with a number of men until you find out what's best for you. Fortunately, there are many levels of intimacy and it is not necessary to expose yourself to more than you feel comfortable with in order to develop this self-knowledge.

THE MAN WHO WANTS TO BE FRIENDS

You should not establish friendships with men who are not able to court you. They divert you from your higher goal. Platonic relationships consume your time. If you have time to spare after scheduling your three search events per week, you would probably do better to build friendships with other women—unless your male friend fixes you up with courtship candidates.

When you cultivate friendships with women, you are building roots that can span years, possibly your lifetime. When you put that energy into developing a friendship with a heterosexual man but are not heading for courtship and marriage, you are building something that is destined to end. Such a relationship won't provide you with the rewards and the nourishment that your pool of women friends will be able to offer. Once your good friend John asks Jane to marry him, he won't have much time for you. She will consume most of his energy, and she will not want him to be with you when he is proposing marriage to her. Likewise, when you meet the man who will become your love and husband, he won't want you continuing a heavily invested friendship with John. On the other hand, your friendships with women should not threaten an emotionally healthy fiancé or husband. It is probably a better use of your limited energy to invest friendship time with other women. Deeply rooted, long-term friendships are jewels worth collecting and polishing. Still, light friendships with men that take only limited energy and time can be nice for networking and professional relationships. Consider balancing both, but limit your investment in male friends.

RELATIONSHIPS THAT DON'T START

What about a long-term, loosely conducted "friendship" that never moves forward? At twenty-three, Louanne had just graduated from Bryn Mawr College and was employed in her first job. She had met a law student from the University of Pennsylvania while they were both college students, and he had gotten into the habit of calling her for long, pleasant phone conversations. Once she attended our workshop, she was no longer interested in spending time nurturing a friendship that was going nowhere. She had thought he was a candidate for courtship, but he never asked her out.

With some forethought, she changed her behavior. The next time he called, they talked for their usual twenty or thirty minutes. In closing the conversation he said (as he had frequently in the past):

"We will have to get together for lunch sometime."

Previously she would have said, "Sure," thereby assuring him that whenever it was convenient for him, she was available. This time, though, her answer was, "Maybe."

They went on to talk further and ended the conversation. Within minutes he called back.

"Is something wrong? Are you upset with me? Did I do something wrong?"
"No. Why do you ask?"
"Because you said, 'Maybe.' What is this 'maybe'?"

She answered that since in the past they intended to get together and it never happened, "maybe" was the more realistic answer to the possibility that they might get together.

He then said:

"Let's make a date. How about . . ."

Right then he named specific times and dates and they agreed on a date.

By not agreeing to his loose suggestion that sometime in the future they might get together for lunch, Louanne triggered his action. Other ways might be even more effective. You might say:

"Great. How about Wednesday at noon."

If he doesn't say yes or suggest an alternate time, it probably makes sense to cut such long conversations short. When a woman gets ready for courtship, she has a great many things to do with her time, all leading to the courtship process. She no longer has time to waste.

THE ART OF APOLOGY

Patricia recounted her distressing story at a recent workshop. She had met a man who interested her, and it seemed to be mutual. They were at a museum opening and he said,

"I would like to go out with you. But there would be no strings attached."

She responded,

"Sure, that's what I want too."

They went out together and had a lovely evening. He wined and dined her, and as the evening unfolded, she found herself enjoying him much more than she had anticipated. A few days later, to her surprise, given his declaration of "no strings," he called her. He said he had enjoyed their time together and asked if she wanted to go out again.

She responded,

"Sure, I'd love to."

He said,

"Great. How about Saturday."

She told him she couldn't since she was going out of town and he said,

"How about the weekend after?"

Here was a twenty-seven-year-old woman being invited out on a formal date twelve days in advance—an almost un-heard-of event in today's single world of casual connections. She said,

"I thought you said no strings. How come you're asking me out so far in advance?"

He sheepishly said,

"Yes, you're right."

The conversation ended without a date agreed upon. Later she felt despair as she wondered why she had behaved as she had. She knew she really liked him and asked for help. We discussed it in the workshop and reviewed the major mistake she had made.

She had not communicated what she wanted. She had not displayed good manners nor made him feel special, manly, and important. While she hadn't rejected his invitation, she had made him feel self-conscious and foolish for having asked in advance. This is precisely what a woman searching for courtship should avoid doing. In searching for courtship, your objective is to make the man feel good, important, valuable. He should be enhanced by your presence, feel his dignity being appreciated and nourished. And you should expect the same in return. Good manners are the hallmark of a courtly relationship. Give them. And expect them.

My advice to Patricia was to apologize. Since she had already blown the start, she had nothing to lose by calling him up with a sincere apology. Maybe she could recover her error. I suggested she call him and say something like:

> "Frank, hi, this is Patricia. I wanted to thank you for calling me and asking me in advance. You got me right in the middle of [fill in whatever it was she was doing] and I really was rude to you. I hope you'll forgive me. I am not usually like that. I would love to see you if you still want to. Could we start over? I have my calendar out. Could we make a date as you suggested?"

Then she should quietly wait for his reaction—and follow it —conducting herself in a courteous way. If she has already blown it, she will know that in a few minutes, but her action in apologizing may restore the delicate balance. It is worth a try. Besides, it is good to learn how to say "I'm sorry." Apologizing is one of the hallmarks of a courteous person, who makes mistakes and tries to make amends. The exercise of good manners takes many forms. Communicating clearly is one of them.

THE MIDDLE OF THE RELATIONSHIP ROAD

WHEN A RELATIONSHIP STALLS

Let's look next at a relationship that has started and reached a point of sexual intimacy but doesn't seem to be going anywhere. This is a common problem for single women.

Once again, the history lessons you study now can help you to build a good future very soon.

There are many variations on the stalled-relationship theme. What determines whether a relationship will progress or get stuck? From what I can discern, all stalled relationships fail to honor some of the eleven courtship principles (see page 10). Listen to some of the stories women told at the workshops.

Being Taken for Granted

Norma described her situation with Phil, who started out courting but was now treating her differently. She felt taken for granted and wanted to know what she could do to be treated with more respect. I told her she would probably have to withdraw, put herself at some emotional distance from him, and get on with her life. Whether she takes herself away from him physically or just by attitude, as she withdraws from him he will feel the loss. The question she needed to have answered was what he would do when he felt her withdrawal.

Most of the time when people are engaged in a relationship and one of them starts to pull away, it shakes up the balance between them and both feel unsettled. If when you withdraw, you do it in a cheerful, self-possessed way, you will be practicing an art of communication that is courteous and subtle. Self-possession increases your capacity to attract and lure. If from this position of being at your most attractive you still cannot engender courtly behavior from the man, you've got your answer. Move on to other prospects.

Norma decided to try withdrawing. She got busy by enrolling in an art course for people who knew how to draw and wanted to learn how to paint. As the course progressed, she got so excited about the class, the new friends she started to make, and the experience of regular practice in painting that she didn't have very much time to pine for Phil. He became a little less important. She wasn't faking it. She wasn't cheating on him. But her new activity changed something subtle in the balance between them. She was enjoying her painting and consequently less available to him. He became more courteous to her. Norma won in two ways—a new hobby and an improved relationship.

When It's Purely Sexual

Catherine, thirty-six, is a successful business executive serving as head of a local, thriving marketing company. For the past year and a half she has been involved with Bill, age forty-three. Professionally Bill enjoys a high profile as a successful executive, and he has a ten-year-old daughter to whom he is devoted. Catherine sees Bill about three times a week. Alone. He rarely includes her in social events and does not invite her to spend time with him and his daughter. She feels distressed but doesn't quite understand what's wrong.

This, I conclude, is a sexual relationship for him. Convenient, necessary, but not particularly good for Catherine, who after a year and a half wants more. The relationship is stuck. He gets what he wants and needs from it—on his terms. She is left confused, off-balance, wanting. She acknowledges that, unlike at the beginning, he is definitely not courting her now. And she wants to be courted. She wants to know if it is too late to turn this affair into a courtship.

It probably is. Bill has learned to see her as a convenient, attractive sexual object but not a candidate for his courtship search. When Catherine completes the exercises and understands what she wants in a candidate for courtship, she is likely to conclude that Bill is unworthy. As she evaluates whether she is now ready for courtship, she will inevitably discover that this relationship is not good for her health. It is demeaning. It erodes her dignity. It takes her energy and diverts it from a path that promotes a wholesome search for courtship. She needs to be part of a family—not hidden as though she were cheating in an adulterous relationship. Bill is withholding his social and family life from her. The sooner she ends this relationship, the healthier she will be. From what she told me, it seems she has not communicated what she wants and needs. Nor has she yet accepted the legitimacy of her own needs.

There is a very slim chance that if Catherine communicates what she wants, Bill will comply. But probably from Bill's point of view, she has already conducted herself as undeserving of good treatment. It is extremely difficult for a man to change his fundamental assumptions about a woman he has been physically intimate with over a long time. I suggest that she use this painful reality as part of her own developmental progress. She should take the effort to figure out all of the qualities she wants in a man and the way she wants to be treated. Then in a very clear, short letter she'll need to communicate this to Bill as she says good-bye. By writing it out, rather than talking about it, she will clarify her own reality and give him a chance to reflect on what she means to him before he responds. Her letter will leave him the option of rising to her challenge. He probably won't.

Meanwhile, Catherine needs to reevaluate what she means when she thinks of Bill's behavior as having begun with a high degree of courtship. According to my definition, Bill was never courting Catherine. He was pursuing her for a sexual relationship. He did not have the attitude that sex and intimacy were necessarily related to commitment and marriage. If he had, he would have included her in outings with his daughter.

Regardless of his intentions, her decisiveness will enhance her dignity and self-esteem. She will be ready to initiate her search for courtship.

When You Practice Marriage Without a License

When you are ready for courtship, you will gain if you set a personal standard to not live together. A man won't treat you any better living together than while courting, but courting time allows for a negotiation for an equitable marriage. In general, living together doesn't set the stage for the optimal treatment of women. Living together doesn't even give you a better vantage point from which to assess your candidate for courtship.

The supporting data have been coming in. Relationships that begin with living together generally do not mature into substantive, enduring marriages. The marriages that result from living together show the highest divorce rates. The reasons why are not known, but some reflection may help to explain the results. The way in which a relationship develops has a significant impact on the direction in which it moves. Consider the women and men you have known who created enduring, stable, and loving marriages. Ask them for reflections on whether living together is likely to hamper courtship and marriage.

Meanwhile, recognize that it is much more difficult to negotiate for courtship and respectful treatment when you already provide a man with the benefits of marriage without its responsibilities. Why should he buy the cow when he's getting the milk for free? From his point of view, there is nothing more to be gained from the relationship. He has it all already. Sexual intimacy is a treasure that should be cherished. Once you are living together, it becomes a losing battle to negotiate for fundamental rights. *Before* you live together, negotiation is the easiest it will ever be *if* a man and a woman are really drawn to each other.

If you want marriage, then marriage should be your threshold. Your man must cross it in order to live with you. Or at the very least, you should be formally engaged with the date set.

THE RELATIONSHIP LIFE RAFT: CLINGING FOR DEAR LIFE ·

Some relationships seem to drag on forever, never getting better. The couples cling to each other, afraid of getting on with their lives. But they are not satisfying each other's basic needs. They are not engaged in true intimacy. Remember the meaning of true intimacy:

a relationship characterized by conscious vulnerability, sharing of confidences and privacy, extreme trust, and sensuality.

113

If your relationship isn't offering you that kind of intimacy, be brave enough to consider why. Has your relationship veered off course from the eleven basic principles? Perhaps you can get it back on track. There is no harm in trying. But, from countless stories I hear, when the principles have not been honored, it is usually too late to fix a relationship. If the Code principles *have* been honored and the relationship isn't working, *it may be correctable.*

Consider Alfred and Laurie's example.

Alfred loved Laurie so much he wanted to be with her all the time. At first Laurie was flattered. Later it felt claustrophobic and she was thinking about ending the relationship. As she touched based with the Code, she thought about principle two, the legitimacy of her own need for space and privacy. She decided to be frank and tell Alfred what she needed. (Communication is principle four.) He listened and he thought about what she was saying. He apologized. And although it was an effort, he gave her the space she said she needed. It took time, false starts, and many little corrections to resolve these interdependent needs. But once they had found a way to communicate and compromise, she no longer wanted to end the relationship. They were able to continue on and had developed a better understanding of the need to communicate.

FINAL ACTS

Dating relationships eventually move on to a conclusion. The bond is formalized and made permanent or it ends.

Whether dragged out slowly or closed suddenly, endings are tough.

WHEN IT'S OVER

The reason to end a relationship is to improve your life. If you decide that you want courtship and you are in a relationship with a man who will not provide it, you have a good reason to end the relationship. When should you end it? The longer you delay, the more of your life you waste. More serious than the time lost is the fact that you become what you do. The more time you spend doing noncourtship, the further you are moving away from the courting life.

> Francine did things the right way. She followed the Code and had a wonderful time doing it. It hadn't always been that way for her, but after attending a workshop and studying the eleven principles, she decided to put them into practice. She began with what was missing from her life—positive solitude and reflection—and took some time after ending a relationship that wasn't going anywhere. She used that time to get herself ready, to decorate her apartment, and to spruce up her wardrobe.
>
> She developed her own fitness program, going out to walk three times a week for about an hour each time. She told me how great it felt getting her body physically fit. Her energy started to increase and she felt much more cheerful, even though when she first began her physical fitness program she had no man in her life. Then she joined a walking club. The group met every Saturday morning and took five-mile walks through Valley Forge Park. Being among men and

women who enjoyed walking exposed her to a new set of friends.

It was on one of these walks that she met Ralph, a man with whom she began to form a wonderful friendship. Early on he suggested to her that it might be nice to get together. She let him know quite clearly that she had reached a time in her life where she was interested in marriage and family. He expressed some surprise, but hearing her communication of what she wanted (principle four), he told her that he also was looking for marriage. When I last spoke with Francine, she and Ralph were dating exclusively. She was enjoying herself and told me that her communication of exactly what she wanted had allowed something very good to begin happening between them. Communicating directly was new for her and she was enjoying the reward of that action.

We discussed Stacy earlier in this chapter. She made the mistake of going to bed with George, a physician, too soon. She concluded four years later that she wanted to learn from her history, and build a better future. She came to a workshop as she was breaking up with George. As she learned further about the eleven principles, she pointed out how her own situation fit them all. Once she understood how her own behavior had affected the outcome of a romantic relationship, she changed it. Her story summarizes what she learned to avoid in the future.

With George, Stacy did not accept that her needs were legitimate and allowed his continual stream of "medical crises" to readjust their plans. Rather than take time to be alone and reflect on what was happening in her life, she was out almost constantly, dating and pursuing other activities. She was

uncomfortable with the relationship always seeming to revolve around George's needs, but she did not know how to
effectively communicate what she wanted. She never took
command of her calendar, allowing his schedule to dominate
hers, usually at the last minute. She saw signs that he might
be dating other women but didn't want to look too closely
and never asked him about it. In other words, she deceived
herself. Sex was never that good, but she rationalized that it
was. After all, a surgeon was a "good catch." Forgetting that
good manners preserve a woman's dignity, she permitted
him to be rude to her (to break dates, to neglect her needs).
As three years passed with George, her naturally positive
self-image slowly eroded.

Stacy became what she did. As she continued in a relationship that assigned her to second-rate status, she began to
lose her magnetism for attracting other, legitimate courtship
candidates. And she could feel George's respect for her diminishing as well. Afterward, when the relationship had
ended, she realized that she had judged him too superfi-
cially. Because he was highly skilled (as a surgeon) and economically independent, she had incorrectly assumed that he
would and could deliver the things a woman needs. As the
months passed, she began to feel despondent. The man and
the relationship that were supposed to be life-enhancing
were far from it. Finally, after attending the Athena workshop, she mustered the courage to get on with her life. When
she confronted her life and studied her history, she saw that
George had not been enhancing her well-being. He really
had not treated her well. Competent, economically secure
surgeons may not be competent, suitable suitors.

Stacy didn't have to decide whether to end the relationship, because George had been seen publicly with another
woman on several occasions. She lived in a small town and

could not pretend this was not happening. (Like Bill, who left Bianca in Chapter 2, George did not discuss what was happening. He just acted in his own self-interest.) In a way, she was grateful he had forced her decision to break up with him. But either way, the use of a history lesson can help a woman get on with her life.

When I next spoke with Stacy, she said she had two dates on her calendar and was in command of her role in scheduling dates. She had rediscovered herself. She was once again emanating a kind of attractiveness men are drawn to. She felt it. Men were asking her out in advance and treating her very nicely. She resolved to use her four-year history with George as a stepping-stone to new knowledge.

Her nagging doubt was that she had wasted the time with George. It isn't necessarily so. She has a great fund of historical information she can draw on. She has a good intellect and a positive attitude to rapidly assimilate what she finds. Now she is ready to form judgments that are productive for her own well-being. She has learned that a "good catch" has no value to her unless he treats *her* as if she is the princess worthy of the prince.

It is reasonable for a woman of the nineties to want to get married. Life is better in a good marriage. The risks of painful sexually transmitted diseases are dramatically reduced. When you make a commitment to marry, your chance for building a lifelong relationship is tremendously enhanced.

The last time I spoke with Stacy, she was planning her wedding to Evan.

SUMMING UP:
THE LESSONS OF YOUR HISTORY

You have *lived* your past and observed the stories of other women. Now *use* the knowledge to guide your future course. Once you have decided that you are ready for courtship, you can take advantage of this information about what kinds of experiences and what types of men did not lead you (or others) onto wholesome paths. Courtship is wholesome. It fills a woman with joy.

The Three Take-Home Messages

1. Use—do not rue—your past. Recognize that your history is a valuable reality. For some women, a period of sexual exploration in the past causes shame in the present. If you feel this way, use the facts to build a better future. If in your "wild period" you didn't do harm to anybody, didn't steal or lie or deliberately hurt anyone, then your wild behavior is a form of history that will have tremendous value to your future.

   But if you carry feelings of guilt, then you will have to deal with those feelings in order to get on with your life. For most of us, the idea of shame is taught in childhood when we do things that our parents want us to know are self-destructive. However, most religions and some parents also teach that when we err we can seek forgiveness. The Christian religion teaches the redeeming power of grace, that if we seek forgiveness by acknowledging our error and resolving to err no more, we will be forgiven. And liberated from shame and guilt. The Jewish religion has a similar message in the idea of atonement for sin. If you have a religious background, use it as you work through these feelings.

119

Shame is taught and built into your conscience as part of your ethical development. It can serve you well when you use it to learn from your history and build a new future. We all make mistakes. But as human beings, we have the unique ability to make amends, to get on with our lives, and to build a better future. If you feel shame, shift your focus to grace, atonement, or some other positive way of accepting your previous errors as fuel for your growth. Consider channeling such negative energy in a positive way; to serving those less fortunate, for example. Volunteer at your local Multiple Sclerosis Society, United Way, food kitchen, or other service agency. As you give of yourself, and react to the value others will come to place on you, you will gain a better self-image. But do not lie about or deny your past—that will only compound your feelings of guilt.

Since no one is without mistakes, recognizing our own errors can help us to understand and be kind to others who have erred. Tolerance is a gracious quality. But if you do get involved in religious, ethical, or community service and still cannot overcome your feelings of shame or the reactions of others, move to a new community. Start a new life. Depending on your neighborhood and its size, such a move may or may not be necessary to build your future.

2. From now on, delay intimacy. Whether you call it chemistry or fate or animal attraction, it's overwhelming and unmistakable. And if you're like some women, you don't want to stop and analyze why you're drawn to a man. Maybe you worry that it would diminish the magic. You'd rather just enjoy it than figure it out. But looking deeper does not destroy the magic. It just increases the chance that you will connect with a man who is right for you in every sense.

3. Avoid unavailable men. The Casanova. The man who cheats. The one who won't commit. The man who just wants to be

friends. These relationships may have confused you in the past. Now, using the insights of your love history, you know how and why. They represent dead ends, not shortcuts to courtship.

Once you have set out on the quest for courtship, you have entered a new phase of your life. Relish the journey—it is a journey to your own true self. With heart and mind prepared for the journey, let's consider the next issue. What every women who contemplates courtship and marriage must discover in her prelude to courtship: finding out where she can meet good single men.

FOUR

Discover Where the Men Are Through Guided Sleuthing

The bullfinch female goes out in search of a male by positioning herself where the one she chooses cannot fail to notice her. If the male is interested, he will get the courtship started with a brief contact. He lightly touches his beak to hers, then quickly darts away. If she reciprocates, he begins his pursuit. Then the courtship sequence unfolds, and with it the beginning of a new pair, one that is destined to last for life.

A girl owes it to her dignity
To wait until she is wooed—*I Ching*

Meanwhile, she can use her time to figure out where the men are.

Despite reports to the contrary, there are many good single men out there searching for a good single woman to get close to. To talk with and walk with and love. To form a partnership with and build bonds of commitment. Our purpose, next, is to figure out what you need to do to find them. If you live in a big city like New York, Philadelphia, or San Francisco, your task is more complex because there are so many more men to choose from. The haystack is so large that searching for the golden needle takes more effort. Still, having more options is often the envy of those who live in small towns. Whatever the size of your town, you will find the men when you use my plan.

If you think your search for courtship is as important as your search for a job or a good college, you will see why a systematic plan is so effective. For a job hunt to be its most successful, you need to know what jobs are available. For college shopping, it helps to know the range of available colleges in your price, location, and academic range. To go searching for courtship, you need to know where the available men can be found.

Your success in locating a number of good men will be greatly improved by a systematic effort. Let's get started.

OBJECTIVES

In this chapter there are three objectives:

1. To explore why my studies of biology have led me to conclude that it is important to appreciate and engage *the feminine* aspect of your nature in order to lure the male into courtship.
2. To instruct you on how to create a *catalog of resources* that will list the many places you can go to find men who are looking for women to date. You will use this catalog to select your choices as you sit down each week to schedule your next three social activities. If you follow my method for developing this list, you will find yourself swamped with invitations, newsletters, letters from men, and calendar listings of interesting places to go. In this section we discover what kind of social

events are available in your town. You will have so many places to meet single men that your biggest social problem will be to make the choice on any given day.

3. To assure you that your searching activities can, and probably should, be done all by yourself. Most of the time it is better to avoid the company of women as you search for the company of men.

MAKING YOUR SEARCH SO GRACEFUL IT SEEMS SIMPLE

As with all high arts, when your search for courtship is conducted gracefully, it looks simple. Simplicity is difficult because single women of the nineties often suffer from role confusion. The mixed messages of a changing culture have not yet settled into a cohesive value system. The feminist search for equality between the genders, for the rights and the dignity of women to be respected, is an important evolution in civilization. Women should have equal access to engaging their energies and their intellect to serve the culture. Women should strive for equal access to financial security. But the imprudent exercise of these rights can intrude on romance and interfere with the high art of male-female connection. A feminist who objects to a man holding the door open may find he won't ask her for a date.

A woman must not ignore the richness of her female nature, that aspect of her being that enjoys the dance between a man and a woman. When you search for courtship, you are going after what you need, as in job hunting or management by objective. With the method I offer, you will sharpen your skills, make a plan, and go out on interviews. As you do this, you refine your sense of humor and play. Searching for courtship should be fun. It should be a celebration—perhaps even an exaggeration—of the difference between the genders. While searching for courtship, it is appropriate to enhance the appearance of the differences.

Engaging your feminine power to lure the masculine. The primary feminine objective in the search for courtship is to attract bees as flowers do. Your goal is to attract more than one man in order to be able to select a candidate from among them. Your candidate will have the masculine role of courting you.

You will engage in the feminine role of deciding whether this is *the man* you can accept for a date and maybe later on for marriage. Consider the dynamic from the viewpoint of my own field, reproductive biology.

Fertilization—the Joining of Male to Female

I think of courtship leading to marriage as a process akin to any other fertilization. When a fertilization is successful, a man and woman join to form a new life, a unity. To a biologist, there is magic in the connection between the male sperm and the female egg. The lessons that fertilization teaches can profoundly affect the way a woman chooses to conduct herself in the mating ritual as she searches for courtship.

The process of fertilization is quite dramatic. Extraordinary biological energy is spent as the egg ripens, moves into position within the ovary, and then journeys out alone from the ovary to the fallopian tube. The single egg, in its grandeur, sits regally, quite still. Hundreds of tiny sperm are the

125

pursuers. Their wriggling tails flick in a frenzy as they beat their heads against the wall of the egg. Hundreds upon hundreds of sperm beat against the egg in an effort to gain entry to its nucleus. It is as if there were a race under way and each of the sperm was competing against all the others. Except in the case of twins or more, only one sperm gains admission.

Biologists have studied the dynamic process enabling the sperm to enter the barrier imposed by the egg's membrane. Apparently, something in the chemistry of the egg permits the admission of the particular sperm best suited to it from among the candidates that got to the site on time. As I see it, she, the egg, selects which of the sperm may enter.

Usually in a successful human fertilization the sperm are waiting in the fallopian tube, anticipating the arrival of an egg. The egg will live about six hours once it has entered the fallopian tube. The sperm last longer—from two to three days. Nature has evolved a process in which many male participants compete with each other for entry to one female. Each time this mating ritual occurs, the drama repeats.

Courtship in many animals involves a similar dynamic. The males preen and prance near the female of interest as they attempt to lure her to a sexual connection. We human females should learn from such basic animal behaviors and play our roles accordingly.

The female's job in the courtship dance is complex. She needs to find the men. She needs to present herself in such a way that they will pursue her in a courtly manner. Then, having attracted enough candidates from which to make a sensible selection, she does the choosing. With the great care worthy of such an important decision, she moves slowly and courteously from acquaintanceship with many to intimacy with one.

Feminine power, exercised with this goal in mind, is a low-stress, high-pleasure experience. When you accept these basic principles of biology as the guiding force for your own courtship search, you will preserve your energy, your health, and your sense of humor. And it will be most enjoyable!

LOCATING THE MEN—
CATALOGING YOUR RESOURCES

The first task in your search for men is to build a resource book—filled with the social opportunities from which you will select your three events each week. Purchase a loose-leaf binder at least two inches thick and a set of at least twelve dividers. You'll need a three-hole puncher, paper, and perhaps a month-at-a-glance calendar to insert in the first section.

It's better to build your skills by trying the lowest-risk activities first. If you fumble on these, you haven't lost a major prospect. Meanwhile, they will give you lots of useful practice. We'll begin by building Section 1 of our loose-leaf binder, reserved for the want-ad reply letters you will soon be receiving.

Personal Ads—Loose-Leaf Section 1

Placing and *answering* personal ads are opposite female/male activities in the dance of courtship. Placing is the feminine act; answering is the masculine role. It is as basic as the sperm and the egg.

Placing an appropriate ad is one way to express the alluring feminine role in the courtship dance. Once the lure has been placed, the men respond. You gather up these responses and make your selections one at a time at your own pace. A personal ad states your availability and requires the men to pursue you. Answering personal ads is a masculine pursuit rather than a feminine lure role. From what I have seen, when women answer the ads men place, they experience the frustration of spending energy with little satisfying return.

Your energy can be better spent setting up lures than pursuing them. Ads are particularly effective when you know how to place the ad in the right way to attract the best candidates. The rules are quite specific.

Most magazines provide a mailbox for an extra fee that enables responses to be sent to the magazine's rented mailbox. The magazine sends you these letters a batch at a time. I do not recommend using this service. It costs more than your own investment at the United States post office and delivers less. When men reply, you will want immediate access; magazines delay the dispatching of replies. If your ad is good, replies will keep coming for the next six to twelve months. The post office box will stay in your name as long as you need it; the magazine box may expire too soon.

Your privacy must be protected before you place your ad. You will want to be sure that your privacy is guaranteed so that any undesirables who may respond are not able to find you. By renting a box at your local post office, your privacy and your security are protected by law. The United States Postal Service preserves your safety. The cost of renting a post office box at a local post office is about thirty dollars per year.

Now select your magazines or newspaper. You'll want to

stick to your own area, of course. Many big cities, small states, and regions have a glossy local news magazine that works well for personals. New York has several that appeal to people with different interests, as do San Francisco, Los Angeles, Columbus, Atlanta, Boston, Detroit, and Philadelphia. *Connecticut* magazine and *Delaware Today* are representative of small states. *Yankee* and *Northwest* magazines cover regional areas. You can discover magazines in your area by going to your local magazine outlet, library, or newsstand and collecting a batch. If you study which ones have ads in the personals section that most closely appeal to your sense of yourself, you will make a good choice. Take a look at the procedures and options for placing ads.

Your objective is twofold: to use the ad to generate pursuit letters from men who will request that you call them to talk further—and to protect yourself while doing so. The ad serves as a barrier and a screen. You do not want to receive phone calls before you have read the letters. You do not want to give away information about where you live unless and until you decide that a particular man is safe.

The purpose of your ad is to develop a collection of good letters to store—a wine cellar of possibilities. Loose-leaf Section 1 will be filled with letters awaiting your selection. You will flip through this section occasionally to select a candidate. Think of it the way wine lists are presented for your consideration at good restaurants. Have you enjoyed the process of flipping through the pages, looking at the labels, and selecting a wine to try? That is the result of a personal ad. You will create a good wine cellar to store letters for retrieval when you are ready to try one.

You will draw on the wine list perhaps once or twice a

month. It will not be your major search activity, but it will serve to assure you that there are many good men out there waiting to meet you.

Many magazines have telephone hotlines in their personals sections. I suggest avoiding that option because telephone calls will not provide you with a "wine cellar." Calls have no substance and no barriers. Letters have both. The search for instant gratification by phone calls will waste your energy.

In most cases, the ads can be placed by telephone or faxed, and charged with a MasterCard or Visa. It is easy to place an ad. But rent your mailbox at the post office first. Then you can pick up your letters whenever you feel like going to retrieve them.

The wording of your ad is important. To write your own, study ads to get an idea of the range of lures people offer and to note which ones you find most attractive. Ads seem to start off either by describing what is wanted or by describing what is offered. Since the man studying the ads is more likely to respond when he sees himself than when he sees you, I suggest you start your ad by describing what you want from a relationship rather than what you offer. Use your own words. Consider the sample ad below:

> WANTED: A man to love and share a wholesome life, and potentially, shared soaring. Pretty, warm, creative, 39-year-old scholar, who exercises regularly, enjoys excellent mental and physical health. Likes home life, dancing, long walks, stimulating conversation, exploring together. Seeking tall, very intelligent, successful man, who, like her, has been lonely and—because he is uncommon—finds compatible partners rare. Please write: Box 100, City, State, Zip.

That ad generated ninety replies. Each was a response from a man who was interested enough in pursuing a possibility to sit down and write a letter. The men ranged in age, in educational status and occupation (high school dropouts, lawyers, doctors, professors, three prisoners, linemen, executives), and economic status (from insolvent debtors to very wealthy businessmen). That ad created a wine list of ninety letters that provided respite from loneliness on many rainy nights. Here are some examples of the worthwhile replies it brought:

Dear Creative,

I'm different. I demand from life things others only dream about. I've always held out for quality, for the diamond in the sea of zircons. The essence of life to me is to share the important things, large and small, with someone who cares. You're similar —you're slender and lean to match my 6'3"—195—42 yr. frame. This S.W.M. [single white male] *professional awaits your call.*

I like your ad—it speaks to my condition. I'm 6'1" 175 BCE (Bachelor of Civil Engineering), MBA with many interests in music, sports, community activities, politics, etc. Please phone we will have much to talk about. If I'm out please leave your number—it's safe.

Hi, we're neighbors! I'm a SWM, 41, co-raising 3 daughters. I'm well traveled, cultured + sophisticated. If interested call home _____.

I really liked your ad, it struck a responsive chord in me, and I felt compelled to reply. I'm 42 years old, divorced, and am self-

employed as an environmental consultant. I'm 5'11", attractive, and in excellent physical condition (I run 4 miles daily and work out). I'm still exploring my limits both personally and professionally and enjoy a variety of somewhat incongruous interests. I'm romantic, funny, self-reliant, vulnerable, and I'm looking for an independent, intelligent, attractive woman with her own life to spend quality time with. If you are interested in meeting, either write me, or if you feel really secure, call me at ————. If my answering machine answers, please leave some sort of message. It's very sensitive to rejection, and won't be worth a damn for days if you hang up on it. Hope to hear from you soon.

From a college professor:

Hi. Yes, I am interested in meeting a genuinely intelligent, accomplished woman who exercises regularly, etc. And who am I? It's difficult to introduce oneself to a stranger so allow me to let some students do the introduction. Enclosed find some student evaluations. The comments should have some element of truth since they were collected and held by a colleague. Only after final grades were posted were these comments given to me.

You can use the replies later to practice your searching arts. Ads offer you a safe place to refine your skills of genteel flirtation, good conversation, exploring for friendship before sex, and learning about what makes men the way they are. They also teach the limitations of stereotypes—the football lineman who writes dynamite poetry, the serious bookworm whose Johnny Carson impersonation can bring down the house.

As you talk with men from a variety of backgrounds, your feminine powers will increase and you will attract more candidates. Learning to accept and enjoy the process of courtship takes practice. Don't think of the ad as the desperate search for the love of your life. Rather, think of it as one of your playgrounds and get ready to enjoy yourself. You can have a lot of fun when you use your wine list sensibly and safely. I know. I placed four ads and enjoyed the pleasure of about four hundred letters that came in response. My friends had similar experiences.

Experiment with your own ads. Try drafting three or four separate ads. Show them to men who are friends, relatives, or friends of friends. Ask them which ones they would be most likely to respond to and you will have tested the market before spending your money. An investment like this, especially if the ad is long and the city is large, will cost you about $150. But it will bring you a year's worth of adventure. A personal ad is a high-yield investment. Chapter 5 explains how to handle the letters men send you. Now let's shift to Section 2 of your *catalog of resources.*

Singles Bars and Clubs—Loose-Leaf Section 2

Clubs and singles bars have a bad reputation because many people misuse them and misunderstand their healthy value. Provided your city has some appropriate bars or clubs, what you do with an encounter determines its value or its danger. Bars or clubs are places a woman can meet men she doesn't know. You will have a chance to polish your skills at conversation, dignity, good manners, positive attitudes, and self-possession. If you preserve your safety, you have not risked much if you make a mistake. And when you get it right, you have learned a powerful new skill.

In Chapter 5 I'll explain how to ensure your safety and

well-being at a bar. For now, I suggest you begin discovering where the appropriate bars and clubs are in your area. Build Section 2 of your loose-leaf into a catalog of good bars and clubs. Reserve a page for each one in your area. Ask friends. Ask people with whom you work. Ask everywhere so you build a long list. Read reviews in the local or city section of your newspaper. In many cities clubs have largely replaced bars as gathering points for single men and women. The concierge at a high-end hotel may be able to suggest some nearby spots. Prestige hotels often have prestige bars. These will be safe. Check them out. Some bars and clubs have regular theme nights that draw single people of similar ages, occupations, and interests, like jazz or Brazilian or country-western music and dance. Find out the sociology of your local bars and clubs and you will expand your fields of opportunity. If you live near or in a big city, ferret out the four or five bars and clubs that will be most useful to you.

Although I know several women who met their husbands in bars and went on to enjoy long and lovely lives together, husband hunting is not your purpose. Use the bar or club as a resource for skill development, akin to the personal ads but activating a different process. When you go into a bar or a club, you are directly engaging in sexual attraction. When you place an ad, you are luring on the basis of your ability to communicate through words. In the early months of your search for courtship, it might make sense to use one of your three weekly social activity dates for bar or club practice. Later, when you've mastered the skills a bar or club can teach, you will probably go only once a month. Chapter 5 describes how to conduct yourself when you enter a bar.

At this point, you will continue to focus on the loose-leaf as you build your list of resources.

Correspondence Clubs—Loose-Leaf Section 3

The Single Booklovers' Club, Box 117, Gradyville, PA 19039, in suburban Philadelphia, is an international club for single people who like books and want to meet people like themselves of the opposite sex. Ruth and Bob Leach developed it in 1970 out of their awareness of the need for people who love books to find like-minded courtship candidates. People who want to join can write to them or call (215) 358-5049 for application materials. The application asks you to fill out a one-page sheet that describes your basic biographical background with respect to your single status, your family status, where you live, and the kinds of books you like. It goes on to ask other questions about who you are. Each member can choose to fill out a phone number, an address, a box number, or any other way he or she would like to be reached should an opposite-sex member choose to make contact.

As a new member, you will receive a list of all the male members coded to protect their anonymity and privacy. The list has a code number, city, state, and two-line description of each member. Each member completes a fuller biography when joining the club. It takes only a phone call or a note and a nominal cost for a member to order copies of the larger biographies of members that interest her. They will arrive a few days later. If a member wants to contact any of these people, it is up to her to telephone or write. With that first call or letter the friendship begins. Once a month single booklovers receive a newsletter with quotes from classic prose and poetry along with an updated list of new members.

Once or twice a year the Single Booklovers' Club holds a cocktail party followed by a show and dinner. This provides a five- or six-hour opportunity for the members to meet one another. Those who live close to the Swarthmore, Pennsylvania, location of these parties are more likely to attend, although national members correspond and go on group-sponsored trips together.

If you are someone who loves to read books, the Single Booklovers' Club is an ideal way to enhance your social life. It has produced many friendships and marriages over the years.

Before you decide whether to join this club, however, you might find it economical to create your own catalog list of other correspondence and social clubs so that you can select those that most closely fit your interests.

Special-Interest Clubs and Groups—
Loose-Leaf Section 4

By referring to the listing of social or singles events in the Weekend section of your newspaper and the classified section at the back of certain magazines, you will find many clubs for single people who want to meet other singles. Call or write them for membership information and build your own list of the resources that are available in your region. Then use Sections 3 and 4 of your loose-leaf to house your reference materials for rules, membership lists, and upcoming events.

Some nationally based clubs (with local chapters) include:

The Single Gourmet
133 E. 58th St.
New York, NY 10022
(212) 980-8788

National Assn. of Christian
  Singles
1933 W. Wisconsin Ave.
Milwaukee, WI 53233
(414) 344-7300

Singles in Agriculture
Rte. 2E 12820 Hwy. 33
Baraboo, WI 53913
(608) 356-3483

Single Persons for Tax
  Equality Assn.
2314 Logan Ave. N.
Minneapolis, MN 55411-1938

National Assn. of Single
  Adult Leaders
P.O. Box 1600
Grand Rapids, MI 49501

Single Parent Resource
  Center
141 W. 28th St.
New York, NY 10001
(212) 947-0221

Parents Without Partners
8807 Colesville Rd.
Silver Springs, MD 20910
(301) 588-9354

Catholic Alumni Clubs,
  International
3523 W. 78th St.
Chicago, IL 60652
(312) 776-9476

Singles in Service
1556 Halford Ave., Ste. 320
Santa Clara, CA 95015
(408) 248-8244

Unmarried Catholics
  Correspondence Club
P.O. Box 872
Troy, NY 12181

Miss Mom/Mister Mom
P.O. Box 547
Moab, UT 84532
(801) 259-5090

Institute of Single Dynamics
P.O. Box 11394
Kansas City, MO 64112
(816) 763-9401

Scientific Marriage Foundation
Hopkins Syndicate
802 S. Washington
Bloomington, IN 47401
(812) 331-7752

National Assn. to Advance Fat
  Acceptance
P.O. Box 188620
Sacramento, CA 95818
(916) 443-0303

Then there are the local chapters of ski and skating clubs. These sponsor local and worldwide trips and outings and other group sporting events such as tennis. To locate your local chapter and get on the mailing lists, write to:

American Ski Assn.
88 Sherman, Ste. 500
Denver, CO 80203
(303) 861-7669

U.S. Figure Skating Assn.
20 First St.
Colorado Springs, CO 80906
(719) 635-5200

Other special-interest clubs—such as the YM/YWCA and the YM/YWHA—attract many single people but are not limited exclusively to singles. Clubs in my city (Philadelphia) are probably similar to yours. They include:

The Philadelphia Canoe Club
Social dancing clubs
Main Line Ski Club (includes tennis, sailing, and canoeing
     activities)
The Professional and Business Singles Network
Philadelphia Swing Dance Society

Representative singles clubs in other cities include:

First Tampa Singles Civitan Club
17539 Willow Pond Dr.
Lutz, FL 33549
(813) 949-7354

Long Beach Single Sailors Assn.
2301 E. First
Long Beach, CA 90803
(213) 434-3552

Gulf Coast Singles Assn.
P.O. Box 267
Biloxi, MS 39533
(601) 872-1717

Pasadena Ballroom Dance Assn.
997 E. Walnut
Pasadena, CA 91109
(818) 799-5689

Texas Assn. of Single Adults
P.O. Box 2090
Harker Heights, TX 76543
(817) 699-7506

Singles Club Assn. of San Diego
P.O. Box 5682
San Diego, CA 92105
(619) 296-6948

All of these are open to people who are willing to pay the annual membership dues. Costs vary from ten to fifty dollars per year for most. Each provides a monthly meeting, which often begins with a social cocktail hour. Sometimes it is followed with an activity, other times with a business meeting. Often this is followed by an opportunity to engage in the activity in accord with the club's charter. Each conducts a calendar of regularly scheduled activities for its members. Whether you want exposure to tennis, canoeing, dancing, or poetry reading, you can probably find a local club. Most charge from two to fifteen dollars per event to cover the costs incurred.

To find out about such organizations in your area, visit your library and thumb through appropriate magazines and newspapers. Initially, developing this resource list will probably consume one or two of your weekly searching-for-courtship time slots. But once you have developed your list, you can begin to engage in your new social life as you make connections with other members of the clubs you choose.

Many regularly scheduled singles events do not even require club membership. As you find clubs that interest you, you can get your name on their mailing lists. In this way, you will soon be receiving notices of a wide range of social events. These will form some of the opportunity menus from which you will select your three socializing events each week.

Develop your own special-interest group.   If you determine that the kind of club you want does not yet exist, consider forming it yourself. In the process of forming your own club, you will make new friends who focus on the activity you have selected. For example, you could form a "great books" club and place an ad to find people interested in meeting once a month to set up a program. For safety, you might not want to hold the first meeting in your home. To rent a hall, call local libraries or houses of worship and ask for help in finding space. In Philadelphia in 1992, for example, an enterprising young man named Jim Scalia sent out a postcard every month or two to his growing mailing list, announcing the next singles dance he was giving at a local pub. Admission was five or ten dollars, and decent dress was required. These Wednesday-night events attracted fifty to one hundred singles each time.

Community Service—Loose-Leaf Section 5

When you give your time to enhancing the culture in which you live, whether through the Sierra Club, your local museum, the soup kitchens that feed the poor, the groups that help people suffering from AIDS, or any one of many groups serving the needy, you expand your opportunities to meet people. To get started, go to your reference librarian and request help in locating a list of nonprofit organizations in your area. Pick one or two and call the administrator to learn more and to find out if there is a need for the help you could give. In election years volunteers are needed to help in campaigns. Choose your candidate and ask the librarian for help in finding who to call to make contact.

There is something profoundly valuable in giving a part of yourself to help others. You cannot give away goodwill without getting back much more than you give. Try it and your life will become richer. As you do it, you will meet others of similar magnanimous spirit.

When you select your friends from among the givers of the world, you will find friends who will give to you as well. Consider building some volunteer work into your social calendar. You will rarely succumb to depression when you give some of your time to those less fortunate than you. Instead of paying a therapist to help you cope with the depression that comes from loneliness, try to donate an hour a week to serving someone else. You might get more and spend less.

If you don't have a lot of time but do have some money you can give away, whether it be fifty dollars, five thousand dollars, or more, another kind of social life can open up to you. Charitable organizations often employ development officers, professionals who raise money for their institutions —often by giving parties to promote cultural events. Museums generally have categories of donation, and according to these categories provide invitations to monthly parties of varying levels of sophistication, fine food, and formality.

Search out your local institutions. Call the development offices. Ask for their literature for potential donors. You will be amazed to learn how many mailing lists you will be placed on. Charitable giving can open new social opportunities. And everyone wins.

To make up your list, look up theaters, theater groups, churches, academies of music and arts, universities and colleges, community service councils, the fund-raising programs of local hospitals, and political groups, and use your list of other nonprofit organizations in your area.

Ethnic Centers That Produce Singles Events— Loose-Leaf Section 6

Most churches, synagogues, and religious temples now recognize the need to provide social activities for their single members. Look into the ethnic and religious centers that match your interests and you are likely to discover a rich social life. In many cases, one does not have to belong to the organization in order to attend dances, picnics, or group discussions. Make some phone calls and put the information you receive in Section 5 of your loose-leaf notebook as well.

Ethical focus groups.   Both within churches and without, groups get together to study the Bible and to pursue other topics of discussion. The list of potential ethical focus groups is diverse. Consider the issues that matter to you— pro-choice, ecology (the Sierra Club), consumer fraud, political issues—and you can enrich your life as you focus on these matters in groups. Some are for singles, others for professionals, others for single parents. Whatever your concern, if you search and have interests, you should be able to find (or form) a discussion group relating to your own needs. These groups pursue ethical questions in gentle discussions. You will meet like-minded men and women in the process.

Consider this activity as part of your spiritual connection as well as your search for courtship. Put the information you find in Section 6 of your loose-leaf notebook.

Dancing and Sports: Clubs or Lessons— Loose-Leaf Section 7

Social dancing presents an important opportunity for single people to gain the physical connection of touching and moving to the rhythm of music. Whether you prefer rock and roll, square dancing, swing dancing, country, or jazz, you should be able to find cheerful people in the age group you prefer. Dancing is a healthful and happy activity when it is conducted in a safe social setting. It provides an opportunity to engage in a social act that gets your body moving in harmonic exercise. And it doesn't require that you talk.

Consider searching for local opportunities for weekly dancing and you will probably find a great deal of joy and health-giving activity in the process. Dancing classes are offered by adult education groups, by businesses that specialize in dancing, and by other community groups. These are often advertised in the newspaper. You may be able to learn about them by calling the adult education center or high school administrative office in your community. You can discover others in your library by asking the reference librarian for help in tracking down community activity lists. Or look in the calendar section of local newspapers and magazines. Most dancing classes do not require you to have a partner. Although they are not limited to singles, you will find a number of single people attending them. Often as the members of the class get to know one another, they go out for coffee and dessert afterward. Dancing can relieve stress and expose you to new friends.

Sports provide a wholesome outlet for recreation, social contact, and meeting new men. Local gyms may offer coed aerobics or swimming classes. Consider water sports like sailing, canoeing, or fishing. Joining a running or mountain climbing group can be a good avenue to fun, good health, and new men friends.

Lessons and Classes—Loose-Leaf Section 8

Local colleges and high schools in many parts of the country offer adult education one course at a time. So do community centers such as local Y's and Township Centers. Look into the educational resources in your area.

By taking a class, you will get out on a regular basis—usually for three to fourteen weeks—learn something new, and possibly make some new friends. Adult education is a marvelous way to expand your social connections and increase the possibilities of finding candidates who will court you in the process.

Whether you want to learn how to cook, read the stars, fix a car, or study Shakespeare, others will also be interested in the same thing. Your local reference librarian or high school administrative office should be able to help you start filling in Section 8 of your loose-leaf. Call the resources you identify and ask to be placed on their mailing lists. Choose courses that interest you, and you will make new friends who share your interests.

Perform the Arts: Sing, Act, Paint— Loose-Leaf Section 9

Whether through joining a choir, a Thespian club, or poetry group, many people like to get together to perform. If you enjoy these activities, there are likely to be many opportunities for you. Singing and acting are low-pressure social activities because you don't need to generate conversation in the early stages of being with new people. As you get to know your fellow performers, you have the chance to select friends from among the group. If some are not single, they may still offer you good exposure to those who are once you have become colleagues. Consider joining a performing group.

Travel Alone
to Be Available for a Partner

In order to be available for a new partner, it is wise to go out to your new activities all by yourself. The more you enter clubs, dances, study sessions, and other places by yourself, the more quickly you will meet new partner candidates. Men will find it easier to approach you when you are alone than when you appear to be already engaged in conversation with another person.

When you learn to go out alone, you will reap a number of benefits:

- By being alone among others, you are focusing on solving loneliness.
- By being alone among others, you announce your availability and increase the number of new people that will approach you.
- By being alone among others, you increase your ability to stand alone. You become competent, whole, independent.

Summing Up

The resources I have suggested in this section should get you started in building your own list. Whether you use my suggestions or search for others that more closely fit your own unique nature, your goal should be to get out of your house three times a week in order to meet new people and engage in new activities. In this way you will improve your socializing skills and make new friends. You will come to enjoy the rich diversity of the world in which we live. When we find ways to appreciate its magnificence, we become magnificent ourselves and we establish our identities. We become what we do.

By participating in activities you enjoy, you will establish your real self and you will be able to be your real self in relationship to a man—not just an object that responds to his needs. It takes practice to establish a separate being. The more of one you have, the more you can offer in stimulation and substance to a new partner.

You begin the searching process by cataloging your resources so that you can select among them. While we cannot predict the length of time we will be granted in our lives, we can usually define how much of our time we will give to different aspects of our living. Choose what you want to do in your three sessions a week and have fun doing it.

With your resources cataloged and your loose-leaf in place, it is time to activate your search for courtship. In the next chapter we will systematically explore how to make use of each of these resources.

FIVE

Going out Alone

For most of the year Uganda kob antelopes live in herds. But when mating season approaches, each female strikes out on her own. She moves from male to male, each of which has staked out its own small territory. When a male sees a female approach, he prances forward to meet her with head held high, displaying his white throat. On the basis of his appearance and real estate (where his territory is located and how large it is) the female makes her decision.

To be wooed, a woman must
Make contact with romantic men . . .

Now it's time to start using your gathered resources to go out and enjoy yourself! Just as when you search for a new job, you do it alone. All by yourself. Independently. Going out is an adventure. You're off to meet men who excite you, engage you, exhilarate you. This is *fun.*

If you have done your sleuthing, your loose-leaf binder is filled with lists of places you can go to find single men. By now you should have discovered *lots* of options. Roughly half the single population is male. Many of the good ones are out searching for a women to love. Now it is time to take a deep breath and plunge in. You may have placed an ad already. While you are waiting to receive your stack of replies, you can browse the other sections of your binder to start planning *this* week's social calendar.

BINDER BASICS

You might start by flipping to the section that lists the singles bars and clubs you may try. You know which ones are safe. (The bar in the most expensive hotel in town should be safe.) Or perhaps you have concluded that your city doesn't have any safe bars and have crossed that option off your list. Bars aren't your only courtship arena. Have you discovered the Single Booklovers' Club and become a member? Or joined a few other singles clubs? If so, you have probably begun to receive a variety of newsletters and announcements for upcoming events. Doing all this preparatory work will pay off. You will find how much opportunity is out there for singles who are ready to socialize.

Let your fingers do the walking to the dance section of your binder. You know where you can go dancing when you are in the mood and have learned the dates and places of the upcoming singles dances in your community. Your research has turned up the types of dancing done, the kind of crowd that comes, how dressy people get, and the fees.

The names and membership rules of local performing arts groups may be in your loose-leaf too. By now you may have looked into the lessons and classes available in your town and tentatively selected the ones that interest you. Start seriously considering which ones intrigue you enough to join. Will it be singing, acting, writing, or painting?

You may have already decided which community service activity you will soon start doing.

Some women find it comforting to build a loose-leaf beforehand and systematically record their discoveries, while others have a different approach. Perhaps you want to do it as you go along. Whatever your style, it helps to realize that you can discover what you need to know when you need to know it.

ACTIVATE YOUR SEARCH

Enough with the paperwork! Now get out of the house three times a week to the places single men are gathering to find single women. The time has come to meet single men with a specific agenda clearly set in your own mind: You are out searching for courtship.

The adventure of searching for courtship moves now from the privacy of your mind to an exterior arena—out in the world of singles. If you have been following my plan, you are ready to start encountering single men in a way that will bring courtship to you.

The clear agenda: You aren't going out to work when you go out to play. This going out to play three times a week is not the same as going out to a professional gathering, a sales meeting, or a cocktail party designed to promote some business goal. It's definitely not an activity you do with your women friends. You need to have a *single agenda* when you walk into a singles event. Your purpose is to transmit your crucial message: "I am single and available." It's a subtle goal, but it isn't likely to be accomplished if some other program has been set instead. When you go out to pursue new customers or to network for business, even if it's a social setting, you are out working. When you try to mix work with luring, you accomplish neither well. If you are working and want to become a successful and economically independent person, stick to business when you are doing business. Once the line from professional to personal has been crossed, it cannot be recrossed with ease or immediacy. Don't mix your messages: When you want to search for courtship, don't try to do business. And when you go out to play, don't focus your conversation on your work life. Before a man will know to ask you for a date, he needs to know that you are available. The attitude you project as you go out to play will tell him.

Basically, we are social creatures. To keep our emotional balance, we need to be among others, enjoying social intercourse on a regular basis. It is unbalanced and it compromises health to be too reclusive for too long. Not only do you lose touch; others lose touch with you. Three social outings a week *among other single people* will satisfy fundamental needs for your social well-being. Socializing regularly will add a sense of good cheer and optimism to your life. You will radiate a spirit that carries over when you are doing other things. The more you do it, the sooner you will successfully connect with a wide range of new single men.

When is a connection successful? When you find a man you like, discover that he is safe, and receive his invitation for a date at least four days in advance.

ACTIVATE YOUR SOCIAL SCHEDULE
ONE WEEK AT A TIME

In Chapter 1 you learned the importance of gaining command of your social calendar. In Chapter 4 you learned how to amass a binder of available social options. Now put the two together. Use your calendar to activate and organize your search. I suggest that each Tuesday night or Wednesday morning you close your calendar to date invitations for the coming weekend. Now with your calendar and your resource loose-leaf at hand, select three events you will go to during the next week. *Write them in your calendar, in ink, as important commitments that you are making to yourself.* If you do the searching each week, eventually you will find a man to court you. If you are going to be away for a week on a vacation, a business trip, or a family matter, just pick up where you left off when you return. This is *your* schedule. *You* are in charge and it is good to be flexible.

Meanwhile, the search itself is going to be fun because all the work you did in getting ready starts paying off. From week to week, as you fill in your calendar, you will probably find it adventurous to select a wide variety of activities so that you can benefit from the diversity. For example, for the first week you might choose to go to a discussion group, a singles dance, and a class. Perhaps you will choose differently: Wednesday night at a bar or club, Sunday afternoon at a singles tennis party, and Monday night to open and answer your ad replies. As you start going out to places where the men are, sooner or later one (and then more) of them will suggest getting together. Each time a man suggests doing something together, you have another chance to practice calling your own shots. Think of this practice as you would the practice of any other skill. The more practice you get, the more you improve your skills. When your skills are good enough, you will find men offering what you need.

If a man asks you to see him tomorrow, the next day, or at a time that you have already committed elsewhere, it is appropriate to graciously activate your power. If you like him, let him know that you appreciate the invitation, will be happy to see him, but need to find a mutually convenient date. For details, refer back to Chapter 1, to the section entitled "Calling the Shots."

As you make wise selections about where to go searching and what standards to live by, your life will get better and better. Good men will discover that you are available because you will be where they can see you. And when they ask you out, they will learn to consider your calendar as well as theirs. You must use your attractiveness to draw available men to you like bees to a flower. The way you conduct yourself largely determines what happens next.

There is great pleasure and power in taking command of your social life. You are in charge of your own curfew. If you are financially organized and in command of your budget, you can come and go as you decide. Searching costs money as well as time. When you have earned your income, you are free to set aside some of it for this basic need to search for courtship. Savor the personal freedom.

In spite of such freedom, I have found that some women are afraid to declare their independence and go out by themselves. If this is your experience, I hope you will stare down the fear and overcome it. Keep rereading the eleven principles in order to internalize the message. If you feel shy at the newness of going out alone, you might create a "basic pep talk" in front of the mirror. To do this, imagine a new man you think you'd like asking you, "What sort of a person are you? What makes you tick?" and a three-sentence answer.

OVERCOMING "FEAR OF THE DARK"

Since you become what you do, start performing acts of bravery and you will soon find that fear diminishes in proportion to the brave actions you take. Just as regular exercise turns flab into a better-toned body, brave actions turn fear into courage. As you start your search work by going out to play three times a week, it will get easier. After all, when you consider the alternative—staying home alone—what choice do you have? Refusing to use the "key" to unlock your jail isn't what you want. You would not be reading this book if you wanted that. I can't promise that your fears will vanish entirely. Sometimes it will be easy; other times harder. It takes courage to achieve a successful courtship. What I can promise is that with practice it will get easier.

ENJOY THE MEN YOU ENCOUNTER

As you go out to play three times a week, soon you will begin to connect with available men. As you do, consider your own growth, your evolving self. Worry less about any faults you might find in a particular man than about what you are doing as a woman living by the Code. Are you exercising graciousness and dignity? How about honesty? Keep practicing. As you improve your skills, you will move closer to a better candidate. Until you have learned to live as the Code advises, you haven't offered as much as you soon will, using the powers inherent in sexual attraction, communicating your dignity, and projecting a positive attitude.

Fortunately, there is no urgency. No need to hurry. As long as you are going out to meet single men three times a week, time is your friend. You can move gracefully without any need to rush. Going out to play should be enjoyable.

With a positive attitude, make plans. Set goals. Get organized. Consider keeping a journal to record the positive elements of your life. When you take time to recap where you are and to appreciate what you have, it will help keep your attitude upbeat. Your rose-colored glasses will help you develop a positive and cheerful personality.

ANNOUNCE YOUR AVAILABILITY

Be honest about your status. To people who ask, announce cheerfully, "I am single—and searching." Imagine how brave, exhilarating, and simple it is to be honest. What a positive way to channel your energy instead of trying to hide your singleness.

What about the single people who seem to spend inordinate energy talking about how much they like their condition? I have often found that this is a defense constructed to hide discomfort. I suggest that you not pretend. Pretending that you don't need a mate, when you do, can sidetrack your search. Pretending wastes energy and deflects you from your goal, just as being ashamed of or irritated at your single state does. Channel negative energy in a positive direction. Get out there and start looking!

Often in my workshops women express concern that if they let people know they are interested in meeting some-one, they will be perceived as a loser or an "old maid"—or worse, a vulture or desperate. Once they activate their searches, however, their concerns evaporate. By being what you want to convey, as detailed in this book, you will feel like a winner, not a loser. And you will exude that magnet-ism to others. When people ask, tell them, yes, you are searching for courtship, but you are also patient, busy, and enjoying life as you go about it. Add, "If you know anybody that you think I might like, please tell me." The object of your search is a deeply loving relationship leading to mar-riage. Be proud of and acknowledge such an elevated goal. As the Code of Courtship principle number six urges:

> You develop your capacity for honesty and your ability to detect deception.

Having announced your availability, get on with your life elsewhere. Don't cling to people. Don't sit home waiting to be fixed up or introduced. Don't demand that others solve your problems. *You* are in charge. Develop new interests and evolve a more interesting "self." By such positive conduct, you will present yourself as you really are, an interesting and active woman, someone who is desirable, a woman a man would want to seek out for connection. You won't be a vulture, and therefore you won't be perceived that way.

You will not appear desperate because you won't feel desperate. An active social life will engage your attention and stimulate your energy as you start going out into different environments. Socializing correctly will evaporate whatever desperation you were feeling. You are going to discover *how many good men there are and how much fun it is to be a single woman encountering them.* When you do it with dignity, competence, and a sense of humor, the search for courtship is a grand adventure.

SOCIAL CONVERSATIONS: GETTING STARTED

When you are standing alone at a singles party, your good posture, relaxation, and smile will signal to others that you are receptive to their initiating a conversation. Sometimes men, in their own discomfort, pose awkward introductory questions like "What are you doing here?" If you are stumped for a graceful response, try being truthful with a sense of humor—and compassion for his lack of imagination and sensitivity. Look at him, grin, and say something truthful that you feel comfortable expressing, something like "I came to meet new people" or "This is my first time and I'm wondering that too" or "I'm searching for a good man to love."

Social conversations at singles parties should be fun. Everyone attending is obviously there for a similar purpose —to make new friends. To lose your self-consciousness, consider the other guy's feelings and try to put him at ease. If you still feel awkward, pretend you are standing in a supermarket checkout line and the person next to you is equally relaxed. What might you do then if you felt like talking? A comment about your shared circumstances can break the ice. If you have an easy humor, use it. If you feel more serious, accept your condition. Above all, remember principle eight—be mannerly.

YOU AREN'T DATING

"Going out" is very different from—and less than—"dating," but it is more than "hanging out at the mall." At this stage of the courtship search, the whole purpose of going out to play is to position yourself. You are going out in order to be seen and approached by men. You are going out in order to interact with them in a way that will lead them to ask you: "Will you date me?"

A date is a formal invitation issued by a man. Your objective is to act in a way that will promote those invitations. Have you ever noticed how common it is for a new executive to say in a newspaper interview that he "accepted an offer to become president"? How do you suppose he elicited the offer? Usually, by sending messages that he was available to be courted by another company or upper management. The same applies in your personal life. Your objective is to elicit the offer for a date. Then it's up to you, as the feminine part of the pair, to say yes. Each time that you go out to play, you are likely to encounter some single men. As you talk with them or dance or socialize in some other way, some of these men will get the idea to ask you for a date. Before he gets the idea of asking you out, though, he needs some suggestion of your availability.

Sometimes the suggestion comes through a friend, as with

blind dates, but most of the time it does not work this way. Most of the time men and women meet each other through one of the social activities they attend. During an encounter, through conversation and banter, the man discovers and expresses sexual interest in a woman. Usually the suggestion is subtle. But, subtle or blatant, *his* sexual interest is a necessary force for real dating. It rarely works the other way around. From my perspective of biology, I have come to a clear conclusion: It is a waste of *your* time to pursue him. Female energy is best spent setting lures. From the pool of men who choose to pursue you, you can begin making choices. If you find you are not luring enough men to form a big enough pool, you are not a failure. You simply have more "luring" work to do. Here are some possible areas for improvement:

You may have to renew and revise your social schedule. If you are receiving enough invitations for dates from men you genuinely like, you are doing things correctly. If you aren't being asked out, don't let that stop you from going out. Soon you will be invited for dates. What you need to do is go out regularly so that men can see you. If none of the men you are encountering are asking you out, you may need to make some changes in the places you go, or in the way that you encounter men. Remember to fill in *three* events for the coming week *in ink* in your calendar. These are dates you have set for yourself to take charge of the socializing you need in order to have an emotionally healthy, balanced life.

You may have to check your conduct. Perhaps you're not connecting because you're not conducting yourself properly.

158

When traveling in a foreign land, it helps to know the local customs. The same holds true for your forays into these "new lands."

YOUR SOCIAL CONDUCT

As you start to go out three times a week for the purpose of searching for courtship, if you are following my plan, you will be walking into parties or bars, classes or dances alone each time. As you walk into the room all by yourself, there are principles to help you make a successful search. These principles vary according to the place you find yourself in. If you are at a dance, the principles are different than if you are at a discussion group or a bar. The pages that follow are filled with reality-tested advice—what I have learned from the workshops, my own search for courtship, and the experiences of many other women. There are ways to conduct yourself to ensure your safety and promote a good time. Some of these ways apply everywhere; others apply only to specific places. Let us look first at the universal principles, the ones you will use wherever you go.

Project attractive qualities.   Develop the essential skills of a woman who is available for courtship, and the time will come when you will find it difficult to keep up with all the invitations that come to you. The most potent attractive qualities:

- A cheerful attitude
- Good posture and physical grace

· A sense of adventure about your single life
· Tact and kindness
· Openness and self-possession (This combination communicates interest, yet stresses that your sexual jewels are reserved for later.)
· Allure—but clearly nonseductive—in your expressions, attitude, and appearance
· Gentle courage, not timidity or fearfulness
· A sense of humor

These are the qualities worth projecting. Practice them and your life will grow better. If you combine these qualities with the ones in Table 2.4, "Building Attractiveness" (page 76), you will be well equipped for your journey.

Getting dressed to go out.　Dressing up is part of the fun of socializing. Allow yourself the pleasure of feeling well dressed for each occasion.

As you're honest in admitting your search, be honest in your manner of dress. Don't dress to please anyone but yourself. Your unique style adds to your overall impression. If you feel that your style of dress attracts the wrong type of men, or gives men the wrong impression about you, you may need to change the way you dress. You might consult a good friend for feedback. If you can't seem to find clothes that are flattering, consider connecting with a professional for help. Check your local department stores—many of the large chains offer free "personal shopper" services. The phone book can help you locate such advisers, known as "image consultants." Or browse a bookstore or library for a self-help book on style.

Search widely. Go places you have never gone before. Meet men who will expose you to new ways of being, new perspectives. As you broaden your horizons, you will increase the fun in your life. And become more interesting to others.

Flirt. To let men know that you are available, you need to communicate your availability. You do this by flirting, engaging in humor, or smiles, a little bit of a taunt, body language, and just plain play. There is something of an art to suggesting that if the circumstances were right, you might be available to a man. When you learn how to make this suggestion without compromising your dignity, men will be all over you with invitations for dating. Men find this kind of subtle seduction irresistible. Flirting well is one of the great arts and powers of femininity. If you don't know how to do it, you will need to practice. Go to the movies and see how it's done. It is very crucial to giving men the correct message—that they should ask you out for a date. The non-verbal communication of flirting encourages a man. When you flirt, you're communicating:

> "I'm interested in you. If you asked me out, and if I said yes, I think we would have a really great time together. I can imagine what it would be like to be near you, filled with the joy, energy, and erotic sensations that we could make together. I'm not sure whether we would ever get physical, but I bet it would feel wonderful if we did. Want to see what could happen between us?"

Develop the art of social conversation. As you encounter men individually, the art of conversation becomes invaluable. In social conversation there is a gentle, easy engagement that switches the talk from one partner to the other. Really good conversation does not consist of a series of questions and answers. That is interrogation, not conversation. Good conversation is fluid, unpredictable, and spins off in exciting directions. It involves listening when the other person is talking, and observing his reactions when you are talking to him.

When you find a man with whom you can enjoy this free and open exchange, you have the potential for some level of friendship. As you converse, show interest in him. A few well-placed questions about his interests, his education, and his work are reasonable, as are reciprocal ones from him. Mannerly people are sensitive to the possibility of intruding; they step lightly. When you see that he does not want to discuss an area, be considerate and avoid it. But be aware— and wary—that many attached men go out to singles events in search of dalliance. Observe his body language. Remember the telltale signs of deception. (See page 21.)

There is a delicate balance between reserve with openness and downright deception. The early stages of conversation with a new man provide good practice in discovering who he is. And he may very well be a captivating conversationalist who is a philanderer.

Many women, in spite of maturity and experience, fear engaging in a conversation with a strange man. If you suffer this way, take heart. Perhaps in the 1950s, a "lady" would *never* speak to a "strange man" to whom she had not been properly introduced. But the nineties are worlds away from the fifties. The practice you get from your many outings will help you to overcome this hesitation. Look forward to a time when engaging in a conversation with a strange man becomes a high art that you enjoy.

Remember the Code principle of honesty, and do not lie at any level. I believe that lying—even "white" lying—compromises the integrity and the credibility of the one who lies. If the man asks you questions you do not want to answer, tell the truth. Say something like "I would rather not discuss that right now; let's talk about the Equal Rights Amendment. . . ." Say no and shift gears rapidly. Practice doing this and you will learn how to preserve your privacy while you maintain the dignity of good manners and your integrity. You might consider developing a collection of all-purpose anecdotes—amusing encounters you or your friends have had. Use them to deflect and direct the conversation when the time is right.

Maintain control of your safety wherever you go. This will require both thoughtful planning and astute observation. Before going into a bar (or anyplace), you should have determined beforehand the safety of the place and what kind of people go there. Figure out the sociology of a place so you can judge its safety. On Saturday nights the lounge in the best hotel in town *won't* feature knife fights and brawls. If it does, move to a different town. Likewise, if you go to a singles dance, you need to be certain that the environment provides for your safety. Plan ahead: Make certain you will be able to go and leave in your own car or a cab. Be sure that the parking lot is brightly lit or—even better—that a valet will bring your car to you at the door. Consider your safety as you would anywhere else. Make sure the backseat is empty before entering your car and driving away. Daytime

163

events tend to minimize these dangers and are equally valid sources of finding good single men.

Go out alone, all by yourself like a big girl. Searching for courtship is an adult activity, just as going out job hunting is.

Ending one interaction to begin another. As you do encounter men, sometimes one man will want more of your time than you should give. Remember, your purpose is to set as many lures as possible. If in talking to one man you decide he is not a candidate, move on. You do not have time to waste when you have decided that he is not a candidate for further interaction. Preserve his ego but move on. Speak to him gently and clearly. You might say something like:

> "John, it was nice meeting you. Thanks for coming over. Now I want to move around the room and meet other people. See you later!"

If he will not permit this, you need to be more forceful. Tell him:

> "Please don't try to detain me. I am sure you will find someone here with whom the chemistry is *mutual.* Good luck with your search."

Then firmly move away. Don't look back. Don't wait for him to give you permission. If he comes toward you later, as often will happen, smile, nod, and move away. Privately take a moment to appreciate your ability to attract men. But keep circulating. If you do this a few times, even the densest man will get the message.

Recognize that even the dullest evening offers a practice field.   Different events will attract a different array of men, and if you are searching widely, you will be continually meeting whole new groups of men. The men that you meet offer you an opportunity to develop your skills. Even when they are dull, obnoxious, assertive, or meek, each man you encounter provides a chance to polish your social skills of tact and grace. Every now and then you might strike fire; but don't worry about how long it takes. Have patience and keep searching. Is it all right to approach a man standing alone at a singles party and introduce yourself? Yes! That's "circulating," not "pursuit."

Focus, as you search, on your increasing power to come and go in full possession of yourself. Enjoy the ever-growing sense of your own developing talents at socializing. Your skills of making other people comfortable as you learn how to grace men with your company will be preparing you for the true elegance that courtship can offer a woman and a man.

Know when to leave.   Most of the social events for singles can be sized up in about two hours. Whether it is a dance, a discussion group, a picnic, or a tennis party, by that time you will have had a sense of the event and the people there. Many of the best events for single people have group sizes of twenty to thirty, and within two hours you will have had a chance to circulate among all the people present. Since socializing three times a week will help build your sense of community, there will probably be many times when two hours will be quite sufficient for you. Discover your own biological rhythm and honor it.

Give yourself enough time to learn how to be comfortable among new people without panicking and running out. But limit your time there so that you can leave and get home to bed early enough to wake refreshed the next day—with further energy for the search. Once you have decided to leave an event, just do it. Enjoy the triumph of being in command of when you come and go. It is a great feeling for many women whose lives have been spent accommodating to other people's schedules.

Take notes when you return home.   Some events will clearly be worthy of engaging in again and again. Others will be less so. If you make notes in your loose-leaf binder, it will help you remember later. For example: "Joe's Bar: Soccer team meets here every Tuesday after their game." Set up a rating system, or note how easy it was to meet new men, the quality of men, how much you enjoyed yourself. As you experience many different opportunities, it may be hard to recall which were the highest-yielding ones. Keep records and refer back to them periodically.

Be yourself.   Wherever you go, whoever you meet, maintain your personal integrity. When you discover a man whose values are different from yours, hold on to yours and feel free to communicate that you perceive these differences. Sometimes the lively discussion of differences initiates a new friendship. Even if it doesn't, you will use your energy well when you learn to be more articulate about your attitudes.

In the process of engagement, some of your attitudes may begin to shift. It is a lot of fun to watch yourself growing and developing.

Learn to convey interest; yet restrain your impulse to pursue. Every now and then you are going to meet a man who sparks your interest. Maybe even inflames it. Now comes the time for restraint. Beyond your clear expression of your enjoyment of him—your smile, your verbal expressions, and perhaps your physical reactions—the pursuit is up to him. Restrain the impulse to pursue him and you will maintain your best self. Let him lead. You follow—by your own choice.

As much as you may want to pursue him, accept the fact that female pursuit is a low-yield activity. Unless you want a marriage in which your power overpowers your husband's, don't pursue such a relationship.

If you disagree with me, go ahead and pursue; but at least know what it is you are doing. If a man cannot get up the energy to pursue you—sad as it is for the moment— he is not worthy of your courtship energies. He may not be the one for you. This is one of the realities of life. The sooner you can recognize this, the sooner you will get to courtship.

LONG-DISTANCE RELATIONSHIPS ARE OKAY WHEN YOU KEEP BUSY IN BETWEEN

A long-distance relationship with someone you meet on a business trip, when there is no possibility of working with the man, can add depth to your search. If you find someone in another state and he pursues you, a romance can be difficult to manage unless one of you is able and willing to move should the romance take off. Mara's experience had a storybook ending.

Mara was a top saleswoman for a major East Coast pharmaceutical company. After a promotion that included a role in training other salespeople, her job took her to California for a training session. There she met Rob, a computer programmer who was single, charming, and kind of sweet. Mara was surprised at how much she liked him because he didn't match her preconceived notions about what "type" she usually liked.

Because he was an out-of-town friend, she was relaxed about letting the friendship take its course. From the beginning he expressed a powerful interest in a romantic relationship with her. In spite of her reluctance because of the distance, she continued to correspond with him and to see him occasionally. He managed to come East, to the suburbs of Philadelphia, for their first shared holiday on Thanksgiving. They spent the four days almost constantly together, and by the time he had left, she was starting to consider whether she might like living in California.

Their romance flourished and they married. For the first year they lived in his house in California. Eventually he transferred his job, and they moved back East to her hometown. The last time I heard from her they were living in Wisconsin, where they had both been able to find good jobs. Neither of them had ever had children, and by age forty-five they were very happy with this marriage, which seemed destined to be a two-person family.

Although these kinds of successful long-distance love affairs may be rare, they do work at times. Don't write off the possibility. If you get involved in such a situation, keep yourself busy three times a week in the meantime.

DON'T CLING

Don't even consider giving your heart away until he has shown that he is ready to do the same, is actively pursuing, and has asked for your commitment. Preserve your integrity to preserve your emotional health. No man enjoys a lovesick female clinging to him when his own feelings have not jelled to romantic love.

AVOID WOMEN WHEN YOU ARE SEARCHING FOR MEN

Nourishing your female relationships is a very important part of your search for courtship. It balances your life and provides warmth and perspective, but it has its appropriate place in your calendar. Courtship searching is not a time for making new women friends or for hanging out with old ones. In order to magnify the opportunities your three sessions a week provide, you will need to direct all your energy to searching for a man or standing alone as you lure one. Avoid falling into the trap of using the two-hour search time for an interesting conversation with a new or old woman friend. Do that other times of the week.

ENGAGING YOUR PURSUERS

Each of the places where single people gather has its own tone. A different set of vibrations. Sensible conduct varies according to the environment. We will look at several environments to show the variations on the theme: bars, ads, classes, and dances.

CLUBBING AND BAR BROWSING

Bars and clubs offer you a chance to practice your skills at flirting, social conversation with strangers, and patience. If you have selected the spots that are peaceful and attract a good crowd, they can be very useful places to go occasionally, maybe once or twice a month. (See Chapter 4 for directions on selecting a bar or club with a theme you find interesting that attracts mannerly people.) Use these places to build your courage and practice your skills. Remember if you flub, you haven't lost much. If you succeed, you improve your skills enormously. Assuming you have found a bar or club that has the right age group, browsing can provide a marvelous opportunity to get out of the house, enjoy social interaction and freedom. To get the most out of this resource, consider using it in four distinct phases: the entry, the perusal, the perching, and the exit.

For your entry, you need to assume a consumer's attitude. Imagine entering a jewelry store or department as if

170

you were going to shop. How do you approach it? Do you worry about what the other people along the counters are going to think of you? Or do you unselfconsciously scan the counters to decide where you would like to look more closely? Do you walk up and down the aisles looking at what is available? Do you occasionally ask to see something more closely if it catches your fancy? And then do you say "thanks very much" and move on when you've seen enough? If jewelry isn't your browsing thing, substitute something that is, and you will get the idea of how to enter a bar or club.

The first two or three minutes of the hour or two you spend at a bar or club require hard work. Hard work because it means overcoming fear, narcissism, and too much focus on yourself and how other people might be seeing you. It really does not matter, for this exercise, whether everyone or no one likes the way you look. What matters is whether *you* see anyone in there who interests you.

Plan to do this exercise with another woman friend or go alone. Going alone is simpler, but for your first visit you may not have the courage. In either event, *enter all by yourself.* As you walk through the front door, move in far enough to clear the path for others who are entering, but go no farther. Then take thirty seconds to *stand still at this threshold.* It may feel like a very long thirty seconds the first time you do it. Do it anyway. Starting to your left, scan all of the men in the bar or club briefly, lightly, in the same way you would scan a jewelry display. (You really do hope to find a jewel—but don't expect that you will.) Should you happen to make eye contact with any one of the men, smile very briefly. Continue scanning. When you finish your visual scan, you will know the room: its size, volume, and age distribution. Now it's time for phase two.

Peruse the place.   After stowing your coat at a coatroom, walk quietly and slowly up and down every nook and cranny to begin slowly dispersing your essence, your perfume scent, or pheromones.[1] You are searching for the place you will perch yourself after you have completed one complete loop of the room. Imagine how you would traverse the place if you were planning to meet a friend, weren't sure which of you had arrived first, and knew that if it was you, you would select a seat—and wait.

Next, perch.   When you complete the perusal loop, which takes about a minute for most normal-size bars or clubs if you walk properly and slowly, repeat the loop again to approach your selected perch. Your hardest work is now completed. Sit at the bar, not at a table or booth.

Having laid the lure, wait to see what it brings—patiently. Stay composed and await an opportunity to give your order for a beverage. If you feel comfortable doing so, engage the bartender in conversation. Whether you order soda or alcohol doesn't really matter. Reflect on your accomplishment. You entered a strange place gracefully, as an adult. You let yourself be observed. As you walked up and down the aisles, men who were there searching for companionship had a chance to know of your presence without being socially

---

[1] Pheromones are naturally occurring chemicals that have attractant properties to the opposite sex. For more on these potent biochemicals, see *Love Cycles: The Science of Intimacy* (New York: Villard Books, 1991).

intruded upon. Whether through scent, sight, or electrical current, the lightness of your being has penetrated the place. Sexual attraction, although reciprocal, demands the man's interest for it to go anywhere at all. Your essence will attract many men once you start engaging the Code.

As you sit quietly, within fifteen to twenty minutes the likelihood is very high that a man will approach and strike up a conversation with you. Be open to this possibility. Keep your eyes level and allow the possibility of eye contact without peering so intently that you overpower him.

An offer of a drink carries no more responsibility than a thank you, and usually the politeness of enjoying a portion of that drink in the company of the person who buys it for you. If you are sure that you have no interest whatsoever in engaging in conversation with the person who offers the drink, say "no thank you" and turn to face a different direction. Your body language should be sufficient to communicate that you do not want to encounter this person. But feel no fear about accepting a drink when you are in a well-mannered environment with an opportunity for a safe exit. Good manners requires that you have a conversation with the person buying you a drink if he tries to engage in one. You don't have to finish your drink if you don't like him, but at least give him two or three minutes in acknowledgment of his generosity.

Engaging your pursuer in a bar or club should be a friendly process in which you hone your skills at mannerly conversation, gentility, and ease of comportment. Should a man behave badly toward you, let him know that you don't like what is happening, and wait to see his response. If it is mannerly and you feel comfortable, feel free to continue the conversation. If poor manners are displayed to you and they do not easily change, move on. Here lies an important opportunity to practice your skills at rejecting what you don't want to accept. A rude man will not get better as you get to know him better. Quite the opposite is true.

Whenever you choose to, end your interaction with any one man so that you can move on to new experiences. You have the right to engage in a conversation when you choose to, and you have the right to end one when you choose to. Exercise this right to increase your sense of well-being and widen your exposure to different men. Keep in mind that in a bar your perch is probably stationary; you won't be able to circulate as you can at a singles party. So turn to your other side, or turn your back to the bar and visually pace the room.

Leave the bar or club. Your departure completes the bar or club "exercise." Leave alone. Always. Every time. Never pick up a man in a bar or club and get into a car with him. Until you have had a chance to know something about a man's character, his values, his ethics, and his attitude toward sexuality with strange women, do not risk the safety of your person with him. No matter how nice he seems, you need time to judge his character.

Other Safety Notes

Leaving with a friend. Until you are sure of yourself in a bar or club environment, it's reasonable to go with a woman friend as long as you separate when you enter. Of course, you have to agree on when you will reunite to leave after pursuing your separate paths inside the bar. Often one person wants to leave much earlier than the other. Negotiate your plan in advance. One solution is to arrive in separate cars at the same time. Then you can leave separately if you want to. At some places you will feel safe leaving alone. At places you go to often, you will soon make friends with others you can safely ask to walk you out to your car when you are ready to leave. Or you and the woman friend you came with can agree on a preset time to leave together.

Time your attendance carefully. As the evening wears on, more alcohol tends to be consumed. Consider scheduling your bar or club outing at the end of the workday and avoiding the second wave at nine or ten o'clock. The sociology of each bar and club varies. When you discover what the drinking habits are at the particular bars, you will be better able to choose the ones you will go to and when you will frequent them. Your aim is to avoid drunk people. The more alcohol a man consumes, the less he will be in command of himself.

In spite of their downsides, bars and clubs provide marvelous opportunities to get out socially and practice your skills. Enjoy them carefully.

A Success Story

And, contrary to popular opinion, you *can* meet someone nice in a bar. Felicia met her husband in a bar and has enjoyed a good marriage for five years. Consider what happened to her.

Felicia was thirty-six when she decided she had had enough of single life and wanted to find a husband and start a family. She tried ads. She went to singles clubs. She went to bars. Felicia was out at least three times a week and had a cheerful attitude about her role in setting standards and finding a husband. She had a "history," but she kept it to herself. And she dressed well.

As a sales executive for a national distribution company, she found herself in Philadelphia at the end of the business day at least twice a week. She got into the habit of stopping into one of the neighborhood bars of that city's Society Hill section, a bar frequented by an after-work crowd of well-dressed men and women in their thirties, forties, and fifties. She developed a camaraderie with many of these regulars and would "hang out" for about an hour when she dropped in. It was fun to stop in, check out the scene, and have a drink as she lingered among old and new acquaintances.

And then one evening it happened. Harold, a casual friend of one of her casual friends, was introduced to Felicia. He was a physiologist who did research at one of the city's major universities. He was smitten instantly and she could see this. The rest is history!

I wouldn't count on finding your mate in a bar or a club, but I have seen it happen successfully.

RESPONDING TO YOUR AD REPLIES

Occasionally, your two-hour event will be best spent at home. Now is your opportunity to take out your "wine list" and search through the letters for the best one to call. You already know that he will welcome your call. He pursued you first by sending the letter!

If a man writes and gives you his address but not his phone number, write back and suggest that he send a note with his phone number in it. If you really want to spice things up and make it simple for him, give him a stamped self-addressed postcard (to your personal P.O. box). Do not send him your address or phone number simply because you like his letter. It is too soon to judge his safety.

Do not give your last name, telephone number, or address until you have been able to conclude this is a safe thing to do. A correspondence can be very pleasant, but protect your safety. Until you have his phone number, you cannot assume that this man is free of commitments. Protecting your safety is an essential part of searching for courtship. Build it into the design of everything you do. As with men you meet in a bar, it takes time to evaluate whether or not he is safe. Try to talk to him on the phone long enough to be able either to reject the possibility of further encounters with him or to accept the idea of meeting him.

If you decide to reject the connection, exercise gracious-ness with a tactful good-bye. Your closing remarks should include elements of the following:

"Well, John, it has been interesting talking with you. Thanks very much for answering my ad. That was very nice of you to do. I wish you good luck in your search for a partner. After talking with you, I realize that you and I are on differ-ent life paths, and for me, a meeting would not be good. I'm going to go now. Thanks again. Good night."

177

Recognize that this will probably cause his feelings to be hurt because you *are* rejecting him. When it comes time to reject someone, do it cleanly, gently, and swiftly. The sooner you do it, the smaller the smart.

If you decide you do like him, continue to converse so that he gets the idea of asking you out. Unless he suggests it, I recommend that you not bring up the subject. Let him pursue. If he does suggest it, arrange to meet him in a neutral safe place, perhaps for coffee, lunch, or a drink. The first meeting should allow you both privacy and safety of entry and exit. There are many such places in any city or suburb. Whether meeting at a coffee shop in a shopping center or on the college green of a local campus, ideally you should park in a place where your car is not easily picked out from among the others if the meeting goes badly and you want to leave quickly. If the conversation continues and he does not suggest getting together, end it. Tell him you have enjoyed talking with him and will have to go now.

If he says he would like to call you sometime and asks for your number, say you would rather not; tell him that if he wants to meet for a coffee hour, you are willing and you can set that up right now. If he objects or tries to force you to defend your position, that's a measure of his lack of respect for your feelings. Stick to your position and tell him that you don't like what he is doing. At the worst, you will soon end the conversation. Meanwhile, you will gain practice in asserting your own dignity. At best, he will apologize and honor what you request. Trust your instincts anytime you feel unsafe. It is better to be too conservative than to risk your safety.

Going out Alone

RONNIE'S EXPERIENCE WITH AD MEN

Ronnie, a forty-four-year-old woman who ran her own art consulting business, attended a workshop to learn how to search for courtship. She was very attractive, successful in her business, but had just about given up on the possibility of finding good men. I told her to relax and just try the ideas we reviewed in the workshop.

About eight weeks later when I saw her at a business meeting, she was glowing. She crossed the room to tell me how much fun she was having with her ad replies. She had placed an ad in *Philadelphia* magazine and was astounded at the quantity and quality of the responses she had received. She told me she had dates lined up for the next three weeks with nine different men. She said she had just gone out with several in the last couple of weeks, and each of them, to her surprise, was courteous, pleasant, and respected the fact that because she had placed her ad he, no doubt, had lots of competition.

Ronnie was going a little overboard, and I guess I couldn't blame her. After a three-year dry spell, Ronnie's use of the ads as her sole source of meeting new men was understandable, but it is not how I suggest you handle your ad replies. A diversified approach will bring you the best results.

Regardless, Ronnie was feeling enthusiasm about her single life and her dating potential for the first time in years. I kept quiet. Still, I look forward to finding out whether she has diversified her activities.

GIVING A PARTY

If you know three single people, you have the basis for giving a marvelous party. Pick a date, especially one that is likely to be desirable for single people such as Thanksgiving, New Year's Day, Christmas Eve, or any other holiday when married people tend to keep to themselves.

Talk to three to seven single friends of either gender. Ask each to participate by finding three other acquaintances of good character. If you are speaking to a woman friend, her task will be to bring one other woman and two single, available men that she personally is not interested in. If your friend is a man, his task will be to bring one other single man and two single women, all of whom are not involved in relationships with one another. Seven friends' acquaintances becomes a party for twenty-eight people. One of your friends does not have to invite another woman since you are that odd person out.

Each of the core group of friends should be assigned a share of the work. One group might be assigned wine, another plates and cups, another crudités and dip. In exchange for your providing the initiative, date, organization, and space, you get a group of people coming to your home who generate the good cheer and the refreshments for the party. Not a bad deal!

When everyone has a stake in the refreshments and the invitations, it enhances the excitement. Consider making it a dressy evening. People who get dressed up for a party bring an extra excitement that goes with the dressy clothes.

Set a time limit for the party, say from six to nine on a Sunday evening or from five to eight on Christmas Eve. Ask for the list of names and addresses so that you can mail out invitations and maps. In this way, you will know who is coming to your home—as you should! Ask for some details about each of the three acquaintances your friends have invited. Then as people arrive, you will have some basis for introductions. Most important: Prepare to enjoy the party just as much as everybody else does.

Try variations on this theme, perhaps three times a year, and you will broaden your social circle as you generate interesting events for yourself and for others. You will also make new friends, who, in turn, may invite you to their parties and introduce you to ever-widening circles of single friends.

JANE'S EXPERIENCE WITH SINGLE PARTY GIVING

Jane was twenty-six when she first decided to embrace the eleven principles and redirect her energies. First she spent several months making her home dramatic. Then she felt ready to create her first party. It was late November, and a lonely Thanksgiving provided the impetus to think about Christmas Eve. She figured that together her living and dining rooms could easily hold thirty or more people. She chose a Christmas Eve tree-trimming and supper party and set about to find her guests.

At her office she had formed casual friendships, and enjoyed a nice camaraderie with George, Henry, and Joan. She invited each of them to come to her party and bring three friends: two of the opposite gender, one of the same gender. She asked each to take responsibility for a specific part of the menu, and they each said yes. She also asked for the names, addresses, and phone numbers of their guests. Her two closest friends, Beth and Glynis, each agreed to participate in like manner. Jane also invited Clara, a fellow student from her weekly cooking class; she asked her to take charge of the desserts. From her women's group at church she had met Frances and Loe, single women of about her age. She invited each of them and asked Frances to take charge of the wine and Loe to supply the cheese and crackers.

In this way, with relative ease, she had organized a nice-size party for thirty-two people to meet new people. She sent an invitation to each and got ready to decorate her home for the holidays. As the weeks passed, anticipation of the party created a kind of optimistic buzz wherever she went—to church, her cooking course, her office. Everyone was excited. Jane had generated good feelings and enthusiasm about the holiday to come and the potential for making new friends. The party turned out to be terrific. Thirty-one people came and filled her house with high spirits and good humor. At her party she met Bob, a man she had begun to date by mid-January.

CLASS AND COURSE CONDUCT

Classes are a marvelous opportunity to expand your horizons without any pressure to perform socially. Consider making a course or two each year an important part of your social agenda.

When you sign up for a class, you can usually anticipate from two to fifteen meetings. Select a course that interests you, and whether or not you meet interesting people, you will have someplace to go once or twice a week for its duration. The longer the course, the more opportunity you will have to get to know your fellow classmates. It often takes two or three sessions before people come to recognize one another, nod hello, chat, and maybe suggest having coffee afterward. If the class members turn out to be the wrong age or gender, relax. The class will serve your other social or spiritual needs. It will be a place for unpressured time in the community of others.

STEPS AT A SINGLES DANCE

Many groups, from ethnic centers to churches to business enterprises devoted to singles, host dances on a regular basis. See Chapter 4 to get started on your list of these. One nice thing about a dance is that it requires no more planning beyond your Tuesday night scheduling. My city, Philadelphia, for example, usually has at least three different dances available exclusively to single adults each week. Sometimes many more.

Select one and go to it. Try arriving within a half hour of the starting time, when not too many people have congregated. It is good practice for you to enter a room where other single people have congregated in hopes of meeting and having fun with like-minded people of the opposite sex. Singles dances are like any other dance—you have a right to ask a man to dance (on the ladies' requests) and to say "no thank you" should a man ask you. Initially, I suggest that you accept when a man asks you for a dance. Getting used to dancing with a stranger will reduce your anxiety. Most men are pretty nice at singles dances. If you are uncertain about a man who asks you for a slow dance, say that you would prefer to wait for a fast dance and then would be happy to give it a try. Slow dancing has the possibility for close encounters.

If a man who is dancing with you holds you more closely than you like, take charge. Use your arms and your elbows to create a distance between you that is acceptable to your comfort level. Or tell him you don't want to be held so tightly. Remember principles two and four:

> Accept the legitimacy of your own needs and communicate what you want.

Don't be embarrassed about asserting your needs for comfort. If you are not shy and you enjoy the physical contact, you can allow the dancing embrace of a strange man in a safe setting. Trust your instincts. After the dance, say thank you and swiftly move away if you are not interested in any further exchange. This is your right. Learning how to exercise this right will build your strength of character and your self-esteem.

Sometimes the same people tend to frequent the same dance clubs, and should you start returning, you will get to recognize the core group who show up frequently. You do not want to cling to these people if they are not candidates for a dating relationship. When such a man approaches you for a dance, depending on the availability of more desirable men in the room, you might say, "No thank you. I am here to meet some new people. I hope you will want to also."

When a man you like keeps approaching you at a dance yet never suggests getting together elsewhere for a date, you should stop wasting your time with him. If you want him to ask you out, indicate your availability, but do not pursue him at the dance hall. The main object of the dance setting is to have a social encounter in which you have graceful physical motion with new men. It's also an opportunity for getting out of the house to enjoy a fun social evening. Maybe you'll even learn to mambo. . . .

SUMMING UP

Now is the time to go out to play. Going out to play is different from going out to work or going out on dates. And the distinction is key to your preparation for courtship. Going out is going public, getting yourself out to socialize with single men. You will fine-tune the important interpersonal skills of conversation, mingling, flirting, and circulating. You will learn to live the Code by practicing it. As you launch yourself into the world of single mingling, you will conduct yourself with dignity, confidence, self-possession, a sense of humor, and joie de vivre. This is *fun*. Going out is an adventure that you will lead as well as follow. You're off to meet men who excite you, engage you, and exhilarate you. Going out is a dress rehearsal for the topic of the next chapter: dating.

SIX

Formal Dating: Rules and Roles

The elegant crane engages in a very delicate formal dance. Like an ancient courtly waltz, the movements are very stylized. Slowly they move back and forth engaging their ritual dance steps as they circle toward, then away and back toward each other. If the moment is right for connection, they mate. Otherwise they just drift away.

With the high seriousness appropriate to so important a life
   experience
The woman searching for courtship engages in formal dating.
This creates the climate for obtaining respectful treatment.

Formal dating is the next crucial stage on your courtship journey. Many woman I talk to insist, "But I have been dating . . . and dating . . . and dating." Perhaps. But maybe you have been "casual dating," an activity synonymous with "going out with," "sleeping with," or "passing time" with men. What I have in mind is far more structured, deliberate, and purposeful, which is why I've termed it formal dating. This type of dating is something quite different from the

186

contemporary behavior of men and women in the nineties, but it is not new.

FORMAL DATING DEFINED

A search for courtship requires a type of dating that has been in existence for centuries. Dating is a social process in which a man asks a woman out for the romantic purpose of getting to know her and becoming known to her. Formal dating is social intercourse expressly intended to explore the possibility of courtship and marriage.

The male pursuit of formal dating is clearly set apart from the male pursuit of a convenient sex object. He conducts himself formally when approaching women for dates, but informally when approaching them for sex. Women as "sex objects" is a discussion topic in the locker room or bar. The woman he dates with the hope of marriage is the one he tells his mother about. He doesn't talk about her in the locker room because she is his jewel. Women who engage in formal dating conduct themselves formally—accepting or refusing a date invitation.

When you are ready to search for courtship, formal dating takes the place of casual dating. You decide what standards to set and follow. You reset them whenever you are ready to direct the course of your journey. In other words, you can decide where you want to go. You can take aim. And you can get there when you take charge of your future.

When you take charge of your love life and engage the rules and roles of the Code, the standards you set will bring good men to you. The rules and roles that help you to date in a way that leads to courtship and marriage are quite specific.

FORMAL DATING: RULES AND ROLES

When you are ready for marriage, you need to date men formally. The first rule is don't rush it. Be patient and hold to your standards. Have faith in yourself and you will make it happen. Meanwhile, as a sophisticated woman, you should recognize that things move most gracefully when they develop according to their natural order. Love grows deeper as a good relationship evolves. Before there is deep love, there is a budding love. As all of nature teaches, there is a developmental stage in the unfolding of each living process. In a relationship that will grow into a long-term bond, growth must evolve at its own pace. Like the blooming of a rose, the shoots come first, then the buds. And the potential flower slowly swells, opens, and finally only with time will yield its full richness.

There is a story about a man who spots a chrysalis in the grass. Coming closer, he notices a butterfly about to emerge. The process is too slow, so he blows warm air on the chrysalis, hoping to speed things along. The butterfly emerges, thanks to the bystander's breath. The man is pleased with himself until he notices that the beautiful creature's wings are not fully formed; it cannot fly. You should fly, but only when the time is right.

The journey from meeting a man to an ever-deepening intimacy with him can offer a valuable life experience. Allow yourself the pleasures that an artful courtship can provide. Take it slow in order to experience it more fully. Meanwhile, as you date formally, keep your life so filled with other activities that you are able to wait while romance takes its course. Use your resource list of places to go, and once a week fill out your calendar to go out and play three times a week.

Think of dating as a highly choreographed dance for the purpose of courtship—one in which the man and the woman both have roles to play and rules to follow. Performed with grace, the reciprocal roles of dating heighten the possibilities for romance. When you set your own rules, requiring that you be treated with respect and honor, you provide a solid foundation for your soft and vulnerable emotions to safely unfold. The rigidity of the rules supports the fluidity of the dance. Choreographed appropriately, dating serves the man and the woman. The rules provide a structure for each of you to evaluate the other's potential as you preserve your emotional security and dignity.

Although in courtship a man pursues a woman, women are in charge, because we can choose. The woman sets lures. Going out three times a week should allow for enough of them. Then the man extends the invitation of a date. *You* accept, modify, or reject his invitation.

Sometimes a man extends a half-hearted invitation, suggesting it might be nice to "see each other sometime," and you are not sure whether he is asking you for a date. When this happens, ask for clarity. Say:

"Are you asking me for a date? Do you want to set a time?"

Although for some women this is an easy question to ask, for others it feels too direct. These women might mellow their question with a preamble.

189

"How nice. It does sound terrific to get together. Is there a specific date you had in mind? Shall I get my calendar out?"

If he says no, whether directly or by a vague non-answer ("Uh, I'll let you know"), you have your answer. He has not asked you for a date. But if he is shy, scared of rejection, or confused, your question about calendars may get the ball rolling so a date can be scheduled. Just remember, it is the man who must get up the energy to pursue the woman. It is futile and a waste of your energy to try to reverse this process. Doing so will consume your time and deflect your path. When you want marriage, focus on men who court you and turn away from those who won't.

How Many Men?

There are no good statistics I can cite. Yet, from what I have seen, I would estimate that an attractive woman engaging the Code in a large city can expect to date about 125 men before she finds her husband. What fun!

Take a look at Table 6.1, which shows a segment of Ellyce's actual journal, covering one seven-month period of her search for courtship. She kept the journal to record her reactions to her private life. She recorded whatever emotions she was feeling—confusion, excitement, for example—or whenever she just wanted to capture a memory. On the inner back cover of the journal, she kept a record of each date she scheduled. This list consisted of the names and the dates she went out with each man. Occasionally, Ellyce would take time to reread her journal and try to draw some conclusions about what and who her life had brought her.

TABLE 6.1. ELLYCE'S DATING LIST

George	6/30
David	7/6, 7/8, 7/14
Eli	7/7, 7/11, 7/13
Stephen	7/9, 8/3, 8/12, 9/9, 9/15, 9/22, 9/23, 9/28, 10/11, 11/2, 11/8, 12/6, 12/16, 12/22
Tom	7/20
Herman	8/4
Phillip	8/8
Karl	8/17, 8/18
Allan	8/19, 8/25, 9/27, 10/1, 10/7, 10/14, 10/21, 10/24, 10/30, 11/7, 12/31, 1/14, 1/22
Jim	10/12, 10/27
Robert	10/16, 10/28
Craig	11/5
Bob	11/7
Paul	1/12
Graham	11/25, 12/1
Hugh	12/28, 12/29, 12/30, 1/1, 1/4, 1/7, 1/10, 1/12, 1/13, 1/15, 1/18, 1/19, 1/21

Although it may seem as if Ellyce did a lot of dating, she went out only three times a week until she started to receive offers for dates. Whenever she hit a dry spell and had no date offers coming, she started going out again to places where single men gathered.

The journal shows that Ellyce has dated sixteen men: from George at the top to Hugh at the bottom. Table 6.1 includes, in the order of occurrence, the dates and times she went out with each man.

Look beyond the apparent randomness of Ellyce's dates and you'll see some helpful patterns. With seven men—George, Tom, Herman, Phillip, Craig, Bob, and Paul—there were only one-time dates. Think of these not as duds or dead ends but as relationships with a finite duration. With four men—Karl, Jim, Robert, and Graham—there were two dates. Two—David and Eli—were triples. And three men lasted longer: Stephen—fourteen dates; Allan—thirteen dates; and Hugh—thirteen dates. Between her second (8/3) and third (8/12) dates with Stephen, Ellyce dated Herman (8/4) and Phillip (8/8)—she's still keeping her options open and meeting new men. Almost a month (8/25 to 9/27) passes between her second and third dates with Allan, but Ellyce is busy—she dates Stephen (9/9, 9/15, 9/22, 9/23). And even when she's dating Stephen fairly intensely and frequently, she nevertheless goes out with Craig on 11/5 and Bob on 11/7.

Does Ellyce's schedule seem incredibly rich and busy? Impossible for you to duplicate? Have faith. I have seen this method work over and over again—in spite of the cynicism, wariness, or weariness with which women began the process.

GETTING THERE

It does take effort and energy to get to the point Ellyce did. Courtship is not something that just happens. It is something you *make* happen. You are the prime mover. Make a commitment to yourself and your future. If you think of this commitment as giving yourself what you're entitled to—a real path to a courtship that can lead to marriage—your only remaining question is "Don't I deserve it?" I think women owe themselves 6 hours, out of their 168 hours a week, devoted totally to their own need for love and romance. After all, it is less than 4 percent of your total time. Isn't filling this major life need worth 4 percent of your time?

Whatever portion of your six hours is not taken up by formal dates should be filled in your date book for its dress rehearsal—"going out to play." And you should go out at least three times a week. Whether dating or "going out," by socializing regularly, you will set lures and emit the vibrations that attract men and, eventually, courtship.

Remember principle nine, *especially* when you feel down.

You recognize that a positive attitude engenders personal magnetism for attracting legitimate courtship candidates.

Getting out three times a week will help keep you cheerful and give you a positive attitude. Imagine walking into a dance hall or a singles party and recognizing at least ten people from previous singles parties you have been to. Imagine the good feelings you can have being among a group of single people who have gathered to play. It starts to be fun. Meanwhile, as you practice and develop your independent behavior and your "luring" talents, you will expand your social opportunities, enhance your cheerfulness, and increase your energy. Your spirits will lift.

Don't be in a rush to get through the dating and courtship months of your life. Live them. Savor them. If you keep an open attitude as you meet men, you will add a new kind of social pleasure to your life. Relish the richness that a variety of men can offer. When you begin dating in a positive way, you are building a valuable history. For women who allow themselves the privilege of discovery, an adventure can unfold. Take a grand, long journey. Enjoy the high art of an elegant, slowly paced process with each man that you meet. When you're happily married, you'll have wonderful times to look back on.

FAST-FORWARD TO YOUR FUTURE

Take a mental journey. Imagine yourself ten years from now and look back on the time when you took charge of your life and started searching for courtship in a carefully choreographed manner. Imagine the pleasure you will feel when you remember all the different men you dated and how much fun you had. Now is the time to cultivate that pleasure so that you can build—into your future—a remembrance of your past for when it becomes your present. A journal will help you sort out your history—even as you develop it.

Rejoice in the opportunity to date many men. Whether you are twenty or sixty, the men you meet can stimulate your energy. As you engage in conversations, spend time alone, and journey with a large variety of men, reflect on some biological fundamentals. Courtship is, above all, a healthy, life-enhancing activity. It should be obvious that it is unhealthy to get too intimate, too quickly, with too many men. A gesture as innocuous as a kiss exchanges bodily fluids. Even "harmless" skin-to-skin contact leaves you a different person. On each person's skin, a particular bacterial flora lives in concert with the human being—his unique dermal environment. When you rub your skin against another person's, you exchange these different bacteria. Recent studies have shown that human skin is continually turning over, sloughing off a top layer of cells and debris into the atmosphere. When you rub up against someone's skin you probably get a lot more than you realize, substances that can affect your own body. Be kind to your body and go slowly with new men. Too many different foreign "adaptations" can overstress the immune system. Physical intimacy should *follow* rather than precede a closely developing friendship.[1]

WRITE A JOB DESCRIPTION

Formal dates give you the opportunity to thoroughly evaluate a man's character and attributes. A shopping list of what you truly value will help to guide you in your search. Think of it as a job description for a *very* important position you want to fill—your husband. Take a look at Table 6.2, "Envisioning Your Mate." Follow its format and evaluate each new man you date. As time goes by, you will probably fine-tune this list of what you really want in a mate.

Remember, intelligent beings learn from experience. As

---

[1] According to the NIH Office of Research on Women's Health, there are between 15 and 20 million women in the U.S. chronically infected with either genital herpes or human papilloma virus (warts). These diseases can spread through skin contact even when no telltale sign of their presence exists. They increase the risk of genital cancers and infertility as well. These are just two of the myriad of skin-transferred diseases that infect the population. A cautious attitude about intimacy can preserve your health.

According to Celso R. García, M.D., emeritus professor of gynecology at the University of Pennsylvania School of Medicine, even monogamous partners who return to each other after a celibate summer apart frequently trigger skin (genital) infections when they resume relations. Apparently the resumed skin-to-skin contact transfers newly acquired airborne infections.

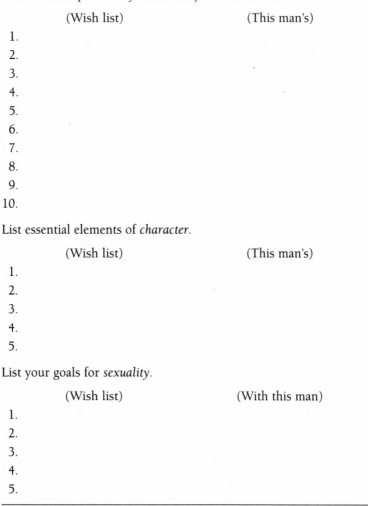

TABLE 6.2. ENVISIONING YOUR MATE (A JOB DESCRIPTION)

Make a list of *personality* attributes you want in a mate.

(Wish list)	(This man's)
1.	
2.	
3.	
4.	
5.	
6.	
7.	
8.	
9.	
10.	

List essential elements of *character.*

(Wish list)	(This man's)
1.	
2.	
3.	
4.	
5.	

List your goals for *sexuality.*

(Wish list)	(With this man)
1.	
2.	
3.	
4.	
5.	

you date, if you are open to new experiences, you will discover new qualities in some men—qualities you never saw before. As you encounter them, you may discover how important they are to your happiness.

196

Let's consider the combined reactions of other women who completed Table 6.2 for the first time.

What Women Want

Some *personality attributes* that women in courtship workshops listed were:

- humorous
- psychologically aware
- self-confident
- financially competent
- healthy
- very playful
- wants children
- handy
- socially graceful
- capable of communication
- a positive attitude toward his life
- not narcissistic
- nonaddictive personality (nonsmoker, not an alcoholic, not a drug user)
- curious
- dignified
- spiritually connected to a religion
- likes his job
- personal cleanliness
- considerate
- in good emotional health

The *elements of character* are more important than the personality attributes. That's why I have classified them as "essential." In the workshops women developed increasingly longer lists of essential character elements they look for. These included:

- ethical
- loyal
- compassionate
- living with integrity
- self-disciplined
- humility
- spirituality
- strength of conviction
- generosity of spirit
- self-controlled, prudent
- respectful attitude toward others
- honest
- reliable

Finally, in their *goals for sexuality* (not relevant in the early stages of dating but important later), a number of qualities emerged. These included:

- patient
- playful (willing to explore new "games")
- communicating during sex
- complementary sizes to enable us to fit well together
- ability to combine passion, spirit, and emotion during a sexual encounter
- his hunger for passion has to be greater than mine
- experimental
- unselfish in bed
- sexually functional (not impotent)

A wish list is useful. But reality testing is necessary.

We list personality attributes first to help you broaden your job description. The wish list is rarely completely fulfilled, but it serves a good purpose anyway. Imagine you were running an office and needed to find someone who would come in regularly to clear away the trash, vacuum, and dust. You would probably write up a job description and put out the word that you were looking, and you might place an ad. Then you would begin interviewing applicants. Meanwhile, as the trash continued to build and the candidates continued to arrive, a time would come when you would stop interviewing and make your choice. So it is with searching for a husband. You make your list. You know what you are looking for. You know what is highly desirable. Then, because life is finite, you decide how long you are willing to wait and what qualities you really must have before you can connect.

Dating Is Not a Commitment

Often when you date a man, you will conclude that it is better to separate. This will keep happening until you find your husband. Each time it does, you will need to end the relationship and get on with your search. Keep clearing the decks and "going out to play" three times a week. This means going back to your resource loose-leaf and filling three events a week in your appointment book. Meanwhile, the men you date will be doing the same thing.

Sometimes a perfectly nice man will decide to stop asking you out. Whatever his reasons, this is his right and it's wise to accept these inevitable rejections for what they can provide: an opportunity to cultivate your humility. The search for courtship continues—either until you find the right man or you decide to stop searching.

Searching purposefully makes good use of your time. The longer you search, the wider your circle of friends will grow, the less lonely you will be, and the more self-possessed and appreciative you will become. I say this because I have seen it work. Among women who are searching for courtship, following the eleven principles of the Code of Courtship, their self-esteem was high and their energy up even during the dry periods when there was nobody asking them out for dates. The very process of following those eleven principles keeps a woman growing, evolving, and cheerful. It increases her dignity and makes her feel strong.

Your Personal Challenge

Keep a sense of humility and perspective. As you begin to make a list of what you want, challenge yourself to see how *you* would be rated by the men you date. This gives you an idea of how fair you are in forming your judgments.

Give yourself time to think about the issues. You need enough information to form sound judgments. What if he suffered an injury that rendered him no longer able to perform sexually? Would you still love to be with him? It's a very important question because life brings unexpected blows. Let them percolate through your awareness.

Be open to changing your requirements as you date more men. Remember, too, that once you find a man to date and he becomes a close and dear friend, each of you is going to change in order to coexist. As you discover the many ways in which you can grow and change, consider that a man *can* change when he knows what you need. Both his personality attributes and his attitudes toward sex should mold to the needs of the woman he courts. As do yours—except for timing. Courteous people wait for their partner to be ready. They don't push for something (like sex) sooner than the slower one is ready.

When his attitude is positive, when he wants to try to meet your needs, and his character is good, you have found a candidate for courtship.

Don't try to change the essential elements of his character. Character is less mutable than behavioral, personality, and sexual traits. Think long and hard about the character elements you require. No matter what he says about his character, judge him by what he actually does. If he says he is honest but cheats on his insurance claims, you have important information about his character.

Consider the conversation and behavior of each man you date to determine whether his character meets your standards. If it does, and he is actively pursuing you, you have a good chance of building something wonderful with him. If he does not have the qualities of character you need, he isn't likely to develop them later. Character is formed over the course of many years. Molded slowly. By the time a man is mature enough to ask for dates in advance, and actively pursue courtship, the elements of his character have formed, solidified, and become the essential part of who he is. Other elements of personality and conduct can change and probably will. In vibrant love relationships people grow and change.

Seek and You Will Find!

The idea in searching is to determine what you are seeking. You reflect, adjust, adapt, and you keep looking. With an open heart, you are likely to find your man. As you learn to modify your requirements, you find what you seek. As an explorer, be open to the discovery of each man's essential being, knowing that you become richer as you come to know different ways of being. Is he deep, kind, gentle, or mean? Keep a clearheaded vision and observe in order to learn. Listen to what he tells you. Ask him questions about the meaning of what he tells you. Ask him what he wants from a woman, what he is looking for. And from what you learn form your own intelligent judgment.

Remember the attitudes:

- Deciding to be in charge of your own life using truthfulness and optimism
- Counting your blessings
- Acknowledging and confronting your pain
- Recognizing that you will make mistakes and learn from them

Unless they are planning to deceive you, most men are delighted to have you know them. When they sense an open attitude, they tend to express themselves more freely. If you can avoid activating a man's defenses, he is likely to tell you what is in his heart. As you suspend judgment long enough to hear him, ask him questions when you are not sure about what you have heard. When you ask for clarification, in a nonjudgmental tone, you are likely to learn what he is thinking. And how he behaves. You will be rewarded with the discovery of the best part of each man. People tend to rise to the opportunity you give them to be known. And to reveal themselves in the process. When he feels known, he will feel less alone. What a gift you have the power to bestow! And look at your reward: a clear look into the soul of the man before you decide whether to entwine your life with his.

Meanwhile, women also have their anxieties, emotional insecurities, and a need to be known. Unfortunately, from my experience and most of the psychological studies, it seems that men are much less able to reassure women than women can men. Perhaps that's one of the reasons why we, as women, need other women friends so much and why men tend not to have friendships that bond each other the way women do. We go where we can get what we need. I think it is good to keep nurturing your women friendships and being nurtured by them as you offer to men the kind of openness and kindness that will help nurture them as well. Whether or not it is fair, for the most part, it seems to be the reality. Men and women are different and have different qualities they can offer to each other.

Behave as if you are self-possessed (even when you don't feel this way), and in time you will become self-possessed. This quality is worth striving for. He may even begin to know himself better as he experiences dating a woman who is self-possessed, clearheaded, kindhearted, and considerate. If he learns that your sexuality is not trivial to you, that its full expression is not on the menu for that day, he may rise to your requirements. Your requirement that a man respect your wishes to delay sex will help you screen for respectful men, exactly the kind you want.

SEXUAL EXPECTATIONS

Don't be surprised when your expectations don't match those of your date. Ask him detailed questions to discover what his expectations are. Consider Susan's experience:

It was the end of dinner, on a first date that Susan had with George. Over coffee, George leaned over, stared deeply into Susan's eyes, and told her:

"I can't wait to go to bed with you. Can I sleep with you tonight?"

Though a little taken aback, Susan looked right back into George's eyes and said:

"How wonderful that you feel that way! What exactly do you want?"

"What do you mean?" he asked. (Now it was his turn to be knocked off-balance!)

"Do you want me just for tonight? [then, puckishly] Will you still respect me in the morning?"

George looked down at his plate. The silence grew thick between them. Finally, after what seemed like forever, he told her that he was attracted to her, wanted to be with her, and had some confusion about what he wanted. Susan looked back at him and said:

"That's okay. I am glad to know you feel that kind of attraction. I do too. But I'm not ready to act on it yet. Sex is

204

something I can't do with a man before I know him well and trust him. He has to be my best friend.

"I really like you. Let's just see how things go and not rush it."

Relieved, George said:

"Okay."

And the tension of the moment began to dissolve.

Susan conveyed an attitude of self-possession, clearheadedness, compassion, and consideration for George's feelings, and a nonpromiscuous nature. If George is truly available for courtship and likes what he sees in Susan, he will be back. If his objective is to satisfy a momentary surge of lust, he may not ask her out again. *Either way, she wins.* She retains her well-being and continues to explore among the men she finds. She will find her man sooner or later.

Dating and Passion

Don't misunderstand. It is fine to want the pleasure of passion. The fire that ignites and overwhelms the senses offers an important life wonder, but passion can be dangerous. You need to be careful so you enjoy passion when and where your safety is assured. Experienced in your best interest, passion leaves you feeling wonderful. Not abandoned or bruised or shocked to discover that last night's consuming physical passion is this morning's breakfast table irritation or embarrassment. Take the time to search carefully and judge slowly. You can't lose when your search is for courtship. If the chemistry is there, the delay will *heighten* the passion when it is finally expressed.

Remember, sexual attraction—or electricity—*is* a prerequisite for romantic love. Although you might delay its flowering, you *do* want to nurture the bud. Cautiously.

How to Test Electric Potential

There is no mistaking it: When the chemistry is there between you and a man, good feelings abound. Just being in the presence of such a man should activate your energy, make you forget about your bedtime, make you feel more attractive, more intelligent, more alive.

Scientists have not pinpointed the elusive nature of sexual attraction, but we all recognize its existence. And scientists are working to close the gap. Research presented at a recent meeting of the International Academy of Sex Research suggested some answers.

For many years Drs. Alan Dixson and Craig Bielert have studied the sexual behavior patterns in primates. What these scientists found may apply to human sexual attractions (after all, we *are* primates). In the summer of 1991, Dixson and Bielert described their experiments to the international assemblage of reproductive scholars in Ontario.

They observed that before mating, animals often gaze intently at the face of their intended partner. If access to seeing the face was denied (by the experimenter), mating was disrupted. Conclusion: Face-to-face contact before copulation apparently serves some biological requirement.

A few days after their formal presentation, I found myself at the same breakfast table with Dixson and Bielert. I asked them for more specifics from their studies. Was it the face or was it eye contact? I wondered. Their answer matched my intuition. *Eye contact,* rather than face-to-face contact, seems to be crucial for a successful sexual connection. They told me that other researchers had discovered that when primates gazed into each other's eyes in anticipation of a sexual encounter, their cortical neurons[2] started firing actively. Primates that are about to have sex excite the electrical firing patterns in each other's brains. Are people wired the same way? Probably, but no research has yet been published to confirm this.

In my own research and codiscovery of human sexual pheromones, I have focused a great deal of intellectual energy on the attractive force between men and women. My conclusion is pretty basic. I think electricity between people is first played out in the brain and nervous system. When it comes to a long-term partnership, it doesn't matter if the initial electric charge is felt in the genitals. (All the more reason to delay sex during dating.) What matters is the charge to the brain. If your "brain batteries" are charged in the presence of a man, don't worry if your sexual response is still dormant. When you live according to the Code of Courtship, you're a long way from needing to evaluate sexual love when you first start to date a man. But know that the electrical charge you feel signals a "chemical attraction."

What does this "brain buzz" feel like? It could be a sensa-

---

[2] The cortical region is the outer part of the brain that forms the bulk of its "gray matter." This region is more developed in the more evolved primates than in the intellectually simpler mammals.

tion in your head, a sudden body urge that makes you stand up straight or inhale deeply. It could be a rush of blood that causes your heart to thump. All of this signals excitement, a physiologic response to the presence of this man.

Enjoy these sensations but don't just go with their flow. Check out his other qualities first. If he doesn't meet your standards of character, a sexual connection could be harmful —or at least divert you from your ultimate purpose. Take the time you need to check him out before you let him into your heart or your bed.

Meanwhile, conveying your attitude is essential. Your conduct nourishes the garden in which attitude and purpose reach their fruition.

DATING ETIQUETTE

Who initiates the date? Who pays? What do you do when your girlfriend's boyfriend asks you out? How do you maintain courtesy in the face of tumult? The answers to such questions define the quality of our dating experiences. Let's examine these and other common problems, using the examples of women in our workshops.

A Date Invitation Is an Honor—Treat It Seriously

Inevitably, some of the men you encounter will ask you out for a date. And these are the men who are worthy of your continued energies. Remember the relevant Code principles as men express interest:

- Principle 1: You acknowledge biology's rules and use his sexual attraction to negotiate for courtship.
- Principle 5: You take command of your calendar (requiring at least four days' advance notice for scheduling a date).
- Principle 8: You understand and live the dignity of good manners.

Scarlett's questions. Scarlett described a series of events in launching a new dating relationship with Barry. It illustrates the self-correcting nature of the Code. You can make a wrong move (or four, as Scarlett did) and still stay on the courtship track. Let's look at the dating relationship that unfolded with Barry, the mistakes she made, and how she corrected them.

Scarlett bumped into Barry in the supermarket. At twenty-nine, she hadn't seen him since her heart-wrenching crush nine years earlier when they were both college students. They had never dated, although they did share a class and had had several conversations. What a coincidence! How nice to see that he remembered her. They chatted for ten minutes and he asked if he might call her. Perhaps they could get together for lunch one day. She expressed delight and they exchanged phone numbers.

Three days later he called and left a message that he would call again. The next day they connected and arranged to meet for lunch the next day. (Wrong move number one: She could just as easily have suggested a date more than four days hence to get him used to the idea of planning ahead.)

They did meet on Friday for lunch. As they caught up on their lives, she had the marvelous sense that the old spark of chemistry was still there; but now she knew she was more in command of her female power. This time she resolved she would not pine away for the campus hero.

As their lunch drew to a close, he said, "This has been really fun. Would you like to do it again?"

"Yes," she said. "I'd love to."

"Great!" said Barry. "Hey listen, I know this is really short notice, but I am having a few friends in for dinner tomorrow night [Saturday]. Could you possibly come join us?"

"I wish I could," she said, thrilled to know how to handle this last-minute invitation correctly. "I am busy tomorrow, but how about next Saturday night? I don't have any plans then." (Wrong move number two: He had not asked for a formal date. Scarlett shouldn't have suggested one because this usurped his male role.)

"I'll call you," he answered noncommittally.

This left her hanging. After reviewing the Code of Courtship and the rules and roles of dating, she realized she had flubbed. She figured out what she had to do to correct it, to readjust her course. Wednesday morning came. She closed her calendar to dates and made plans to go out that night and two other times. She filled in the dates in ink in her calendar, lifted her chin, and resolved that she was going to be out Wednesday night when she suspected Barry would call.

Wednesday evening arrived and Scarlett had not yet heard from Barry. She forced herself to go to the singles dance she had selected that morning. She dragged her feet—it was hard to get dressed and to go out when she really wanted to be talking with Barry. But she knew that going out would lift her spirits and make her more attractive and buoyant. It turned out she had a great time dancing. And when she returned, her message was waiting.

"Hi, Scarlett. This is Barry. [He had called at 9:00 according to the timer on her machine.] Just called to see how everything was going. I'll talk to you later."

Scarlett wanted to know: "Should I call him back?" (Potential wrong move number three.) "When we talk, and if he suggests we get together on Saturday night, I realize I cannot be free to see him. Shall I tell him that I am sorry but I am going to be with my aunt?" (Potential wrong move number four.)

My advice was quite specific. Let him call you again. Enjoy whatever conversation unfolds. Then when and if he asks you, say something like this: "How nice of you to ask! I wish I could, but I can't. I have plans for then."

Don't bring up specifics—no matter how mundane or exciting your plans are. The point here is that you want him to think you have the most exciting private life that his capacity to fantasize could possibly imagine. Without knowing what exactly it is that you are doing. Is it a date with another man? Did he miss the boat by leaving you hanging when he had the chance? Had he better start asking you out sooner if he wants to get to see you more often? Never say what you're doing that prevents you from accepting his invitation for getting together. Let him wonder. Enhance the mystery and you will increase the enchantment and the feminine power. This is fun. Allow him to generate the energy for pursuit. Heighten his interest with your cheerful self-possession and vivacious personality that are currently unavailable to him, but may be, if he follows your lead.

When you do receive a formal invitation for a date, your courteous response will reflect your character. An invitation for a date deserves a thank you as well as a clear acceptance or rejection. When you accept an invitation, be sure to thank the man for asking you out. Then make it clear that you are happy to go out with him and are looking forward to the time you will spend together. Set the date and time right then. If you find this awkward to initiate, just say:

"Wait a second, I will get my calendar."

Then open it and suggest the time and date if he does not.

When you do not want to accept an invitation, courtesy requires that you reject his offer immediately. Be clear and compassionate. There is always a way to tell the truth with minimal injury if you use courtesy and tact. One of the simplest ways to do this is to say something like:

"No thank you. I'm sorry, but this just isn't working for me. But thanks for asking me out. I appreciate the compliment. Good-bye now."

Don't wait to hear protestations. Put down the phone. Or nod and walk away. All rejections are painful. Make yours short, sweet, and courteous. Then move on.

Regrets and Second Thoughts

Sometimes when you reject a man, you may be left wondering if you made a big mistake. Perhaps he was the one, and you just didn't recognize it at the time. It is perfectly natural to be curious about what might have been, but brooding over it diverts you from your ultimate purpose. Instead of sabotaging your self-confidence by doubting yourself, allow yourself to feel accomplished for having made a decision. Whether or not it turns out to be the optimum one is not the point. Once you have made your choice, focus your energies not on what might have been, but on what will be now. Rise to the challenge and apply your clever imagination to making the best of your situation.

Is It Safe to Accept a Date?

There was a time when growing up in a community ensured that a woman could track and trace the character of any man who might approach her for courtship. Not anymore. The ever-increasing mobility of populations has changed this, and most women will marry a man who was once a total stranger. In many cases, she was not introduced to him by a family member or trusted friend but had to form a character judgment herself.

Dating requires the man to escort you to an event and bring you back home safely. The assumption underlying this custom is that your date will protect you. In order to accept a date with a man, you must be able to trust him. You are going to have to develop your skills at detecting deception until you can rely on them. Check a man out in several different ways before you give him your phone number or address. When you do give a man your phone number or address, you deserve to have his. Try to make sure these are genuine before you accept a date with him. Also, get his number at work and make sure he really works there. When you have made the proper checks and believe a man is safe, you can accept his offer for a date.

Who Pays?

The person who extends the invitation pays for the date. On the first date, since he invites, he pays. You can help by being considerate and aware of his means. A date's courtship potential is as valid whether he spends a lot of money or a little. A walk in the park and a picnic can be almost free.

Remember, reciprocity is the hallmark of good manners. When a man spends money on you, he is extending a gift, and you must find a way to reciprocate. The exception is if his invitation followed a response to your personal ad, because you paid for the first connection (the ad) and he is reciprocating. Otherwise, think of ways to show your appreciation. A thank-you note is a nice touch. Or if you make as much money as he does, buy some theater tickets or share the costs of dates. When you get to know him better, you can invite him to your place for dinner. Or make him some homemade jam.

Courtesy and expressions of appreciation are worth cultivating because they enhance your life as well as the lives you touch. Work on it everywhere. Try to be courteous even to rude, boorish people and you will come away elevated. Your conduct reflects on you. By conducting yourself beautifully you exude beauty.

What About Female Competition?

Women friends are a resource to treasure. Women friends can enhance each other's lives, support each other in times of difficulty, provide respite from loneliness, and can just "be there" for each other. If you are fortunate enough to have six or seven good women friends, your life is enriched. Blessed. If you don't yet have such a cadre, work on it. Develop women friends—but separate this goal from your three-night-a-week date schedule. Women friends provide needed balance. Find them. Treasure them.

Sometimes the goals of attaining women friends and the search for courtship appear to clash until you apply some thoughtful analysis. Consider the story Melissa told at a workshop:

> Melissa and her friend Sharon went to a party together and Sharon told her ahead of time that she was very interested in one of the hosts. He made her pulse race and her heart quiver. George, the man Sharon mentioned, was handsome and personable. From the time Sharon introduced them, he pursued Melissa with great interest. She liked him, and when he asked for her phone number she assumed he was bluffing and gave it to him. Within the next week he called three times and was in fervent pursuit, creating a very tenuous situation between Melissa and Sharon. She suspected she had done something wrong and wanted to know how to gracefully repair the damage.

Melissa did make a mistake. She compromised Code principle eight—living the dignity of good manners—by giving the appearance of enticing her friend's dreamboat. I believe that when a woman friend tells you she is interested in a man, you should consider that man off-limits until she informs you she has released him. Although many will disagree with this, I think that in the long run, setting such boundaries is your best course of action. Women friends are hard to find and keep, and it's not worth risking them for the tenuous possibility that a particular man who expresses interest in you will eventually court and love you.

Rather than feeling desperately that this man is your one last chance, take a more self-confident view. Understand the value of communicating to your friend that her interests are more important to you than a stranger. By doing so, you are building what might be an enduring friendship, a safety net for the times you are down-and-out and need a friend to turn to. So when George approached her, Melissa should have said something like:

> "Thanks, George, I appreciate the compliment. I like you a lot too, but so does my friend. I don't date men under this circumstance. Thanks very much. It really is great to know that you like Sharon enough to like her choices in friends. Maybe the two of you could develop something good together."

An attitude like this expresses humor, generosity, self-confidence, loyalty and friendship, and a self-possession that will increase your self-esteem. It shows a woman of high character. Most important, you will have done "the right thing" by your friend. In time, Sharon and George's relationship will or won't evolve. Meanwhile, George is going to think, What a terrific woman Melissa is. If he can't have you, he might invite you to his parties and introduce you to his friends. Your circle will enlarge as you behave with consideration for your women friends and with self-respect in your conduct with men.

Melissa still wanted to know what she should have done if she felt "chemistry" for George. The answer would still be to decline. Chemistry is not enough of a reason to put your interest in a new man before those of your friend who introduced you to him. When you go out three times a week to places that good single men gather, you will discover many men with whom you can feel "chemistry."

If you feel chemistry for the man, tell him that if your

friend tells you she is no longer interested in him, you will consider his pursuit. But until she tells you that, your answer to him is "Sorry, I'm not available."

If he is interested enough, he may decide to help your girlfriend find a man. Then the coast will be clear.

Grow Better Men

You are bound to encounter men who are not worthy of your dating time or even your playing time. If they pursue you, let them know why you are rejecting their offers. If their unworthiness can be corrected for the next woman who encounters them, you have done single women a favor. A man who is rude to you or uncaring about the feelings of your friends is not of good character—unacceptable as a friend. If you let him know *how* he was rude or inconsiderate, you may give him something to think about for his next encounter. Women should be growing better men as they say no. Leave the man's sensitivity finer and more well-honed than before he met you.

The same applies to ongoing dating relationships that have gone sour. Rejection is the only signal that sinks in with certain men. Only after you reject them do they finally begin to believe that they have to change their behavior. Unfortunately, it is usually fruitless to take back someone you have rejected. If you take back such a man, he may not believe that he really has to change. This is not a hard-and-fast rule. Only your experience with a particular man can teach you how to make that judgment. Some men do change.

Once you have concluded that you must reject him and cannot reconsider his pleas, the finality of that rejection may be sufficient to cause him to change. The changes he makes will not reward you directly, but what goes around, comes around. You will have helped the next woman he encounters. And you will have helped him as well. Think of it as fertilizing the soil, for the next woman.

THE QUESTION OF SEX

Since sex is such a precious resource, it is sensible to postpone its fullest expression until you find a man who is your best friend. Since you cannot know whether a man's character meets your standards until you get to know him, give yourself time to form judgments. A date who asks you to "take a chance" and dive into sexual intercourse before you have assessed his character is not respectful of your needs. He denies your right to protect your self-esteem, your health, and your personal integrity.

Men are different from women. Most men are willing to use sexual intercourse for recreation and release of internal pressures without any need for commitment. Be forewarned. Many will invite you to bed, although few will be truly interested in courting you.

Communicating Your Worth

Women often ask:

"How do you know when a man no longer considers you a sex object?"

Men are the initiators in romantic encounters, and what gets them started is that spark of sexual attraction. It is also what keeps them coming toward you. Appreciate the high art of banking the embers of that sexual fire as you make yourself known to him, revealing your good qualities, earning his respect. Slowly the ratio of sexual interest to respect in his attitude will change. His initial impetus to approach you and connect with you may be sexual, but he will come to restrain it in order to spend time with you. When you sense this, he no longer considers you a sex object but a complex being, worthy of respect.

The self-respect you convey to a man and the restraint you show in the expression of your sexuality will give out subtle signals to him. There are many men who place women into one of two categories: the whore and the madonna. Women must fight back against such trivialization of their complexity and their sexuality. One of the ways to preserve your self-esteem is to convey that until he has met your standards, you cannot even consider the possibility of being sexual with him. In the early stages of dating, sex is inappropriate for a woman who is on the way to marriage. It may have been appropriate when she was exploring, getting to know about men, wanting to learn about her own reactions. Her standards change once she decides that courtship is her objective. When she knows she is ready for marriage and looking for a man who will make a good husband, she will recognize she has no time for sex as sport nor for taking a chance. These activities divert her from the goal of courtship.

WHO IS A CANDIDATE?

A good man who wants to be a candidate for your affections will meet the standards you set. He will not insist that you risk anything before you have had a chance to evaluate him. The ones who ask you to risk your mental and physical health to meet their needs are not worthy of your consideration.

I suspect from talking with many men and women that unless a man feels sexual attraction for a woman within the first five or so minutes of meeting her, he is not likely to experience it later. His excitement is the essential trigger that causes him to get up his energy to pursue her. From then on a negotiation is under way. Your critical job is to focus on these men, the ones who want to pursue you. In this way, you will sound out candidates for courtship.

Once you are formally dating, your field of focus narrows to one or two men. Let's turn to Chapter 7, "Forging a Friendship During Formal Dating," for details on intimacy negotiation—and on getting physical.

SEVEN

Forging a Friendship During Formal Dating

During active courtship, the bowerbird is very attentive. He presents his prospective mate with gifts—little shiny objects or colorful flowers—laid at the threshold of his nest. He regularly replaces the dead flowers with fresh ones to keep things spruced up. Many males bring food as a gift, laying it in front of the female of interest.

Mutual respect forms the fertile soil
For growing a deep friendship.

When you have started formal dating and you find yourself continuing to accept one particular man's offers for dates, the time is ripe for discovering whether you can forge a real friendship with him. Yours is a specific objective—to transform a man's formal dating activities into a warm and respectful friendship. Put it in perspective. Forging this friendship is not your whole life but an important step along the way to courtship. Ideally, your experience with a man should round out a complex life, one already filled with your involvements in work, family, community, and friendships with women.

221

Nor should you exclude other men. Remember, when you haven't yet agreed to exclusivity, you are free to date several men and to be gently public about what you are doing. You wouldn't want to parade the fact that you have other "friends" to the man who has begun to pursue you, but you don't have to hide it either. It's a matter of good manners. Meanwhile, you have every right to forge several friendships at a time. So does he.

How many friendships can you expect to form? Time will probably be the limiting factor. From dating several men, you will eventually progress to friendship with one or maybe two.

If you don't have any dating condidates for friendship right now, hang on. It's a common experience when you are single and searching. Go back to Chapters 4 and 5, scan your resource loose-leaf, and go out to play three times a week. If you keep on going out, the dates will follow. It is inevitable. When you go out alone to places where single men gather, they will be able to find you. Because *men need women,* they are out looking for them. Once you find your peer group, they will want to go out with you.

Let us assume—as you read this chapter—that either you are at the stage of relationship where you are dating one man, or you are reading ahead to discover what happens when you get to that stage. (Remember that you may repeatedly move through the stages as a relationship ends and you go back out to play.) The cycle of searching, going out to play, dating, and beginning to forge friendships will repeat until you marry. See Figure 1.1, page 27.

With a gracious attitude and a sense of humor you can find good men to build friendships with. How do I know?

I've watched it happen again and again. So many good women who began acting out the principles of the Code with deliberation found the power it had and the fun it produced. In fact, the Code was designed to serve as a kind of pole to vault you over the hurdles. Remember Code principle eleven:

> You realize that there are many good men searching and muster the courage to end all romantic relationships that are not leading to courtship.

When you have had enough of dallying and are ready to find a life partner, the Code will take you to him. Mistakes are inevitable; nobody learns without them. Learn the Code principles so that you can make fewer. The fewer the mistakes, the fewer the detours and the shorter your journey.

The men who ask you for a date will usually do it because they are sexually attracted to you. And if they have a healthy libido, they will be pushing for what they want: to take you to bed. As soon as you will allow this. Your challenge as a traveler to courtship is to restrain this natural impulse and exercise Code principle one:

> You use his sexual attraction for you to negotiate for courtship.

When a man you like is hot to bed you, recognize how wonderful this is. Tell him that you like him and appreciate his interest. Tell him you look forward to the idea too. Tell him you want to start a friendship *before* you become sexually intimate. This takes artistry in order to prevent misunderstandings or hurt feelings. It is a skill you can learn with practice. The object is to let him know that you share his feelings but aren't ready yet.

Veronica's experience shows how you might like to handle such a situation. Veronica was thirty-eight when she returned to Philadelphia from her clinical training program in psychology. Equipped as a therapist, she had already refined her skills in asserting what she wanted in a gentle manner. When she met Bob she knew she liked him. When he pursued her she was delighted. And when he quickly let her know that he was dying to be intimate with her, she told him how pleased she was, that she felt the same way, and that she wanted to wait until she knew him better. She told him that sex was very precious to her and she hoped it would be right for them both in time. He did agree to wait until she was ready. And she held off until she was sure that she liked his character and could trust him. Something in the exchange itself may have served to build bridges of mutual respect and appreciation. Today they are married, and as far as I can tell, they are happy with each other.

If he is unwilling to do it your way, if he won't consider becoming your friend before you consider becoming his lover, move on. He does not qualify. Mannerly people wait till their friend is ready; they restrain their impulses and do not resort to force—physical or psychological. In other words, they behave respectfully when they care for you. If a man you are dating cannot respect your wishes, you are fortunate to discover this early on—long before he thinks he owns you.

Caution: The world is a dangerous place. Women need to protect themselves against brutality and violence. The newspapers are full of stories of beatings, rapes, and murders in "romantic" relationships. The pattern is tragically familiar: The man lacks the capacity to respect the feelings of his (often former) sexual partner. She is an object of his need rather than a friend whose feelings he considers or respects.

Use caution now—and determine that you will connect sexually with a man only after he has met this friendship hurdle. Before you have become sexually intimate with a man, your clear but kind rejection of his pursuit is unlikely to evoke the rage that can come later with such a bad character. Make sure a man has demonstrated *by his conduct* that he can and will listen to what you say and respect your wishes. The reward? When you do find a friend, you will better preserve your safety and your emotional health. You have the right to plan for and insist upon your personal safety. And when you are out socially with a friend, *he* should help protect your safety.

YOUR CRITICAL CHALLENGE

Forging a friendship during formal dating is the last challenge before permitting a man to court you. When you call for a friendship before you permit an intimacy, you are not only protecting your own safety and interest but are also stimulating a man's potential to try to win you. It is when he must meet a challenge that he may begin to think that you are valuable, a woman he cannot live without. And then he may decide that you are a woman whose friendship he wants and whose further partnership he wants to explore. If you asked four or five men how they feel about pursuing a woman, you would probably get the same answer from all of them. Men love a challenge. They love to feel that they won a woman due to their own actions.

THE MEANING OF FRIENDSHIP

Friendships are treasures, worthy of your thoughtful attention and appreciation. The term *friend* has become devalued in recent years. Think of how often people deprecate a relationship with a man, saying they are "just friends." Don't make this mistake. In courtship terms, a friendship brings you a step closer to your goal. In courtship, a friend is a personal resource and a treasure.

The man with whom you are forming a friendship is a well-known companion whose "track record" has earned him the special standing to be confided in, relied on in an emergency, and asked for substantive advice. When you have a friend, you have someone you can trust, feel safe with, and enjoy. Within limits, you participate in your friend's ongoing life, his activities and his feelings. And he participates in yours. A friend will do things *against his self-interest* to help you because of your connection. You have someone who wishes you—specifically you—well. He wins when you do. And sometimes when you have a friend he wants to help you be your best self, to grow and to bloom.

Forging a friendship means receiving and giving these special qualities. When you begin to connect with a new man and start accepting his offers for dates, look for the blooming of friendship as an important criteria before considering further intimacies. A man who doesn't want to develop a friendship should not get your valuable time. The theme repeats again and again. You move slowly—from formal dating with men who will ask you for dates at least four days in advance to friendship with the ones you like the best.

When you set standards for yourself, you eliminate people who do not meet those standards. Nature does not permit a vacuum. If you can manage to keep out the men who would waste your time, you will make room in your life for the kinds of men and experiences you do want. This liberates your energy and lets you sharpen your focus on the men who treat you well and are candidates for friendship.

It is a kind of gentle and natural process of elimination. There isn't any fighting. There aren't any demeaning put-downs or bad behavior. As a woman who is searching for courtship, you have set such clear standards that you can move gracefully in a predetermined order: from searching to connecting to accepting offers for dates to dating and then to forging a good friendship. Give your search the same patience you would give to any other long-term, important goal. If you do, you will get the reward you seek: a good man to court you.

Most Dates Will Not Be Friends

Most dates will be short-term connections. Only a few will become friends. These are men who, as the months go by, will form your stronghold—men who will provide you with opportunities to talk, play, and share as well as test out personal ideas. Where does love fit in? Sooner or later you will connect to your ultimate goal of love, and the love that emerges with the mutual admiration and respect of a friendship establishes a stable foundation. One or more of these friendships is destined to move closer into the realm of courtship. One of these courtships will progress to marriage. Until then each friend is a treasure, a person worthy of your thoughtful consideration.

Men Friends Are Different from Women Friends

First, face facts: Most good friendships with men are destined to be wonderful memories rather than ongoing connections. Only one man can be your husband; the rest will become "the men who were," or "history." Why are most friendships destined to be temporary connections? It's really quite basic.

Once you have found him, your fiancé will not want you to sustain a deep and abiding friendship with an ex-beau. (Just as your ex-beau's new wife or girlfriend will not want him calling you to share the personal details of his emotional life.) It is sad but inevitable. When you find the man to love and marry, the rest of the men with whom you enjoyed friendships in the dating experience will probably thrive best as treasured *memories* that add richness to your personality. You carry them inside you but you no longer exchange intimacies. To prevent the unpleasantness of triangles, you will be wise to forgo lesser intimacies with old beaux. As pleasant as they are by themselves, they can confuse you, making you uncertain of your loyalties. Worse, they can threaten your primary relationship by making your spouse feel like an outsider.

When you find the love of your life, either your old beaux

will recognize the change in your availability or you will be forced to widen the distance between you. Letting go of friendships with men who "almost made it" is one of the major challenges of establishing sexual intimacy and monogamy. You need to do it to conserve and focus your intimate energy on your beloved and to prevent a confusion of loyalties. It is a lot easier to avoid temptation than to work at fighting its power. Everyone wins when your paths diverge and you separate your lives.

Friendships with women can endure. Relationships with your women friends can last. The woman who was your friend when you were single can become a deeper and everlasting treasure even after you have been married for ten years. You can still call each other and share levels of intimacy that would be unthinkable with an ex-beau.

WHAT TO DO WHILE YOU WAIT

Some diversionary tactics may be needed if you can't seem to light a fire under the object of your interest. Since, according to the Code, it is a man's role to pursue a woman, you may find yourself in the position of waiting: waiting for the man you like to call you for the next date, waiting while he sorts out his own life and relationships, waiting for him to pursue you more actively.

Remember the fundamental biological principle—you can slow him down, but you'll be at a dead standstill if you try to get him to move faster. Wanda's story illuminates many of these issues.

Wanda had been dating Christopher about every other week for several months. The relationship was moving tortuously slowly as far as she was concerned. Every time he called, he was courteous. He would ask her out in advance and she was very happy to accept. The dates were wonderful. He would wine and dine her, take her to concerts, and in general find all sorts of exciting things to do. Occasionally she would invite him to share her theater tickets. He was always delighted and would take her out to dinner on those nights also. They enjoyed each other's conversation, but she felt herself being put on hold as she waited for him to pursue more intensely.

Meanwhile, she began to test his values. In the conversations that were growing ever more meaningful, they began to tell each other who they really were. She learned that his wife had suddenly left him and he had felt bewildered and abandoned. She sensed that his cautious development of a relationship with her was a sign that he was trying to protect himself from another injury. She knew that she liked him. The more time they shared, the more she hoped he would move faster, but she recognized that she could not speed up this relationship, and so she worked to endure the delays with as little anxiety as she could. She used the waiting time to "build a raft" by developing one of her hobbies, poetry, and showing the results to him. Initially she didn't want to pursue other men and go out to play, and I couldn't fault her for this. She knew that she was exchanging some loneliness for what seemed to her the intensity of a terrific relationship. I did not agree that she was doing the best that she could for herself, but it was her life. Meanwhile, she commanded his respect and found his respectful attention to her delicious.

Forging friendships is a highly personal journey. I can suggest some ways that could maximize this journey, but each woman takes her journey all by herself. Think about what I have to say, but take the parts that fit your life, and good luck to you.

If you are involved with a slow mover and want to be more active, you can do two good things for yourself: nourish your female friends *and* keep searching for courtship. Within several months, Wanda's loneliness did drive her out to play. And later when I spoke with her she was cheerful and feeling more patient with Christopher's slowness. Even later I received the news of Wanda's wedding to Christopher. When you like a man who is moving slowly, your best interest will be served when you go out three times a week. Inevitably you may find that more than one male friendship will begin to flourish.

THE RIGHT NUMBER OF MEN

The number of friendships you can forge at one time depends on your energy and your emotional needs. Until you are ready for exclusivity, a natural outgrowth of the decision for sexual intimacy, three dates (or outings) per week will probably be about right. You might find it helpful to refer back to Ellyce's dating list, Table 6.1 on page 191. If you look at it closely, you can see that there were times when she was juggling several friendships as she accepted dates with new men. At other times her energy was focused on one man.

Women are great givers—of warmth, affection, acts of kindness. In return, they are blessed with the joy that comes from their generosity and the appreciative reactions of others. In a social sense, generosity draws people to her—as flowers attract bees. But be aware that feminine giving often leads to exhaustion. Watch for exhaustion and use it as a signal that you are giving too much. Pushing your energy near your limits can lead to collapse. The time you then need to recuperate delays your return to the searching process and can leave you lonely in the short term. You must learn to pace yourself. When you can't feel cheerful about your social life, it's a warning signal. Pull back and conserve your energy.

But as long as you have the energy and men are asking you for dates, go ahead and enjoy the fun that your conduct brings.

TREASURING ALL YOUR FRIENDS

Whether with a woman or a man, a great friendship can offer a full spectrum of experiences, from joy to mystery. When you treasure your friends, you will enhance your experience of them. To do this, treat them well. Recognize that what you bring to your friendship will form the atmosphere you experience it in. Avoid polluting the friendship. Don't bring your dirty laundry and you won't spend your friendship time doing chores. Bring humor and gifts of consideration and you will find yourself laughing and being enjoyed.

Each time a new man starts actively pursuing you, you will find yourself shifting where your spend your time. Women friends will miss you as you connect with a man and begin to give most of your energy to him. That's fine. It is to be expected. But in these times it is especially important that you take a few minutes to remind your women friends that you cherish them. You might send a humorous card in which you scribble a note that says, "I'm checking in—thinking of you. It's kind of crazy right now, but I want you to know I will be back soon. Please wait for me because you count." A phone call or a card that communicates such a message will be greatly appreciated by your woman friend who suddenly finds herself abandoned because of the new man in your life. Sooner or later that new love in your life will cool down and you will find yourself needing your women friends. Preserving the connection even when you can't take time to get together is good insurance for you and basic consideration for your friends. If you can remember your women friends while dazzled by the brighter light of a new romance, your subsequent nights will never be too dark.

As you begin to forge a friendship with one man, you may need to reposition your other suitors, those not ready to be called "history." Perhaps you will find yourself in the confusing position that Mary Lou described.

I was dating George, Bill, and Harry when the relationship with Harry kind of took off. Harry is consuming all my free time and I love it that way. But what do I do about George and Bill? What if Harry doesn't work out and I want to go back to George? I don't want to reject these two nice men, but I can't continue to see them because Harry and I are testing out our future.

She wanted to know how she could preserve her "safety net" and still maintain her integrity.

I suggested she remember principle six and tell the truth. She could tell George that she had become involved with someone, and though she didn't know what the future held, couldn't continue to see him under these circumstances.

Then she could tell him how much she liked him and ask if he would like to hear from her if she finds herself free again.

If you found yourself involved in such a situation, you could go even further. You could mention that the relationship never did get a chance to develop. That maybe someday in the future, if both of your paths cross in similar circumstances, it will. Probably he will say yes (because he has nothing to lose). Then if the relationship with your current flame fizzles, send the other man a card and let him know that your situation has changed and you would welcome his call if he finds himself free at the time. Do the same thing with all the men you put on hold.

A courteous expression of your true situation is always appropriate. It may be that your old beaux won't be available to see you again. Then again, there might be someone waiting in the wings for you when you need him. The bridges are not burned. Send such men a card on the holidays, and a year or two down the road you might have a chance to explore a relationship with one of them again. And if your paths never bring you back together again, that's okay too. It means that life got better.

NOW THE DATING RULES CAN SAFELY CHANGE

As the man-woman friendship deepens, some of the dating *don'ts* become *do's*. The rules change because you no longer need the emotional protection they once provided. You can take the lead—you can call him, set up dates, initiate activities, deepen the friendship—without danger of being misinterpreted.

Why? Well, he knows you better. He is beyond the adolescent whore/madonna mind-set and he can see you more fully, not as a cliché. When? That depends. The greater your restraint in getting to that point, the more time you will have to nourish the friendship, learn about each other's personalities, intellectual needs, and styles of being. One good way to do this is to imagine your future together. Take some time to complete the exercise in Table 7.1.

When forging a new friendship, it is useful to imagine what your marriage would be like. Imagining your ideal will help you evaluate the appropriateness of the man you spend time with. You might—and probably should—change your projected ideal over time, but laying out your thoughts gives you something to work with.

TABLE 7.1. IMAGINING YOUR MARRIAGE

When I think of my marriage I envision . . .

Spending____hours per day together
____part of the day together
____hours per week together
____part of the week together

Doing the following activities together

235

Vacationing together in the following ways

Living in an environment that looks, smells, and feels like

Sharing this environment with the following beings

Making our priorities as a couple

When you have articulated what you want, you can begin to reality-test your ideals. Talk them through with each man you become friends with. Ask him what his attitudes are about how much time to spend together. Is he a sailor with six-month bachelor cruises? Learn what kinds of activities he would like you to do together and how he would like to vacation. Does he want pets? Does he hate children? Do your needs match? Are you the "odd couple"—you meticulous and he sloppy? Can either of you adapt? The answers to these questions will help you know whether to continue this particular friendship. Either he will adapt, you will adapt, or you will part. Regardless of the decision, keep searching for your courtship partner.

YOU SET THE SPEED TO INTIMACY

Finally, if the relationship continues, the time will come for you to uncover your sexual selves to each other. When does this happen? It depends on him, but it also depends on you.

Consider what happens on a summer day when you go to the seashore and stride toward the surf. The air and the sand are hot, but the water is cold. At the point where the sand becomes damp, you slip off your shoes and step over the line from dry land to damp sand. At first the sensation of coolness against the heat of the day can be shocking. But after a short while your feet adjust and you no longer feel cold. As you start to edge deeper into the water, the incoming tide splashes against you every now and then. Icy water sends a thrill—and a chill—into your feet. Maybe up your spine. A little while later, as you adapt, it no longer feels quite so icy. Entering deeper into the surf continues the breathtaking sensations. And now you have a choice. Some plunge into the water to acclimatize, to get it over with. Others inch in slowly. In each case, once you emerge from the water, the salt will dry on your skin and make you uncomfortable. Or at least conscious of having splashed into the surf.

The development of intimate relationships is much like an encounter with the ocean. If you tiptoe, and move slowly,

237

you can enjoy the water and retain your sense of comfort. If you get in a little too far and find you don't like it, it is easy to back up a little. Not too much salt to deal with. But if you plunge in and quickly swim out past the breakers, you might get caught in the undertow and find it an enormous drain on your energy to recover a safe stance at the shoreline. And when you do come out, you will feel sticky.

When you are not sure about a man and you decide to tiptoe, you can often discover whether or not you want to go further. And you do this with minimal stress. If you move slowly into the intimacy and find it's wrong for you, sometimes you can back up with minimal stickiness, allowing the two of you to retain the friendship. In time, intimacy might yet bloom. But if you plunge into intimacy with a man that you like and find your actions bring you distress and displeasure, the fracture of the friendship can leave you drained and lonely.

Remember this metaphor when you are dating a new man and are considering friendship with him. Should you take it nice and easy or take a chance and plunge? If the power of love, chemistry, and passionate attachment is there, your caution won't hurt anything. But imagine the difficulty of having enjoyed such passion and then discovered things about his life that made your attachment to him unacceptable. What if you discover—after the sex—a prison record, a debt-ridden future? Or the thorny problems of his children?

It never hurts to progress slowly to greater intimacy. By moving slowly—and then only to the level you're sure you can handle—you treat each other respectfully. And you risk less. Once you cross a line and expose a more vulnerable part of yourself, the line has moved. It is hard to cross back again. It's usually too late. The relationship that is inappropriate at a deeply intimate level will usually fracture entirely. When a break occurs, it is often permanent. When a man ceases to perceive you as a valuable "prize," it is almost impossible to change his attitude.

GETTING HIM TO PRIZE YOU

This represents the high art of forging a friendship, because friendships should be prized. If you stay alert to subtle changes in manners, you will usually be able to correct a problem before it looms too large to be fixed. Every behavior is yet another step on a path, taking you either toward or away from your goal. If your new friend begins acting unfriendly, inconsiderate, or indifferent, this is a very important signal that the relationship is in danger. About the best thing you can do is tell him—quietly, simply, clearly. Then back away and wait to see what he does with the information. If he cannot give you what you need, it's up to you to cross back and stay further away. Remember principle eleven:

> You realize that there are many good men searching and muster the courage to end all romantic relationships that are not leading to courtship.

Maintain whatever level of friendship sustains courtesy and respect for you. When the respect slips, step back from him and stand your ground.

If you have moved slowly, you may be able avoid the hurtful fractures. You won't sustain all the relationships you start, but you can learn to command respectful treatment. You should be able to leave in your wake an ever-widening circle of positive feelings. Ideally, people should feel that having met you was a gift, that they encountered goodness and were enhanced as a result.

SEXUAL CONNECTION

Since sex is critical to forging a friendship that leads to courtship, the question is relevant here: Is passion evergreen or perennial? No scientist has yet reported on the nature of this intimate cycle—how long it lasts and just how crucial it is to marriage. One thing is certain. Passion rarely lasts at full blast for very long. Imagine trying to sustain the energy required by an initial love affair as you go about developing your career, raising children, balancing economic responsibilities with time for play and family life. Someday it may ebb and flow according to its own seasons, naturally, the way deciduous trees change during the course of the year: leafing out in spring, reaching their fullness of green in summer, turning vibrant color in autumn, and standing bare and proud in winter. Whatever the season, sexual connection is the glue that attaches a man to a woman. It is the private secret they share and nourish. It matters.

When you find a man you like so well that you think you might want to be with him permanently, you are almost ready for healthful sexual intimacy. When you know that he cares about your feelings, considers your needs, and loves to be with you, the time approaches for sex with love.

Before you get there, there will be intimate dalliances along the way. From your first kiss to ever more intimate hugging and petting, you are on a private journey. Intimate relations should heighten your sensations. When a sexual relationship is blooming, the world looks different. Colors appear richer. Sounds more distinct. Sensations of fabric on skin, smells, taste are heightened.

Don't forgo these delicious sensations in a headlong rush to sex. There was a time (when I was growing up) that "fast girls" plunged into sex and were secretly gossiped about by the girls who didn't admit to such behavior. The more proper girls enjoyed intimacy too, only with slower resolutions. Petting, stroking, fumbling with arousal while fully or partially clothed provided extraordinary adventure as well as sexual passion. It also provided intimate knowledge without exposing everything. It was not so much the *act* as the *attitude* of intimacy that brightened the environment. Relive this ardor. Try it yourself—bring back this petting to climax in your life and you may discover why it had such value, such resonance.

Hold back on the full expression of sex until its partial expressions have been traversed and thoroughly explored with pleasure. If you do, you may discover a level of artistry to enhance the friendship and promote a more elevated courtship experience. The man who must travel an enormous distance to reach your inner being is likely to appreciate you more. Such is the stuff of myth: the search for the Golden Fleece, the Trojan War to rescue Helen of Troy, the building of Camelot. They all share this theme. The great lady was to be won after many deeds of bravery, patience, and restraint.

Imagine being treated as a woman of such value. Your

conduct can take you there. It begins when you learn how to command respect.

COMMANDING RESPECT

As a woman out in the single world, you will have many opportunities to exercise restraint in order to command respect. From what I have seen, a variety of disrespectful behaviors are common and may be increasing in frequency. But you can take action to command respect. It is not difficult once you get the hang of it. Think of it as an interesting feminine challenge. The following examples show what I mean. Each of these stories is true. Sometimes the woman's solution was effective. Other times I suggested one that might have been.

THE GOLF COURSE ASSAULT—AVOIDING A RAPE

Louise, an attractive woman of forty, was doing all the right things to search for courtship. She had placed an ad that produced many replies. She was going out to play three times a week. And she had started to meet many men.

One of these, a lawyer named Bill, pursued her with apparent interest. She liked him but was not sure. As she got to know him, she began to discover some values that made her a little uncomfortable.

Still, after their third date she invited him to her house for dinner. After a pleasant meal they agreed to take a walk. After about a mile they reached the edge of a golf course. The next thing Louise knew, she was flat on her back on the green with Bill straddling her, holding her down. Shocked, she couldn't quite believe what was happening. As far as she knew, she had given no indication that she was interested in physical intimacy. She started to fight him to push him off, but that only seemed to make matters worse.

With a line right out of a grade-B movie he said, "Do you know who's on top of you, Louise?"

She looked him in the eye and asked him to get off. He seemed not to hear her, and to her horror, began caressing and kissing her. Then she quit fighting him and made herself go completely limp. Once she stopped playing his game, he jumped up off her, filled with apologies.

Somewhere there had been a miscommunication. Bill apparently believed that she was having a good time and was play fighting. His quick retreat when she went limp showed this miscommunication. He did not consider himself a man who rapes women. He thought his "macho" behavior was arousing (and acceptable) to her. Apparently, he thought they were engaged in a game, but it was a game that she neither agreed to nor wanted to continue. It was by going limp that she was finally able to communicate her displeasure.

Would such a tactic work every time? I doubt it, but it did work here. Although he was profusely apologetic, Louise did not go out with him again. In fact, she couldn't stand the sight of him and wanted no further contact with him. Undoubtedly, the whole event left him embarrassed. Perhaps the next time he is confronted with passion, he may listen harder to the woman. As for Louise, she now recognizes that neither his professional credentials nor her apparent comfort level are any guarantee of her safety.

What should a woman do when a man is imposing himself on her? That depends on the circumstance. According to legal statute, unless a woman resists actively, her passivity implies consent. Louise's act of going limp might be judged as consent. Screaming and fighting, yelling "police," "rape," or "fire" are effective approaches if you are where people can hear you. It is a calculated risk, and each woman must decide in her own way. I have read true stories about women who resisted a rape and suffered terribly as a result, while others went along with their rapist and survived with their lives. And the reverse can happen. The safest thing a woman can do is avoid being alone with a man until she knows his character.

It takes a long time to accurately judge someone's character, even if you like him, even if he is known in the community. Women must be alert to danger in order to protect themselves. The saddest thing of all is needing to protect yourself against possible assault from a friend. Yet these are the realities. A clear vision can preserve your safety.

Handling an Aggressive Man Who Isn't Listening

On a less intense level, Dana revealed her story.

> Toward the end of Dana's first date with Frank, a man she had rather enjoyed being with, he reached out to kiss her good night. She didn't want to and said so. Frank began to argue: Why wouldn't she kiss him? Didn't she like him? Dana tried to explain her feelings; that she doesn't like to kiss a man until she knows him better. That she didn't feel comfortable kissing Frank right now.
>
> She also told him she had enjoyed the evening. They continued to talk a little while longer, and as he got to the door to leave he turned to her and said, "So what do you want to

know? Ask me some questions. I'll tell you the answers and then you'll know me."

She felt uncomfortable, pushed at, at a loss for words. She knew she liked him. She knew he liked her. But somehow at that moment she was not able to get from him what she needed.

My feeling was that Frank was not treating her with respect. He was not listening to what she told him she wanted. He seemed to consider his needs important and hers irrelevant. The quandary—teaching manners to a man cannot and should not be done with a set of lectures. I suggested a light touch, a reality-based approach such as:

> "Thanks, Frank. I think you're attractive too. But it takes two consenting adults and I'm not consenting now. It takes time, not questions and answers, for me to grow comfortable with a man. I hope you can be patient with me."

In saying something like this, she would be making it clear that an interrogation wasn't what she needed. She would be telling him that it takes her time to get to know a person. And for her, kissing is something that follows rather than precedes "getting to know each other." She would also be giving him one last chance to show that he could and would treat her wishes respectfully—even if they didn't match his.

Not everybody feels so reserved about a kiss. To some, a kiss is no more intimate than a handshake. When it comes to commanding respect, what is appropriate is that *your* feelings be honored.

The acid test of respect is whether what you say is appreciated or ignored. Telling a man who you are and what you need is very helpful in promoting a mutually respectful relationship. Learning how to stand your ground, particularly when you do so graciously, is a high art worthy of your practice. As you exercise this art, it will get easier, and you will attract men capable of the kinds of relationships that allow for rich friendships. And quickly free up your time from being wasted by those who are not. If you keep sitting in the car, he'll get the idea you want him to open the door for you.

But courtship hurdles are not only about sex and passion. Other things can pop up.

THE CHILDREN CONUNDRUM

Children enrich our lives, but wanting, conceiving, adopting, and stepmothering them can all present courtship hurdles.

Helen had developed a career and, at thirty-nine, found herself wanting to find a husband and start a family. But the men she met didn't share her feelings. Men her age either had children and didn't want any more, or if they wanted children, wanted younger women. She wanted to know what could be done about women who want to have their first child in their forties.

When we reviewed her situation in a workshop, it seemed clear that Helen had several problems. The first was whether it would be possible to find a man who wanted to start the responsibilities of parenting with a woman of forty. Another was whether infertility would be a problem (infertility increases in this age group).

I suggested that she keep going out three times a week, diligently searching for courtship. It may be that when she finds the right man, the two of them will agree on a path. It may also be that Helen's intentions will change when she finds a man worth marrying. I suggested she keep her mind open and keep her wishes real. Helen will discover, out in the world of courtship searching, whether her goal is worth pursuing. As she no doubt realizes, her time of fertility is running out. By the age of forty-five, pregnancy is rare even among those who are actively seeking it.

The other problem, the availability of men, will likewise be resolved out in the world. Although it is true that some men seek younger women, many discover that women their own age have more to offer on a long-term basis. And women in their forties sometimes find that younger men are eager to connect with them.

I was intrigued by what Philip Sarrel, M.D., a professor of gynecology and psychiatry at Yale University, told me. In his research in England on perimenopausal women—Helen's age group—he found that married women in their forties often report some sexual problem in their marriages. The exception was those married to younger men. It seems that everything we do in our lives has a risk and a benefit. You must choose from among your options as best you can.

ANOTHER TRIANGLE—
YOU, HIM, AND HIS CHILDREN

If you love other people's children and enjoy managing their lives and needs, the question of his children may be irrelevant to you. But if your own life consumes the lion's share of your energy, if your work excites you, or if you have raised your children and are relieved that the job is done, take time to consider what you want and need. In a marriage with children, all the adult experiences are different.

Stepmothers, I'm sad to say, are frequently disliked by their stepchildren when their biological mother is still alive.[1] Regardless of their own behavior, stepmothers often have disappointing initial experiences with the families they join. I'm not sure exactly why, but have some ideas. In his single state, Daddy may have seemed so accessible—generous with money and time for his children. Children grow accustomed to having their single father this way. When Daddy falls in love, his focus shifts and his children's lives are bound to change. Whether she was the bimbo who stole Dad from Mom or wasn't even around till after Mom left and moved in with her boss doesn't seem to matter. The children usually blame their stepmother for their loss of family cohesion. From what I have read and heard from newly married women, the Brady Bunch is an illusion, a television fantasy. What is more typical is jealousy, rage, and hostility. Children can make a stepmother's life tough.

The father in these scenarios often finds himself caught in the middle and confused. He plays the pivotal role in a terrible triangle. He cannot win everywhere and he usually waffles.

If you are considering forging a friendship with a man with children, take them into consideration, especially if

---

[1] This theme repeatedly appears in therapist literature, the popular press, and the words of women attending Athena Institute workshops.

they are still young enough to need daily and nightly parental supervision or financial support. What happens with them is vital to your own well-being. If his children are hostile to you, you can be in for some challenging times.

Positive solutions can be found, provided you can get Daddy to agree to a set of values and rules. Recognize that *he* will have to play the pivotal role in establishing how your role will fit with his when it comes to his children. If you can develop a dialogue with him to work this out, you should be able to assure your rightful place as his Number One. A parent has an absolute right to maintain a connection to his or her children. A stepparent needs to be treated with courtesy. Establish both of these agreements in your social contract, and eventually the new family will develop its own history, warmth, and close ties.

Meanwhile, getting to know a man's parents, siblings, and children gives you a wonderful opportunity to learn about him. They all know, from a different perspective, what you are trying to learn—who he is. And if he is to become your life partner, the relationships you forge with each other's families can enrich your lives.

You will get a chance to judge how your suitor juggles the very hard job of allocating his affection, energy, time, and money among you and his children. Have some sympathy. It is difficult, as you may know if you are a single parent. Although stepfathers tend not to get such a raw deal, a woman should be sensitive to the way her children behave with their stepfather. Teaching one's children to honor their stepparents will help them learn to cope with the realities of their new lives.

Part-Time Parents—A Two-Sided Marriage

Another stepparenting situation to consider is joint custody. Consider the case of Dolores.

Dolores is an attractive woman in her early fifties, enjoying her husband Darrell's recent success. He lost his job in a corporate buyout and started his own business. The business is flourishing, and they have moved from the East to the Midwest. Meanwhile, Dolores told me about her twenty-five-year marriage. It was a second marriage for both of them. He had four children, now in their twenties but then in early childhood. The marriage was marvelous, but life was tough. They both worked full-time from Monday to Friday. Then every Friday evening for twenty years he picked up the children at their mother's house while she shopped for food.

The children would arrive and consume the weekend. But they built a family structure, these six people, and as the years went by, the children began to warm toward Dolores. Meanwhile, every Sunday night as her husband drove the four children back to their mother, Agnes, Dolores stripped the beds, did the laundry, and returned the house back to normal. The next morning she was up again by six and off for another week of work.

Only recently, a year after Darrell's first wife's death, did Dolores learn what the children were experiencing weekdays at their mother's home. Poison. Agnes hated Darrell and Dolores. From Monday to Friday the children were assaulted with invectives against their father. It was only after Agnes's death that the children learned that Darrell had sent her financial support for twenty-five years. It was only then that they began to describe what had really been going on.

Dolores told me that although she and Darrell thought

250

they were taking the high road and *never* said an unkind word about their mother, the children wished they had stuck up for themselves. Now they are telling her how hard it was for them to try to sort out right from wrong when all they ever heard was one side of the story. Now they tell her that if they had only been able to speak up, they might have gained some perspective. They said it was a kind of brain-washing, and not really recognizable by young children as it was happening, but it kept them from freely loving their father and stepmother. It confused them.

Think long and hard before getting into a relationship that involves stepchildren. Read the growing number of books on the subject that advise how to negotiate for improvement. When they are ready to be intimate and married, a man and woman should place each other *first*. Ask your friend whether he agrees. Ask him where his ex-wife and children will rank in his list of priorities. If he firmly believes that his children will always come first, consider this a signal of a serious problem for you. If children know that their step-mother comes last, chances are they will make her life mis-erable. Even without their biological mother egging them on, stepchildren present enormous mine fields to new mar-riages. And it is usually the stepmother who suffers the most.

Tell your friend that you are not willing to pursue an intimate relationship with him if you must play second fid-dle to his children, and if his character is good, he may decide—after several lonely weekends—to rethink his priorities. There is always hope—especially when you take a stand. The sooner you take it, the sooner you can resolve the problem and the longer your time of good feelings.

When children recognize that this new parental team is bonded so closely that courtesy to their stepmother improves their own family life (because Dad will not tolerate anything less), the growth of a new set of relationships can begin. Eventually, the children may discover that Dad's choice was a good one and they are fortunate to have their new stepmother in their lives. A good man is worth some stress from his children. Particularly when he is willing to work with you to establish a set of rules for building a new family life, you can develop a loving marriage and maybe a loving stepchild. Dolores and Darrell achieved it. In retrospect, they recognized that clearing the air earlier with their children may have resolved the situation sooner.

INCREASING INTIMACY

A friendship with a man, when it is growing and good, will lead to an ever-increasing intimacy. When you have found a man who behaves as if he treasures you, someone with whom you want to imagine a future, the question of sex will inevitably loom. With your heart and mind prepared for the journey, let's consider your body next. Every woman who contemplates courtship and marriage should understand sexual basics and sexual ethics. The next chapter explores the range of information you should know when you are ready to be sexual in the context of monogamy and commitment.

EIGHT

Sexual Basics,
Sexual Ethics

Doves and pigeons share in their parenting duties. After the
female lays the eggs, the male and female take turns sitting
on them while the other has a chance to fly free, collect
foods, and return to the nest. Mutual responsibility forms
the basis of dove and pigeon pairing.

A woman has the responsibility to exercise her dignity
whenever it is challenged. This preserves her erotic pleasure.

When your goals are courtship and marriage, the way you
live out your sex life can help or hinder you. Maybe in the
past your attitudes about sex were liberal. Or maybe they
were more modest. Maybe you had lots of experiences with
many different men. Or maybe you have no experience.
Whatever your history, the specific details belong in your
private past. It serves you best when you use the lessons it
can provide but maintain discretion. Now the sexual life you
lead can move you toward or away from marriage.

When the friendship you have forged is moving toward

intimacy (including sexual intimacy), your candidate for courtship holds promise if he has waited. When he is a man you want to get close to, sex is inevitable—sooner or later. If you can agree to an exclusive partnership for as long as the two of you see each other, courtship is looming. A shared attitude that considers intimacy precious can bring joy and health to your life.

In the last fifteen years a tremendous amount of information explaining how sexual behavior affects the inner workings of the body has emerged. Particular patterns of sexual behavior produce particular kinds of effects. These recent discoveries about human sexuality have changed the map of knowledge as we know it. Update yourself for your safety and well-being.

First of all, healthy sex is good for you. Knowing the difference between healthy and unhealthy sex is vital.

SEXUAL BASICS

YES, HEALTHY SEX IS GOOD FOR YOU

Healthy sex is physiologically invaluable.

- It creates harmony in the hormonal system, enhancing emotional stability.
- It promotes hormonal levels that reduce the risk of cystic breasts and uterine fibroid tumors.
- It facilitates healthy bones by promoting adequate levels of estrogen and progesterone.

- It may help to prevent cardiovascular disease by generating the kind of hormonal environment associated with cardiovascular health.
- It promotes and preserves fertility.

My initial research from 1974 to 1992 led to some of these conclusions. I worked with fellow scientists at the University of Pennsylvania, Stanford University, the Monell Chemical Senses Center in Philadelphia, and the department of gynecology at the School of Medicine, Hospital of the University of Pennsylvania, and the Athena Institute.[1] Meanwhile, investigators in Sweden, Germany, Colombia, the Netherlands, the United States, and a number of other countries had been investigating the nature of orgasm, arousal, sexual health, and disease. Some of these studies have shown relationships between sex and physiology that led to important conclusions about bones, the cardiovascular system, and health. Some were the natural outgrowth of separate research.[2]

Not all kinds of sex are healthy. In each of the studies women who engaged in regular weekly sex[3] exhibited the healthiest vital signs. Their menstrual cycles were more regular and approached the most fertile timing—every 29.5

---

[1] For details in nonscientific language, the reader might want to take a look at my last book, *Love Cycles: The Science of Intimacy* (New York: Villard Books, 1991).

[2] The studies of aging, bones, and cardiovascular health in relation to the sex hormones are reviewed in two of my other books: *Hysterectomy Before and After* (New York: HarperCollins, 1988) and *Menopause: A Guide for Women and the Men who Love Them,* Second Edition (New York: W. W. Norton, 1992).

[3] "Regular sex" criteria required that they *never* had a week without a sexual encounter when they were not bleeding. Sex during the days of menstrual bleeding may be potentially dangerous.

255

days. Their estrogen levels were higher. Their basal body temperature charts showed a healthier rhythm. When you are ready to settle down, find courtship, and build an intimate relationship leading to marriage, you need to get your body in sync with your goals. Even if you have been getting the physical benefits of regular weekly sex, there may still be the question of how many men. If you are a sexually active woman with more than one partner in your life, making substantial changes now will bring you closer to the goal of commitment and marriage. A feast-or-famine or multiple-partner sex life is bad because it consumes your energy, energy you need to search for and build a monogamous intimate relationship. If you are a woman who is searching for courtship, the implications are clear:

- Until you find a dependable partner, sex can be a detriment to your physical and psychological health.
- If you can't have regular weekly sex in a stable relationship, you are probably better off being celibate. Intermittent (feast-or-famine) sex can be unhealthy.

CONSIDER CHOOSING CELIBACY WHILE YOU SEARCH

A woman who has a good sexual appetite while waiting for courtship will get to courtship most quickly if she abstains from sex. Even if you have a good friend (or two) who is happy to have sex with you providing things don't get too committed, my suggestion is simple. *Don't.* Not once you've decided you are really ready to search for and commit to courtship. You need to focus—not dissipate—your energy. When regular sex with the same partner (often enough to never miss a week) is not an option, celibacy is the next best choice. The studies of young women in their twenties tell it clearly. They show that about half of the women who had an intermittent (on-again, off-again) sexual life had severely disturbed endocrine systems. In the premenstrual weeks, these women had very low estrogen levels—characteristic of menopause—while still in their twenties. A sporadic sex life was causing their bodies to age before their time. The impact was less extreme in celibate women. The "celibates" showed moderately low estrogen levels in comparison with the "weeklies" but were spared the extremely low levels of intermittently active women.

The Consequences of Long-Term Celibacy

Scientific studies cannot tell for sure how celibacy affects women, but judging from the results of my work with the Stanford Menopause Population Study, I can infer the likely outcome. In that group, some women in their forties reported having been celibate for long periods of time—five or ten years. Apparently, when a woman stops having sex, her estrogen levels move moderately lower and stay low.

If you are past forty and take hormonal replacement therapy, or between thirty and forty and take oral contraceptives, you will probably manipulate your estrogen and progesterone levels to your benefit. You should be aware that studies have not yet been published to address the long-term effects of celibacy without hormonal therapy. During long periods without a man, estrogen, progestin, and testosterone hormones, taken appropriately, can enhance your health and well-being.[4]

In women in their twenties celibacy is not nearly as disruptive as intermittent behavior; celibate women did not show the extremely low levels of estrogen characteristic of half of the sporadically active women. Hormonal support is probably less critical during celibacy before age thirty or thirty-five. At all ages, celibacy seems to put the body into "low gear."

When you've recently ended a relationship, celibacy is also a good idea for emotional reasons. It helps to give yourself some time—for mourning, for reestablishing your equilibrium, for taking stock. At the conclusion of two or three celibate menstrual cycles, you will be calmer and more ready to resume your search for a sexual partner who will court you. Giving yourself the gift of celibacy can prepare your body and mind for a fresh start. Meanwhile, there are plenty of other things to do to prepare yourself for the search.

WHERE TO FIND REGULAR SEX

Since the healthy kind of sex—regular, at least weekly, relations with the same partner—is so important, a single woman needs to analyze what promotes and what inhibits it. One simple fact is clear. Men who are available for long-term relationships promote it. The ones who come and go promote intermittent (feast-or-famine) patterns. Usually

---

[4] See *Menopause: A Guide for Women and the Men Who Love Them* or *Hysterectomy Before and After* for details on taking hormones safely.

you can avoid placing yourself in sporadic relationships by being slow to start intimacy with a new partner. This decision to move slowly will reduce your exposure to flash-in-the-pan relationships. But taking charge demands a thoughtful strategy.

Delayed gratification can translate into sexual satisfaction because it gives you time to learn about sensuality—yours and his. Just because you're not having sexual intercourse doesn't mean you're not having sensual experiences. If you broaden your definition of sex, your social life can offer a lot of intimate pleasure. Sex is more than a distinct event—"the act"—it's a continuum of events, feelings, sensations, to be enjoyed and shared. It is particularly elegant when it's not only stages of progressive excitement but of physical involvement and emotional vulnerability.

INTIMATE KNOWLEDGE—
WHAT YOU NEED TO KNOW

For women searching for courtship, intimate self-knowledge is one of the first steps to take. Some of the knowledge is physiological; other aspects are emotional. It is important to know how your own body responds to arousal and to orgasm. Honoring your own needs is a basic principle of well-being.

Unfortunately, many women allow their bodies to be used without reciprocity. They pretend sensual pleasures they do not feel. This is terribly unfortunate. Such "white lies" are probably delivered out of a misguided wish to make their partners feel competent. But, in the long run, if you fail to achieve sexual satisfaction, this will inhibit the development of a satisfying sexual relationship for *both* partners. Pretending to enjoy hurts the pretender and the pretendee. Faking orgasm violates four principles of the Code of Courtship:

- Principle 7: You acquire basic hormonal and sexual facts.
- Principle 6: You develop your capacity for honesty.
- Principle 2: You accept the legitimacy of your own needs.
- Principle 4: You communicate what you want.

In most of the media hype and cultural mythology about orgasm, one simple fact is rarely mentioned: Orgasm is a simple reflex, not much more physically complex than a yawn. Knowing that it is a basic biological function can diminish anxiety about orgasm: whether you've never had one, can have one only under certain circumstances, or wonder if you're having the "right" kind. Triggering your orgasmic reflex requires self-knowledge and enough trust to communicate certain relevant information to your partner about the way your body is "wired." Once you know how your physical reactions work when you are alone, you can integrate this information into your search for shared intimacy with your lover.

FEMALE SEXUAL RESPONSE— A FLOW CHART

A woman's sexual response is most sensuous when all four essential elements are working in concert. The four components are similar in men. The continuum begins with

- *libido* (the desire for sexual encounter), progresses to
- *sexual arousal,* moves on (sometimes) to
- *willingness* to engage in intercourse, and is followed by ever-increasing arousal that leads to
- *orgasm* (the muscle spasm that reflexively, automatically follows properly timed stimulation).

When a new relationship moves slowly, the four elements flow in a continual process in which you travel smoothly from one stage into the next. But intimacy doesn't always move smoothly. Often some of the sexual-response elements are present and others are missing. For instance, it is possible to be *aroused* but for a variety of reasons to be *unwilling* to engage in intercourse.

Likewise, a woman can experience no arousal (during periods of hormonal dips) but still achieve orgasm. By the time women are in their forties, close to half no longer experience libido; but 75 percent are now fully orgasmic. A 95 percent figure was the result of actual research with healthy women in Denmark and is described in *Love Cycles: The Science of Intimacy.* Our own research at the Athena Institute suggests a lower figure of 60 percent after age forty who almost always achieve orgasm at coitus. In other words, a woman can have no interest in getting started, but if she accommodates her partner, she can have no problem in experiencing an orgasm.

Libido, the desire for sex, is very different from orgasm, the ability to have the reflex muscle contraction. When you have forged a deep friendship with a man you love, the circumstances are ideal. Both libido and orgasm can be very pleasurable. But think of libido as the appetite for the meal, and of orgasm as the ability to enjoy the flavors. They are different but closely connected aspects of sensuality.

Even when you have found a loving and sensitive partner, a variety of conditions affect the four response components differently: the time of the month, your age, stress, and general health; your level of fitness, your previous sexual experience, your particular man, your use of drugs or alcohol, and your emotional state. Let's look more closely at the workings of these four physical elements of sexual response.

LIBIDO—
THE DRIVE TO GET SEXUAL

Although it's a normal part of life, libido can produce difficulties for single women. If you accept the idea that celibacy is a choice you make to focus time and energy on a courtship search, you'll have times when your libido is burning but your willingness is not. Celibacy won't make your libido disappear.

Fortunately, you can put your normal drive for sex to good use to discover and practice your sensuality while you search. Learn about your body by studying your own anatomy, physiology, and sexual responses in the privacy of your own home. A number of good books can help you learn how to stimulate yourself to find out how your own body functions. With enough practice you will probably discover the facts without much book study. Self-stimulation will relieve sexual yearnings and teach you about your capacity for arousal and orgasm. It will also prevent vaginal atrophy, a problem of many celibate and intermittently active women.

Both external and internal genital massage keep the vagina and labial skin healthy and the cellular substructure intact. Masturbation is very healthy.

Having a sex drive is natural and should be appreciated for what it is, the drive for life. What you do with your normal sex drive helps determine how healthy your future will be. But sometimes a woman's sex drive makes her feel uncomfortable.

How Men React to a Woman with a Strong Libido

When a woman wants sex a lot and really enjoys it, some men will be pleased but others may be intimidated. It depends on the man. People vary in their appetites and capacities. If you enjoy sex a lot and have a relatively high drive for it, you will want to find a man whose appetite matches yours as closely as possible. Such a man will be grateful to bond with you. Likewise, the man who is intimidated by your drive won't be a good candidate since he is unlikely to be able to meet your needs. A man's libidinal level and responses will give you valuable information about how good you would be for each other. Observe his reactions.

How Couples Can Manage Her High Libido When His Is Low

The person in the opposite situation from her man can expect to confront many challenges. If you are in a relationship with a man who doesn't have as much sexual need as you do, you should carefully consider this fact. Your solution depends on how you feel and the reason for this gap. Maybe he needs seductive education in the romantic arts. Or it may just be that his sex drive is much lower than yours. If that's the case, it doesn't bode well for the relationship. One of the worst combinations I have seen in marriage relationships is a woman with a high sex drive bonded to a man with a very low libido. She can feel like she's climbing the walls, and he can't understand what's the matter with her.

The older the man, the longer you should wait before judging. Older men can have lower levels of libido—or they may just be more patient. A more mature man may be seriously searching for a marriage partner, but with more deliberation, slowly. If all other elements of his personality and character make you feel that he would be the ideal husband, a wait of six months is reasonable.

If he is in his early twenties and you are seeing him two or three times a week and have a healthy libido of your own, two to three months is usually long enough to evaluate whether your drives for intimate connection are compatible. A young man who is interested in seeing you that often but is not interested in sex is likely to have a libido that will leave you wanting.

Unfortunately, there are no simple answers and each choice we make has its own risk. And its own rewards.

SEXUAL AROUSAL—
GETTING PHYSICALLY READY

Sexual arousal can begin in the brain or in the genitals. But center stage—where sexual response is physiologically mediated and felt—is the pelvis.

A woman's pelvic anatomy is rather miraculous. As important as it is to know how to drive a car or make a pot of coffee, it is even more important to know your own anatomy when you are ready for courtship and marriage. If you can identify your clitoris, the highly sexually sensitive external "button," your urethra, from which urine is expelled, your vagina, the access route to the uterus or womb, and your anus, the exit from the rectum and intestines, you have some necessary basic information. If you are not sure about the location and basic function of these female parts, you can get that information from many responsible books, including my own.[5]

For healthy sexual intercourse, the vagina is the only pelvic cavity that a penis should enter. In spite of 1990 data showing that anal intercourse is experienced by one in every three American women, the practice is a health hazard. The thrust of a penis into the anus can make hundreds of tiny tears in the intestinal lining, causing pain, distress, and making you more vulnerable to infection with HIV— the AIDS virus. The shearing pressure can also cause hemorrhoids.

What activates female sexual organs? What starts the process of arousal? What turns you on? Scientists have not been able to figure out the magic that sometimes ignites between a particular man and woman. It's probably a combination of physical and psychological attraction. Leslie described a situation common to dating encounters.

---

[5] *Love Cycles: The Science of Intimacy* (New York: Villard Books, 1991) (see Chapters 4 and 7). See also *For Each Other: Sharing Sexual Intimacy* (New York: Anchor Press, 1982) by Lonnie Barbach.

"I meet men I like but have no physical attraction for. I don't even want to kiss them. I want to gracefully get out of any physical contact but keep them as a friend or date."

When a man wants intimacy and you recoil, you probably can't manage a sensible dating experience with him. Sexual attraction is the basis for courtship, and courtship is the basis for the long-term male/female intimate relationship. When you get ready to search for courtship, your energies should be directed to finding a sexual match. But before you are sure that you feel no physical attraction, give yourself some time to dance with him and, if appropriate, to hug and kiss him good night. Many women find that in spite of thinking they feel no attraction for a man, the very act of a touch or kiss triggers the electric feelings of sexual arousal. Still, you can't expect a long-term relationship to flourish if he doesn't make you respond sexually when you do get close enough to kiss. If he can light your fire, it's a good sign. If he can't, he may be the wrong man for you. The chemistry is not working.

All Systems Go

As a woman becomes sexually aroused, her body sends her blood flowing in a different pattern. Blood is shunted from general circulation (all over the body) specifically to the pelvic region. As the blood rushes into the pelvic blood vessels, the tissues of the vagina, the labia (lips), and the entire pelvic cavity become suffused with blood. This swelling produces a series of sensations that are associated with arousal, erotic pleasure, and sexual focus. In other words, when your emotions are in line with your physiology, your blood flows to your pelvis and the sensation is erotic.

The flow of blood to the pelvic region also leads to genital lubrication. This moisture is a signal that the vagina has reached a state of sufficient arousal. It is physiologically ready to receive a penis. Lubrication protects against the friction, pain, and tissue damage that dry intercourse would cause. And lubrication enhances the pleasurable sensations that a rhythmic genital massage can offer.[6]

When I consider the exquisite symmetry of the design of a woman's pelvic region, I am awed. Sexual arousal promotes the conditions that facilitate fertility. As sperm enter from the penis through the vagina, they move up into the uterus and up the fallopian tubes. In part, the sperm do the swimming, but the uterine contractions a woman experiences during orgasm help to propel the sperm on its journey. Meanwhile, sometime later, an egg enters from the ovary. The sperm and egg enter the fallopian tube from opposite ends for a possible meeting near the middle, a possible fertilization. A kind of consummation at high noon.

The anatomy makes biological sense. The arousal and orgasm mechanisms make sense. Nature's system is not haphazard. The design of new life reaches its fruition in the act of sexual intercourse. It is therefore not surprising that regular sexual intercourse triggers physiological changes that contribute to a healthy mother, one who can establish a

---

[6] Not all wetness is arousal, however. The vagina is a self-cleaning organ. Daily secretions help keep organisms from gaining a toehold. Any form of vaginal infection will result in an excess of fluid as the body attempts to wash out the infection. Also, around the time of ovulation the cervical region produces a copious fluid that bathes the genitals. This monthly increase continues until menopause approaches.

healthy pregnancy. And even if you don't care about pregnancy, fertility reflects hormonal harmony in the premenopausal woman. Every system functions at peak level.

WILLINGNESS

Willingness to engage in sexual intercourse is legally required for adult consensual sex. In other words, if you are spending time with a man but are unwilling to have sexual intercourse with him, it is your right (and also your responsibility) to communicate that fact. It is your legal right to expect that he will stop advancing whenever you ask him to stop. But be warned. Rape is rampant. Men often say they misunderstood the willingness of women. As a single woman going out a lot, meeting many new men, it is essential to be aware of the danger. To protect your own emotional and physical safety, you need to learn how to make yourself clear. Enlist Code of Courtship principle four:

You communicate what you want.

And you need to know how not to compromise yourself. Be on guard against the possibility of misinterpretation. You give the wrong signal about willingness when you isolate yourself with a man before you want intimacy with him. Since men tend to be stronger than women, you need to protect yourself with knowledge. Until you are ready to have sexual intercourse with a man, it is probably smart to prevent his private access to you. Whether in a bedroom, apartment, or other secluded area, access can communicate willingness. Even when you don't mean it.

Once you are sure that you can trust him, the rules change. But remember, it takes time to evaluate a man's character. You won't know that he is willing to respect your stated wishes until you have known him for some time. His profession, economic circumstances, and educational level won't tell you about his character. Read the newspapers to prove to yourself that even men of wealth, power, and education commit rape. And read on to see how often they say (they believed that) the woman *wanted* sexual intercourse. If your kisses do not include a consent to intercourse, don't engage in kissing unless you have control of the situation. A kiss in a park when others are nearby communicates a less willing message than a kiss in his bedroom. Be alert! Use common sense.

But if you do come to trust him, trust that your desire for physical connection with him will grow.

ORGASM—NOTHING TO SNEEZE AT

Orgasm is sexist. This neuromuscular reflex is required for normal fertility in a man. For a woman, orgasm is required only for her own well-being, not for procreation. She can conceive and give birth years before she ever discovers orgasm. The reflex of orgasm is relatively simple, but moral and emotional inhibitions overlay simple biology and are often very complex.

Let's first consider orgasm's simple reflex nature. Orgasm in a woman is something like a yawn. Think of the way, when you yawn, muscle tension builds in the throat, opening its walls wider and wider until it concludes with a spasm. A similar sequence occurs in the vagina. For a man, orgasm is more like a sneeze—a tickling of nerves until an explosive discharge releases the tension.

On the physiological level, it's an automatic chain reaction for both sexes. When the sensory nerves[7] are stimulated by appropriate rhythmic stroking, the stimulation of nerves builds tension in nearby muscles. The sensory nerves set in motion another set of nerves called motor nerves. As these motor nerves fire electricity, they cause muscles to contract. As muscles contract, muscle tension builds. Then when the tension reaches its maximum, a spasmodic release discharges the tension—in the genitals it's called orgasm.

I use the commonplace yawn and sneeze to explain orgasm because when all goes well, orgasmic release becomes as inevitable as the release of a yawn or sneeze. Unfortunately, many different kinds of inhibitions can block that release and build tension without resolving it. If the rhythm of stimulation is out of sync, the tension can begin to dissipate before it successfully resolves in the spasmodic pleasure of an orgasm. One value of self-stimulation is that it teaches awareness of this simple reflex mechanism. Once you're familiar with your biology and associated feelings, it gets eas-

---

[7] Nerves transmit electrical energy and signal information into the spinal cord. Different nerves have different kinds of endings, and the ones that are activated here are particularly sensitive to pressure and touch. There are hundreds of nerve endings just underneath the clitoris and inside the vagina as well as at the tip of the cervix. Under the normal course of sexual stimulation, either by touch or penile thrusting, the sensory nerves are pressed against, and this triggers a firing pattern that is transmitted to the central nervous system and brain.

ier to achieve satisfaction with a partner. When the relationship is good and the partners can communicate with each other, they can take the time they need to overcome inhibition and discover their mutual biology.

GETTING TO KNOW HIM

If you want to enjoy the pleasures of erotic arousal, it helps to understand the basic mechanisms of sexual pleasure. Knowing your own body provides half the equation. Women need a basic education about men too. And it is never too early. Even if you haven't found him yet, it is helpful to get ready now for when you do.

When it comes to sexual connection, anatomy clearly shows the exquisite design for fitting together male and female. As an informed woman, you should understand what a normal penis looks like. You should also know what variations to expect. Some men are circumcised, a surgical procedure usually performed in the first few days of life, where the foreskin of the penis is cut away for religious or health reasons. The circumcised penis looks different from one that is uncircumcised. Both are "normal."

If the man you love has an uncircumcised penis, he needs to give greater attention to hygiene because the fold can accumulate secretions. The fold can attract various irritants and transmit infectious diseases. The newest research studies indicate that an intact foreskin (an uncircumcised penis) may predispose men to infection with the HIV virus.

For sexual relations, the foreskin of the uncircumcised penis is folded back to reveal the head. Whether the penis is

271

circumcised or not, the head (or glans) is exquisitely sensitive to rhythmic touch and pressure, especially on the underside of the penis where glans meet the shaft. (The anatomical counterpart to the glans of the man is the clitoris of the woman, which has the same remarkable sensitivity.) The younger the man, the more sensitive the penis. In young men, simply rubbing the penis against their underwear can be sufficient to trigger an erection. Sensitivity declines with age. As a man ages, it takes ever-increasing stimulation to promote the same degree of sensation. The same goes for women.

In a man, as in a woman, sexual arousal can begin in the brain or the genitals. Once sexual arousal is triggered, a predictable series of events follows. First the blood flows from general circulation into the pelvic region. In women, the blood flow is diffuse, producing swelling throughout the labia, vagina, and pelvic region. In men, the blood flow is focused, channeling into the penis and producing the characteristic and undisputable arousal signal of a stiff penis (also called an erection or tumescence).

At full erection, the penis achieves its maximum size. Books give a range from about two and a half to over twelve inches in different men—all healthy variations of "normal." The average erect penis measures between six and eight inches. The depth of the vagina of women is equally variable. When you consider the size of your partner and know your own size, you will be equipped to improve your sensual life together. The greater the discrepancy in fit between penis and vagina, the more sensitive the partners will have to be in learning to meet the needs of each to promote sensation and avoid injury. If his penis is too small to fill you easily, you can explore together the things you can do and the positions that will satisfy each of you. If his penis is too large for you, you can develop habits that protect you from pain by discovering how deeply he can enter you without hurting you.

Arousal, which leads to an erect penis, allows penetration for intercourse. This thrusting into the vagina massages and stimulates his nerve endings. When sufficient stimulation builds harmonically, the tension it produces is followed by a spasmodic release of the tension, known as orgasm, which is obvious in your partner by the pulsing release of fluid ejaculated through the urethra out of the penis.

After ejaculation, depending on the level of testosterone in the blood and his age, the erection will be maintained for some minutes. It is not uncommon for an erection to last five or ten minutes after ejaculation in a young man, although as men age, the detumescence (loss of erection) usually occurs more quickly. If he is still hard after he tells you he had an orgasm, it does not mean you have not satisfied him.

THE RHYTHM OF PLEASURE

Whether stimulated by masturbation or by thrusting within a vagina, the unskilled man, in most cases, moves to the rhythm of his own pleasure. He doesn't think about the rhythm but *knows* when to press harder, lighter, faster, or slower. So it is with vaginal or clitoral masturbation when you are alone.

Intercourse can be just as orgasmic as masturbation in *both* partners. Often more orgasmic, once the skills are developed. Male and female are remarkably similar in their separate approaches toward orgasm. Regular rhythmic thrusting of the penis will inevitably produce an orgasm in the man and the woman *if the rhythm and pressure are correctly applied.*[8] The problem for many couples is that his rhythm isn't hers; it takes time for him to learn what rhythm she needs. And usually *he* does the thrusting, since his biology is designed for this role. It is physiologically difficult, or at least uncomfortable, for the woman to control the thrusting. That would require her to do the equivalent of deep knee bends positioned above the man.

Regardless of who's on top, it is the rhythm, as well as "hitting the target," that matters most. Women vary in the location of their target region of vaginal sensitivity. Depending on the way you are "wired," face-to-face or some other sexual position may be needed to allow the tip or ridge of the penis to hit your target. Most men easily achieve orgasm during vaginal stimulation because most men are in charge of the thrusting pattern—hitting their own targets at the rhythm that is just right for them. In a sexual encounter the couple should learn together to achieve mutual pleasure. Since the man will lose his erection shortly after he ejaculates, many couples find that by attending to the woman's needs first, both can be most easily satisfied. If

---

[8] Different women have different areas of sensitivity within the vagina. But studies show that each woman has a place that is particularly sensitive to regular stimulation. For the majority, it is located at twelve o'clock high, about one and a half inches inside the external opening to the vagina. But some women have their sensitive region at four o'clock low, or six o'clock, or somewhere else.

she has already reached orgasm and he continues to thrust toward his own, she may be able to have another orgasm as well.

On the topic of orgasm, many women feel as Sara does.

"I don't really care to reach an orgasm every time we have sex. I agree that I should not fake orgasm, but sometimes I don't want one. I don't see anything wrong with telling him to just go ahead and take his turn because I don't need it."

Be aware that there is something wrong with this attitude. The thrusting of the penis in your vagina is going to produce stimulation. With stimulation, the body is either being aroused or abused. If it is being aroused, it is building tension and the tension should be discharged in order to have a satisfactory sexual encounter. Once you learn how easy it is to reach orgasm, your experience will change. Your orgasm should become as inevitable as your partner's if you both learn how your body works. It will help reinforce the relationship's value to you both.

Although I am not familiar with the research on this subject, I suspect that undischarged tension is unhealthy for a woman's pelvic physiology. *I suspect* that fibroid tumors and other diseases of the pelvis may derive in part from the unresolved tension that builds up. I don't think a woman should submit to being put into a position where mounting tension is not resolved. If he ejaculates before you reach orgasm, he can manually stimulate your clitoris or vaginal target area to help you reach yours. Courtship, love, and marriage should enhance your health when you are doing it right. Learn how.

THE EXQUISITE FIT

The male and female sexual organs are designed to fit together, but there is more to sex than the fit of penis in vagina. The high art of sexual pleasuring is worthy of learning. This is a lifetime education, not to be achieved at the first few encounters. Human sexual response is complex. Since your sensuality changes with your hormonal rhythms, it takes time to experience and learn harmony with your partner. Monogamous connections permit the development of the high art of really knowing each other.

If you want extraordinary sex, you should expect to study about it, be willing to practice, and to develop a sense of humor when you bumble. You will need to find a lover who will want the same thing and be willing, with humility, to engage in the extended process of learning who you are, how your sensuality works, how you fit together. It really *doesn't* just come naturally.

HEALTHY SEX IS YOUR RIGHT

As delicate and lovely as sex can be when it's right, when it is wrong it can be dangerous to your health, your well-being, and even your life. Sex can be deadly. The threat of sexually transmitted diseases (especially AIDS, which according to the Centers for Disease Control is on the rise in heterosexual women) means you should take basic precautions when it comes time to have sex. That means that single people should use a condom every time they have sex. It's a black-and-white choice: life and love or despair and the risk of death.

276

To get the greatest possible protection from condoms, both women and men should know how to use them. Condom labels have instructions, but you need to learn about the correct use long before the condom is pulled out during an intimate encounter.

And you should have your own supply on hand. Condoms come in more sizes, shapes, colors, and textures than you probably ever imagined. You may want to get a few types and experiment. The safest types are made from latex, a material that appears to be impermeable to HIV viruses as well as the organisms that cause hepatitis B, herpes, chlamydia, gonorrhea, and syphilis. Natural lambskin condoms —made of layers of porous collagen—are a bit riskier. Escape-minded organisms can sometimes wriggle through the minuscule airways of a lambskin condom. Also not safe-sex condoms are the short stubby "caps" that cover just the head of the penis. These may be dislodged during vigorous thrusting, and since they do not cover the shaft, genital to genital contact and therefore the potential for disease exposure occurs.

Whether or not you have used condoms before, it is crucial to your health and your very life that you do so from now on. If he won't, don't have sex with him. A man who would ask you to risk your life for sexual pleasure is not a man who can court you.

When He Objects to a Condom

When a man says, "I have never worn condoms. I'm safe. Why don't you believe me?" consider telling him this: "I do believe you that you think you're safe. I think I am too. But people can carry AIDS, even test negative, and still have the disease.

They can feel great and have the disease. They can be virgins and have the disease. I am not going to risk my life for sex. I am going to give my husband (when I find him) the gift of having used condoms every time I have sex until I am married to him."

When a man says, "It hurts to wear a condom," tell him to try a different size or shape till he finds the brand that doesn't hurt.

When he says, "It cuts down on my sensation," or "I'm allergic to condoms," or "I can't stay hard with one of those things on," tell him you understand that he can't use condoms, and if the two of you are to build a love relationship, you are willing to wait for him until you marry. That as much as this may be a sacrifice to hold off on sexual intercourse until you marry, you are willing to make this sacrifice in order to protect your health and that of your future husband (and maybe children). Tell him that there are plenty of good sensual activities the two of you can enjoy until you marry or he overcomes his problem with erection, or sensation, or so forth.

And when he won't wait for you if you insist on condoms, wish him well and say good-bye. He may be back when he realizes that you mean it. But even if he does come back on your terms, would you want a man who will only give you what you need when you threaten to leave him?

"CONDOM SENSE" SEX

Before using a condom, read the instructions on the package. Here is a brief review of the rules.

When to put it on. Put the condom on as soon as erection occurs. Unprotected vaginal or oral contact is unsafe, so the condom should be put on the man's penis before it gets near any body opening. You want to avoid exposure to any body fluid that may carry infection.

How to put it on. A condom looks something like a rolled-up balloon (see Figure 8.1). It has a ring on the outside. This ring is placed over the tip of the penis, as shown in Figure 8.2.

Remember that the purpose of the condom is to hold the biological fluids that are released both before and after the

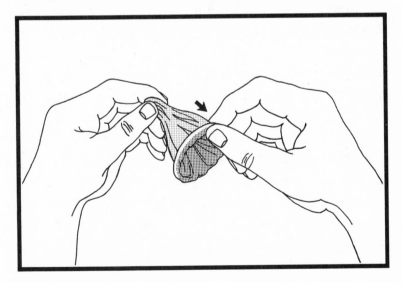

Figure 8.1

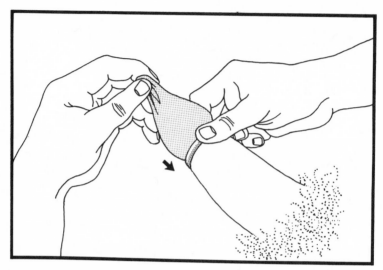

Figure 8.2

man reaches his orgasm. Therefore the tip of the condom should not be tightly placed against the tip of the penis. It is important to leave some empty space (about half an inch) for holding the fluid. Or choose a condom with a reservoir tip.

Figure 8.3 shows how to unroll the condom. Squeeze the tip gently so that no air will be trapped inside it as the unrolling proceeds. A person putting on the condom needs to hold the tip as the condom is carefully unrolled all the way down to the base of the penis. If the condom won't unroll, it is on backward and should be thrown away. Then a new condom should be put on according to the directions just given. If you've never put a condom on a man before, practice by unrolling one on a carrot, candle, cucumber, or zucchini.

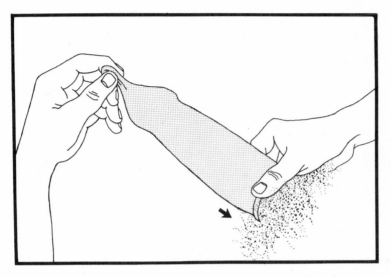

Figure 8.3

How and When to Take It Off

After sex, once the man has ejaculated, the condom should still be on his penis. To be sure that he does manage to keep it there, it helps if, after ejaculating, he withdraws slowly while his penis is still hard. He should use his fingers to hold the condom in place at the base or rim of the penis as he pulls out. This avoids spilling semen and other biological fluids on the woman's genitals. Ideally, a man and woman should be physically separated and facing away from each other as the condom is removed, and it should be thrown away. Then if there will be more sexual intimacy, a new condom should be put on as described above. Figure 8.4 shows how a man should place his hands to hold on to the condom as he withdraws from a woman's vagina.

Successful condom use is enhanced if you:

- Wash hands and genitals (penis, vagina, and surrounding areas) before and after sex to reduce the risk of infection.
- Avoid condom contact with any kind of oil such as petroleum jelly, baby oil, or mineral oil. Keep a condom away from talcum powder. These substances deteriorate the rubber. Use lubricated condoms to reduce friction and prevent tearing.
- If you are going to use a lubrication aid, opt for a water-based product such as K-Y Jelly. (Read the label of the product to make sure it's water-based.) Condom manufacturers recommend using a foam, cream, or gel sold in drugstores for female birth control, which serves as both a lubricant and as additional insurance against fertilization. The active ingredient in these products, nonoxynol 9, helps kill the HIV virus as well as other viruses and bacteria.
- Store condoms in packs in a cool, dry place. A wallet is a bad place to keep a condom; body heat and friction can damage it here.

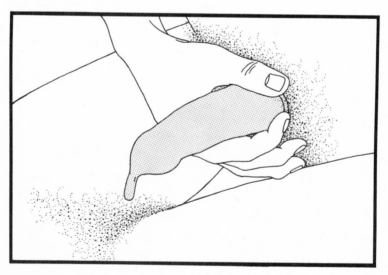

Figure 8.4

· Throw away any condom that feels sticky or stiff or looks damaged in any way when you unwrap it. It is not worth the risk. Also, discard any condom that is too old. (Check for the expiration date on the package.)

When It Is Okay to Stop Using a Condom

When you know it is safe, you can give up condoms. And you will know it is safe when you are ready to get married, have been monogamous for a reasonably long period of time, have evaluated each other's character, know that you have been honest with each other, and are not carrying a sexually transmitted disease.

COMMUNICATING ABOUT SEXUALLY TRANSMITTED DISEASES

A problem like herpes must be discussed. Even if it does not flare up very often, you cannot keep it to yourself because it is unethical to avoid disclosure. Remember principle six of the Code:

> You develop your capacity for honesty and your ability to detect deception.

An intimate relationship built on lies or deception is destined to cause tremendous suffering. The truth will eventually come out. And the longer it takes, the greater the shock. When you are ready to be sexual, if your objective is an honorable relationship, you will have to tell him. If you have had a disease that flares occasionally but hasn't erupted for a long time, you might reasonably decide to tell him after the first or second intimate, condom-using connection. You have the right to measure your own willingness for continued intimacy before you divulge your own dark secrets—provided you have taken precautions to spare him infection. If you need a sexual encounter to make that decision *and* can assure his safety (through careful use of condoms), a short delay is reasonable.

EMOTIONALLY SAFE SEX

Protecting yourself against the dangers of sexually transmitted diseases and pregnancy by learning about effective condom use is not all you need to know about safe sex. The essential need still remains for protecting yourself against emotionally dangerous sex. Consider one common type, a man who doesn't appreciate feminine sensuality, who makes a woman feel bad when she is sensual. When you are searching for courtship and marriage, such a man is not worthy of your energy. He cannot court. He cannot love you enough. Keep searching elsewhere, and you will find a better life without him.

Other forms of emotionally dangerous sex are more subtle. Many women find they have been deceived. A man has "come on" to them with apparent romantic interest and hopes for a long-term future. They decide to accept his pleadings, trust him, and "take a chance." They go to bed with him and then endure the humiliation of not hearing from him soon—maybe never. This kind of sexual behavior is dangerous to a woman's well-being. It eats at her dignity. It reduces her self-esteem. It makes her feel like an object.

Return to the rules described in the Code of Courtship. Conduct yourself by its principles and you will protect yourself. It isn't easy to hold fast to a guiding set of principles. The price will be exercising restraint, taking charge of your health and well-being, and making decisions based on your own well-being. Nor is it easy to suffer the humiliating pain of postcoital abandonment. Sex is powerful stuff. It can magnify the goodness in your life or destroy you.

SEXUAL ETHICS

THE RIGHTS, RESPONSIBILITIES, AND PRIVILEGES OF SEX

Intimate connection carries with it certain rights, responsibilities, and privileges. When you accept the Code of Courtship, you have the right to expect honesty, monogamy, and availability from your partner, and you have the responsibility to give the same. It's good to know that somebody is there for you when you need him and that he welcomes your calls, but if you want a man to be available to you, you need to make yourself available to him. If you want to be treated with courtesy and respect, you have to treat him in the same way. Your intimacy should add strength to you both.

WHAT TO DIVULGE ABOUT
YOUR SEXUAL HISTORY

Sexual connection between grown-ups is part of the search for courtship. It can be an appropriate risk to take in the journey toward marriage. But even after they have become sexually intimate, a couple may decide not to marry. This is natural. You have to expect that as you search for a life partner, it will take a certain number of false starts, exploratory journeys, and partial successes before you figure out what you want. But what do you tell—or not tell—the next man with whom you become intimate?

Deciding what to divulge to your lover will shape the elegance of your love life. When you become close to a man, it is natural to want to share details about your histories, facts about who you are, stories about where you have been.

When confiding in a trusted, caring friend or lover, it is always okay to tell him how you feel. It is never okay to describe in any detail personal information about another man with whom you have been intimate.

Your previous love might not want his private exposure to you divulged to a man he does not know. Consider how *you* would feel. Decency and good manners demand that sexual intimacy remain forever private between the consenting adults who shared it. Mannerly people respect the privacy and dignity of others. If their relationship does not continue forever, at least the intimate details of their private connections should be privately held forever.

Fred will never have the standing to know what you did with George before Fred came along. If you tell him, you will be telling him more about *your* character than about George's. You will be telling him that you are not

286

trustworthy and that, should you and he not make it, he can expect you to tell your next man intimate details about him.

Recognize that in being discreet the sexual sophistication you display tells a lot. It conveys that you are an experienced woman. That is enough for him to know. If he asks you about your history, be dignified. In your own words, say:

"I'm uncomfortable discussing this because I respect the privacy of my previous relationships. Those people were in my past—what counts now is you, in my present. And I would be very uncomfortable hearing *your* sexual history."

A woman has the responsibility to exercise her dignity whenever it is challenged. You have the responsibility to teach men how you expect to be treated if a relationship is to continue. When you are out searching for courtship, you can be the leader. You can define the elegance of the relationship by establishing your own ground rules. Take the high road and restrain the impulse to tell all. Don't expose details about your prior consensual sexual experience.

But if your private history includes sexual abuse or having been raped, that is a different case. That is not something you should necessarily keep from the man with whom you share your life. You may need and want his emotional support to help you, and if you feel you can trust his maturity, to turn to him for understanding and kindness.

One of the rewards of behaving like a dignified person is you will be treated like one. A good man will rise to the standards you set. If he cannot rise to your standards, move on and find someone who can.

One woman worried:

"I know you say that I should not divulge the intimate details of my sexual history, but the fact is that I had a pretty wild period and am well known by a number of men who move on the outer edges of the social circle in which I now circulate. When I meet a new man, I'm afraid of what will happen if he hears about me from other men."

If you have this feeling about your own history, you can take action. In the early stages of your relationship you might consider telling him a general history of your past. Perhaps something like

"When I was in my early twenties, I went through a pretty wild period. I learned how I did not want to live in the future. It was part of growing up and I am glad that I had some experience, but I am no longer interested in wild connections. I thought you should know that I have outgrown this."

Then if he hears about you, he will have some understanding of who you are and where you have been without having to know the details. This will preserve your dignity and your nondeceiving character. Both are qualities of your adult character that you want to communicate to him.

When the Man You Love Will Not Sleep with You

Once sexual intimacies have started, other sticky situations arise. Consider the case of Alice, who described her confusion over sex without sleepovers.

"Peter and I have been seeing each other for six months and recently we have become sexual. My problem is that Peter does not want to sleep over. After we have a passionate experience, he will stay with me for a half hour or so and then insist he is uncomfortable, wants to sleep in his own bed, and tells me he has to leave. I am left feeling terrible and I don't quite know why."

This problem came up again and again in our workshops. And it is relatively easy to solve. When you are searching for courtship, sexual intimacy will be part of the process of moving toward ever-closer connection. From this perspective, such a partner's behavior is a red flag warning you that he is not interested in courting. When a man wants to have sex with you but does not want to sleep with you, his behavior is telling you that he does not want to become too intimate, too committed. Although he may tell you that when left alone overnight his dog is incontinent and his geraniums wilt, in courtship your needs must come before his dog's and his geraniums'. Discuss this with him, and if he is unable to change his behavior, end the relationship. This is not courtship.

SEX FOR RECREATION?

Some men and women consider it okay to use sex for the release of tension and other good feelings it provides. "Sex as sport" is a common behavior of a significant percentage of the single population. If such behavior is a part of your history, keep your own counsel about your past experiences.

They are no longer appropriate once a search for courtship is under way. In courtship, sex is not sport. It is part of a growing love and commitment experience.

In courtship, by the time partners become sexual, they want to sleep together and they want to see each other in the morning. When you are ready for courtship and marriage, don't settle for less. Preserve your energy for where it will yield its best and highest use, an intimate relationship with a man who is actively courting you.

DELAYING THE START OF SEX

From the workshop participants, I learned that women vary tremendously in how soon they feel ready to become sexually intimate. Some women like to start a sexual relationship only after they have a long period of getting to know the other person. But while they are waiting, physical affection is very important. They want hand holding, hugging, and cuddling, but they don't want to take off their clothes and get sexual too soon.

If you feel this way, nothing is wrong with you. You should respect your feelings and look for a partner who will be willing to honor them. There is no correct formula of how long it should take an individual to be willing to expose herself and stand naked before another. Your attitudes are defined by your history, how well "trusting others" has worked for you in the past, and your general state of being now. Don't worry about it. Accept yourself and the way you feel. And look for partners who will do the same. Your attitude will be enchanting to a man who can love you.

Another way is to have a noncoital but very sexy experience.

Suggest a Sleepover

A planned noncoital sleepover can be a wonderful comfort zone between being nonsexual and becoming sexual. By suggesting a pre-sex sleepover, you allow a man who may be nervous about his ability to attain an erection a chance to be close with you first. And you might prevent the possibility of a relationship where a man wants sex without a sleepover. If he wants sex with you and is willing to sleep over, he is providing an important signal about his intentions. If you request a sleepover first, you will give yourselves a chance to get used to the intimacy of closeness without the pressure of sexual performance. If everything goes well, you always have the right to change your mind and go further into intimacy than you had planned; but by agreeing to go slowly, you preserve your comfort and put yourself in the position of entering into deeper and deeper intimacies one step at a time. Once one step has gone well, it is easier to move on to the next one.

But the modern reality of parenting among single adults may limit the possibility of sleepovers. Many ethical questions emerge in such a situation.

HANDLING SLEEPOVERS WHEN THE PARTNERS ARE SINGLE PARENTS

Single parents who are ready for sleepovers should be sensitive to the feelings of their young children, preteens, and teenagers living at home. You should carefully consider whether you should tell your children about parental sleepovers or keep them secret. It depends on your values. If you reserve sexual connection for serious potential marriage partners, there may come a time when you want to be forthcoming with your children about your sexual life. However, the more slowly you can expose them to the fact of your sexuality, the more you will preserve family cohesion and prevent disruptions.

If your children sometimes stay overnight with their father, it is sensible to have your sleepovers with a potential mate when they are away. But if your children do not have alternate sleeping arrangements, you will probably have to go very slowly in initiating a new sexual relationship if you want to keep your children's emotional life stable.

COSMETIC SURGERY

What about cosmetic surgery? Is it worthwhile to enhance your sexual attractiveness in this way? Is it ethical?

Some women wonder whether it is dishonest for a woman to augment her breasts or to have other types of cosmetic surgery, but I see nothing wrong with doing whatever you want to do to make yourself more attractive. The more attractive you are, the more candidates you will have to select from. If you have confidence in your attractiveness, chances are you will exude a magnetism that attracts men to you, regardless of the size of your breasts, or having a less than perfect body. But if you don't have such confidence and the surgery will help give it to you, the choice may be sensible.

However, any cosmetic surgery, such as a face-lift, breast augmentation, liposuction, or rhinoplasty, has biomedical risk and potentially serious health consequences. Your doctor or women's health resource should be able to give you advice.[9] Be sure they can support any safety claims with scientific data published in peer-reviewed medical journals.

AGE DIFFERENCES

The ramifications of going out with younger men (a difference of ten years or more) are complex. Men have gone out with younger women for centuries, and women have the same choice.

But it isn't that simple.

In terms of sexual basics, there are pros and cons. Men who have reached their mid-forties tend to have a much more severe decline in their sex drive than do women of the same age. As a consequence, for many sexually interested women in their late forties and beyond, the major limitation to an active sex life is the availability of an interested and interesting partner. Younger men can offer more sexual activity than older men. In fact, research conducted in England by investigators working with a Yale University[10] medical

---

[9] I am unable to render a scientific judgment on the safety of all of these procedures, as I have not yet researched the biomedical literature—and doubt it is even sufficiently documented yet. At the time this book went to press, the news of silicone damage had been exploding in the media. Breast augmentation with silicone had become a major public story, something to avoid.

[10] Dr. Philip Sarrel, professor of gynecology and psychiatry, described his research at a recent scientific meeting.

scholar asked exactly this question. They found a consistent response. Once they have reached the menopausal transition years (mid-forties), women who married younger men had much more active sex lives than those who married older men.

But the downside of connecting with a younger man should also be considered. In our culture, an aging woman may begin to feel disproportionately older than her younger partner. If she has cause to worry about his continued interest in her, the quality of the relationship may erode. Older men who marry younger women often have the same concern.

THE REAL MAGIC OF SEX

Sex is more than just "doing it." Sex among consenting adults is powerful behavior, but sex should be more than just the act. Sex is good when it provides trust, commitment, emotional and physical openness, as well as communication. All these intangibles enhance the physical experience. For sex to be truly magical, you need the joyous participation of both partners. Sex is a gift, something a loving, supportive partner can give with loyalty and dependability. Interdependent rather than independent, each partner plays a different but equally important role. And each partner brings special abilities, responses, and reactions to the mystery of the private loving connection between a man and a woman. The deliberate, unguarded exposure of one's intimate self is its essence—intentional and mutual vulnerability.

Sometimes you need to say no to sex. There is a world of difference between a "quick fix" and fulfilling your real sexual needs. The quick fix is a dead end for courtship. Sex without a mutual commitment sets you up for abuse. It delays you from finding a search candidate. And it can have negative repercussions on your internal health. Say no to intermittent sex. Say no to using a man as a sex object. Say no to sex as sport. Instead, opt for celibacy. It calms your endocrine system and your nerves. It allows you time and space to rally your energy and strength for the intelligent search for courtship.

Self-knowledge is sensual power. A woman's body, as well as a man's, is designed for sex. It is part of your birthright. When you learn the high art of your own sensuality, you will be richly rewarded. You will have more to bring to a lover and in return can attract more quality from him. And as you are able to bring your feminine sexuality to a new relationship, you will add one more alluring, even irresistible, quality. Your sensual awareness will increase the number of candidates from which you can make your choice.

When it comes to sex, time is on your side. Intimacy is a journey, a gentle unfolding. Take it slowly, one stage at a time. You will preserve your health. Reveal and share yourself at whatever pace feels right to you; it will not necessarily be the pace of the man pursuing you. If you need to move more slowly than he would like, trust your feelings. His willingness to be patient gives you important information about his character and his "husband potential." If *he* needs to go slowly, be patient with him.

Take good manners into account when selecting your companion. Good manners are a mark of one person's ability to respect the needs and feelings of another. A man who has them will give you much more joy than one who does not.

Next, having grasped sexual basics and sexual ethics, our focus shifts to courtship. In courtship, as in sex, women have tremendous power in negotiating the move toward a marriage commitment.

NINE

The Dance
of Courtship

Some partners, destined to stay together, perform elaborate courting ceremonies. One remarkable ritual is the singing of duets. Some birds sing the same notes in unison or time their rounds to echo each other. Others sing a more elaborate duet back and forth, with alternating refrains which they then combine to make music together. Duet singing has been noted in primates as well—in the ape-like Sumatran gibbon. Human beings are primates.

To every thing there is a season . . . a time to mourn and a
   time to dance . . . —ECCLESIASTES 3

When you have found a man whose courtship you accept, it's
   time to dance for joy.

Spiced with erotic connections, the dance of courtship should be special, sensual, monogamous, and it should be fun—a time when you establish the private, unintrudable space of an intimate partnership. It *will* work this way if you have been following the Code of Courtship, especially these principles:

- Principle 1: You acknowledge biology's rules and use his sexual attraction to *negotiate for courtship.*

- Principle 5: You strengthen your capacity for self-control *by taking command of your calendar.*
- Principle 8: You understand and *live the dignity* of good manners.

If you have developed these three skills and put them into practice, the only men you will get close to will already be geared toward courtship.

WHEN COURTSHIP BEGINS

Once your search has led to *one* special partner, courtship begins. Courtship is a wonderful time, with all its special feelings, sensual moves, and erotic experiences. This is the time your love blooms. It has a birthday, anniversaries, special days—the day we met, the night we cooked lobsters, the time we made love on the coffee table. It is a time to fill with extraordinary private experiences—pet names, inside jokes, favorite restaurants, secret trysting places, your private language, and the world seems to be yours alone because it symbolizes the uniqueness of your love. As time goes on, you accumulate memories and forge a shared history. With this firm foundation, a man and a woman can confidently face a future together as partners.

The couple glues itself together with intimacy, trust, and commitment. It constructs its own miniature cosmos, a private world with very different rules from those of the public world in which the two also move. In your courtship cosmos, the roles of men and women thrive on exaggeration of their differences in roles and talents. In courtship—and later in marriage—you want a counterpart, not a clone. You need someone who will play man to your woman. Someone who makes you feel sensual, feminine, utterly compelling and desirable.

FEMININE AND MASCULINE SEXUAL POWER

I define power as the capacity to get what you need or want. When you are searching for courtship, you probably want a loving partner who is sexually competent. You have the power to achieve this aim. But it is a very special kind of power. Elsewhere I address the separate issues of power in economics, work, and character. For now, coital power is the relevant issue.

Nature has evolved an equation in which male dominance (sexual erection and penetration) coupled with female submission (sexual receptivity) promotes sexual reproduction (perpetuation of the species). She lures him and yields to his sexual pursuit. At a basic sexual level, I'm talking about permitting a man to take control, perhaps to sensually sweep you off your feet. I'm not talking about who runs the boardroom. I'm talking about what can occur in the bedroom. You can have a richly sensual romantic life, an egalitarian relationship, *and* an active career life if you want them all. But to have the romantic partnerships, you must have some understanding of the biological principles. The dramatic social changes of the past thirty years have obscured some of these.

Since it is the male who must "stand at attention" for sex, it is he who must generate the erotic energy and interest for a sexual encounter. He can't be passive. And he can't fake it. As I consider it from the perspective of science, this biological pattern seems natural. It's not only the way of animals —human societies have also embraced this way of being.

In Eastern culture you will find the same story. The Oriental philosophies have long expressed the idea of the yin and the yang, the female and male principles, which together are necessary to complete a whole being. It is not so much that one is boss and the other is servant. It is that there are different powers that fit together to promote life. Apart they look different, but when they are connected correctly, the current flows.

The Sexual Problem of the Nineties

The notions of "male/assertive" and "female/receptive" run counter to much contemporary thought. From what I have observed at the Athena Institute workshops, in the works of women novelists, as well as from social commentators like Gloria Steinem and Susan Sontag, many women raised in the postliberationist era are finding themselves caught between a rock and a hard place when it comes to their pursuit of power and self-realization on the one hand and their longings for romantic love on the other. Many believe that the man and woman should be equal, that women should have as much strength, power, and as many "rights" as men, that for a woman to submit to a man on any front is to deny her being, that women are just as strong and dominant as men, that it is demeaning to the dignity of a woman to permit a man to be stronger than she or dominant to her. An entire generation of women are living out their adult

300

years with these assumptions. So hard won by their mothers and grandmothers, these attitudes have changed the landscape of romance—sometimes to our detriment.

But the belief that a powerful man should encounter a powerful woman head-on with equal force can hinder romantic love. It's like trying to connect two plugs without a socket. What good is that? No current can flow between them.

For romantic love, a woman can encourage a man to feel the surge of manly power that will stimulate his courtship drive—the drive that protects and serves a woman. She does this with her feminine power. Female power is different from male power. Sometimes it is greater, other times lesser —but at least in the sexual sense, it is never equal. While equality in career development, intellectual life, and economic access to goods and services may represent fair play and right action in those domains, the sexual arena is different. Here feminine power consists of a kind of magnetic strength luring the male to want to serve her. Masculine power provides the greater physical force. The greater her feminine power, the more he will want to use his power to serve her, to please her, to protect her. The lesser her feminine power, the more he will seem to dominate her.

I see a generation of single women and men trying to apply "equality" to a biological principle designed to merge differences. They may want romantic love, marriage, and family, but they cannot seem to get them using the same sexual equality ethic that is appropriate in their public lives. It's a similar problem among the "single again" women of forty plus years who correctly broke out of a bad marriage only to confuse sexual harmony with an equality of power.

Confusion and distress are the natural outcomes of such conflict, as are lonely, unpartnered women and men.

A Biological Solution

Biology teaches that the activity of courtship is different from all other social pursuits. It demands and deserves its own space. Here the sensual dance of power and penile dominance is a joy to be cultivated. Dominance, as I use the term, means to grow bigger, to stand over and take care of the needs of the submissive one. I think that the nature of biology endows a man with a need for a certain kind of dominance in the sexual encounter. When he feels bigger, he grows bigger. His erection follows. The object of all this dominance is to use his greater physical strength for the security of the pair and their progeny.

When you, as a woman, can go out into the world as a strong, intelligent individual and pursue a career, yet still enjoy the greater physical power of the male who is your romantic partner, you are on your way to a magnificent courtship experience. From this perspective, feminine receptivity means receiving the courtly treatment of a man who is working to win you. If this idea is contrary to your values and your history, why not take a thoughtful look at it. See how it might fit your own future. Give it a try. Those who do can discover, often to their surprise, how much fun it is to use feminine power to harness the power of a man.

Behaviors that accentuate the differences between male and female have a higher probability of promoting love, marriage, and family. It is an interesting secret some very successful lovers have: that your true power sometimes lies in your confidence and ability to refrain from asserting it. Let him take the lead sometimes, while you lead at others. Listen and receive him sometimes; other times talk and penetrate his being with your will. Allowing him to open a door, carry your packages, or haul the lawn furniture can build his pleasure in serving you. Such couples recognize that *each* is very powerful when the pair is building a loving, rich life. The powers are different but equally important because in fitting together, the partnership grows stronger. Both win.

My purpose in describing the dance of courtship is to suggest *a way* of enjoying the experience of searching wisely and doing so as a high feminine art—an art in which the artist takes control of her medium. Research (and common sense) has made it clear that when you feel some control over what happens to you, your health and well-being improve. I think women should be in charge of what happens to them. Why not use your natural faculties? Use feminine power to attain the satisfaction of your needs, and I believe you will find it works. And you will have lots of fun!

Using Feminine Power in Courtship

Appreciate his biological need for dominance in the erection. Promote his sense that when it comes to sex, he is predominant physically. Choose your man carefully and grant permission each time he approaches you sexually. You will be amazed at the power you will gain. When the man has first met your standards through dating and forging a friendship, you are en route to remarkable sensual pleasures.

If after trying this path you conclude that you are unwilling to continue on it, at least you will recognize that this is not what you want. With an open mind and a sense of adventure you might change your perspective after you have had a chance to experience different forms of conduct. That's fine too.

The Leader Must First Follow

The dance of heterosexual genital intercourse is biologically driven and neurologically choreographed. In every case, the male has to perform, but the female exerts considerable control. He generates the rhythm, but she first triggers it through the lure of her essence. Consequently, she had the power to guide his force.

In the high art of courtship, partners use their strengths to nurture the partnership rather than to oppose each other's power. It is a win/win situation. People who love each other should use their separate powers to serve their love. If he is stronger, you can harness that strength for the benefit of the relationship, because in courting love he welcomes making this contribution. If one of you is wiser in the ways of money management, you can harness that skill as well. Money isn't sexual. But "masculine" and "feminine" as qualities of sexual being can enhance the erotic part of the match. When lovers enhance the differences between them to serve their sexual pairing, they put these masculine/feminine differences to their best use and private benefit. Whether through claiming certain skills as "his" or "her" domain or through clothing accentuating her curves and his straight shape, or any other acknowledgment of differences, they can appreciate each other's unique contribution to the pairing. Two genders offer a beautiful set of differences—to be celebrated because both are necessary to the well-being of the whole—the relationship.

"Masculine" and "feminine" culminate in the sexual encounter. Enhancing your "masculine" and "feminine" in the dance of courtship *promotes* a sexual relationship. When it goes well, you feel more womanly; he feels more manly. Woman and man are defined romantically in relation to each other—in counterpoint. Different, rather than the same. Each time male connects with female the boundaries of each self dissolve, though neither is lost or diminished. On the contrary, each is affirmed, enriched by the union.

THE ROMANTIC COCOON
OF COURTSHIP

As you enter courtship, now is the time to become vulnerable to each other. In the early stages of dating you win when you exercise self-restraint. In a friendship you protect yourself and avoid investing your emotions until he has passed all of your tests. In courtship the rules change. Now you can let down some of your reserve. Now is the time you begin to commit pieces of your emotional life to him. And he does the same. You spin a lovely cocoon around your partnership to form a safe haven for each other. Now is the time when a breakup would have to be painful. It is the price we pay for vulnerability and the reason the Code counsels to withhold vulnerability until you have had a chance to evaluate each other—till you know he has the strength of character to play fair.

The Rules Dissolve

Now the rules that have protected you from the pain of abandonment or ill treatment are no longer necessary. When you accept his courtship bid, you can let down your guard because you have followed the Code of Courtship and he has passed your critical tests. Once he has generated the energy and declared courtship, you have new rights and roles. These roles are so fluid and flexible that there are no specifics I can list. Except this one: The basic understanding is that your social life will be together—unless otherwise agreed.

Unlike in the stage of formal dating, now the partnership decides the rules. By now the question of who initiates time together should be irrelevant. Once you have engaged in a sexual relationship that includes courtship, your access to him should be as unobstructed as his access to you. Now you ought to be feeling protected and cared for. When you telephone him you should feel that your call lights up his being. If you find yourself feeling that you are an intruder when you call him, take a look at that and figure out why. You may have been deceived about his courtship intentions. Or you might be calling too often, intruding on his need for a separate space. Or something else.

WHEN INTIMACY FEELS LONELY

Twenty-two-year-old Hilda described her recurrent feelings of loneliness in her relationship.

"Although my boyfriend, Jack, and I are very intimate, I
often find that he drifts off to another planet and I am shut
out, unable to tap into what he is thinking. This makes me
feel that I am somehow not privileged to his problems or
thoughts."

Hilda wants to know if there is any way to draw Jack out
of his separateness. But it may not be so good to try. People
need separate selves, and that may be what is happening
here. Perhaps Jack sometimes needs his separateness, while
at other times he is able to engage in intimacy. Healthy
adults ought to develop personalities and strengths that
allow them separate existences. A certain amount of separateness will help promote respectful interactions in a relationship. But the degree of separateness is what counts. If
Hilda often feels shut out, this may be a sign that Jack is not
really interested in a closer relationship.

Perhaps the two of them did not have a chance to forge a
really good friendship before they became sexually intimate.
Hilda might ask herself whether if sex were eliminated from
this relationship, there would be anything left.

She might even consider telling Jack that she would like
to continue to see him *without sex* for a few months because
she is not certain of her feelings and wants to refocus on the
friendship first. If he can rise to that challenge when she tells
him her reasons, she may very well overcome the distance
that is plaguing her. But if he rejects her request or if he
tries it and she finds there is nothing else there, this as an
important signal that it is time to separate from him and
resume her search for courtship. Each relationship is unique
and what people need and find cannot be defined by a simple

formula. One young woman I know did try this abstinence and found it strengthened the friendship. Months later, when sexual intercourse was resumed, she felt closer to her lover than she ever had before.

One thing is sure. You ought to feel comfortable with the man with whom you share sexual intimacy. If you don't, try eliminating the sex *until* you feel comfortable. In other words, retreat and go back a few steps to see if you can forge a better friendship. The cocoon should feel warm and safe —not cold or lonely.

FOCUSING IN, NOT OUT

As you become a couple, increasing shares of your time will be spent with each other—as it should be. But recognize that the time must be taken from somewhere else. Others may feel shut out, displaced, and hurt. Often the erotic connections of courtship temporarily blind people to the negative reactions of their friends and family. In the wild, heady experiences of early intimacy, the man and woman can easily lose touch or lose the sense of closeness they previously shared with friends and family. Caught up in the demands on your time that work and the new courtship create, everything else can seem to be expendable. It is fine for this to happen temporarily, but eventually you will have to compensate your friends and family for this period of distancing.

CONSIDER YOUR FUTURE TOGETHER

The erotic days of courtship are the ideal time to begin to tentatively consider the hurdles to a permanent relationship.

These early, tentative looks will solidify later and have to be resolved if the relationship is to continue. But early in a courtship it makes good sense to gently consider the areas that will need to be negotiated. Think of it as reality testing. By doing it now, you will maximize your marriage, if marriage follows. Or you will discover you cannot find a compromise that satisfies you both.

Age can play a distinct role in the capacity to find compromises. Sometimes older people are less flexible in their ability to bend and mold themselves to the needs of another. Sometimes older people are wiser, more able to discern who is and who is not a good candidate. I suspect that these qualities balance out, equalizing the difficulty of the search. What you lose as you get older, you gain with your growing wisdom.

Your topics of negotiation will differ from another couple's, but all will probably share several common themes. These are

- Discovering what basic premises you each have about sharing responsibilities and decisions (money, work, chores).
- Who should do what (cook, clean, launder, haul trash).
- How will your inevitable differences be negotiated? Is one of you going to be "the boss"? Will you take a vote? Will you keep fighting until you come to an agreement?
- Hammering out the basic rules of "fighting fair." Can you establish them together?

Although the answers to these questions may not come in the first months of courtship, the fact that the questions exist is worth recognizing. Play with these topics a little bit at a time, and you will begin to forge the reality that courtship is intended to lead to—an enduring, loving partnership that nurtures each of you. Why early? Because there will never be a better time to establish a pattern of equity than when your man is hot for you. Begin ironing out any sexual wrinkles in the relationship now too.

SEXUAL WRINKLES

Some frequent difficulties in women's experiences of sexual intercourse might be helpful to review.

If He's on a Different Wavelength

Arlene, a twenty-year-old junior at Bryn Mawr College, described the problem she had with sexual intimacy.

> "During sex, it seems that Andy is doing all the work and I start to feel very detached and passive. If he is on top of me, I don't know how to participate and feel like an equal partner when his sexual power is stronger and I take longer to attain orgasm. Instead I feel passive, like he is in total control."

It sounds as if there may be a more fundamental problem here. Two courtship principles apply:

· Principle 7: You acquire basic hormonal and sexual facts.
· Principle 4: You communicate what you want.

When men are young, penile nerves are hair-trigger sensitive. They fire readily. Sometimes too readily. These sexual sensations can be so powerful that they overtake his awareness. While he is engaged in sexual intercourse, a young man's brain and sensitivities may not function very well. (He couldn't do algebra, for example!) But that doesn't mean he can't learn how you work. Be patient with him. Read the sex chapter of this book together, so that you can both be sure you have the facts. Then try relaxing and let him do the work if that is what he wants to do.

Many men do not want to have foreplay when they have an erection. It delivers too much sensory stimulation, especially when they are young. Young women are different. They need a lot of foreplay because arousal and lubrication develop more slowly. It is good to recognize and celebrate these differences in men and women.

With the passage of years, his reluctance for foreplay may change. And your needs for extended precoital stroking will probably decrease in your thirties and increase in your forties, fifties, and sixties. As your hormonal secretions change —from your twenties through your seventies—so do your sexual sensitivities and responses.

In the meantime, save your sensual gifts of touch for later —when you are sharing affection rather than sexual congress. From your point of view, it may help to think of this as foreplay, on a different time scale. It occurs hours or days before your next sexual intercourse.

If He's Remote After Sex

A frequently mentioned concern once courtship and intimacy occur is "distancing." Men sometimes become remote during and especially after sex. If you are always communicative and open in conversation but during sex relate to each other less openly, as if it were a separate space and time, it may help to understand some physiology.

After a sexual encounter it is reasonable to feel peaceful, passive, almost detached. There is nothing wrong with enjoying the sense of satiety that sexual intimacy ought to deliver. If after his orgasm, he is feeling satiated and drifting off into peaceful sleep but you are left tense and needing to talk, it may be that he didn't properly understand or take care of your sexual needs. Particularly with a young or unsophisticated partner, it is likely that during and especially after sex he is so engaged in the erotic stimulation he is experiencing that he doesn't fully notice what you are experiencing. Young lovers need time to learn the high art of sensuality. Men often take *five to ten years* of sexual activity before they begin to perceive what is going on in the woman —unless she helps him out and gives him the information. Sit down with him and read the sex chapter of this book and you will be on your way toward communicating better. Meanwhile, be patient with him. If he is always communicative and open in conversation when you are not engaged in sex, consider letting him have his way here.

Another Man in Your Husband's Bed

Not every intimate problem involves sex. Eleanor, a fifty-two-year-old widow, described her experience.

> "My husband, Vernon, died eighteen months ago after a wonderful thirty-year marriage. Now, with Harold, I feel squeamish about violating my marriage bed. I don't want our first time together to be in Vernon's bed."

Eleanor's reaction is understandable. If this is your situation, take charge. By having forged a friendship first, you can enjoy the special pleasure of planning for a romantic interlude. Together new couples can select their own special first night, make hotel reservations, and create a magical memory of their first time together. Once you have built an intimate partnership, your feelings will probably change. But if they don't, why not give the bed away[1] and buy a new one?

HANDLING PROBLEMS

In order to cultivate a loving life, you will always be rising to new challenges. A relationship is like a garden. It can grow beautifully if you tend it. But neglect it and weeds will soon overtake it. Fortunately, most weeds are easy to pull up before they have taken root. Search for yours while they are still small.

Problems in courtship come in many forms: Sex, money, attitudes toward healthy eating and drinking behaviors, and kids are some common ones. Face such problems so that you can resolve them. Next we'll explore some solutions to problems you might experience as part of a new couple.

Sexual Dysfunction

Some sexual dysfunctions can be cured by love, others cannot. Here are two things you should know that may help.

---

[1] Perhaps to a homeless shelter or a battered women's shelter.

First, if a man past the age of forty-five is having erection problems, either establishing them or maintaining them, they may be due to a prescription drug. About twenty-five commonly used drugs have now been shown to produce erectile dysfunctions in 15 to 30 percent of their users. If this is your man's problem, the prognosis is good. Usually his physician can substitute a related drug that does not produce sexual dysfunctions.

The other scientific discovery about male sexual dysfunctions is psychological. Apparently, healthy men get more erect when you tell them what you want in bed. But sexually dysfunctional men are intimidated and tend to lose their erections when a woman tells them how to perform or what she needs.[2]

Whether you or the man you love has a problem with sexual function, if you cannot solve it yourselves, consider searching for a sex therapist.

How to find a good therapist.   Sandra Leiblum, Ph.D., professor of clinical psychiatry and codirector of the sexual counseling service at the Robert Wood Johnson Medical School in Piscataway, New Jersey, and president of the Society for Sex Therapy and Research, gives the following advice:

> You might try writing to the American College of Sex Education and Counseling, 435 North Michigan Avenue, Suite 1717, Chicago, Illinois 60611, which is the accrediting

[2] For details on this study see *Love Cycles: The Science of Intimacy* (New York: Villard Books, 1991).

agency for sex therapists in the United States. Any therapist who achieves accreditation has had at least some workshop training as well as demonstrated knowledge of research discoveries.

However, the mere fact of accreditation does not mean that the person has the sensitivity you need or that they will be compatible with you; so this is just your starting point.

You might try calling your state psychological association, or if it is not listed in the phone book, call Washington, D.C., information for the national office of the American Psychological Association.

The association can refer you to local professionals who meet its standards.

Once you have assembled a list of therapists, the next step is to schedule an interview. State your purpose when you make your appointment. Explain that you want an interview to discuss your needs and the therapist's methods and training, and let the therapist know that you are searching for someone with whom you will feel comfortable. Expect to pay a fee for the therapist's time. At the interview, ask questions about the therapist's methods and training, and trust your own feelings about whether you feel comfortable with this person. When you feel right with a therapist, you will know it.

Rates vary. For each forty-five- to sixty-minute session, 1992 fees ranged from ninety to one hundred and fifty dollars. Under some circumstances your insurance company may cover this, especially if a physician prescribed the treatment.

How long can you expect to be in therapy? That depends on the nature of the problem. At first, it is best to be patient.

The need for patience cannot be overstated. By the time a couple begins work with a sex therapist, they have usually been carrying a problem for a long time, and it takes time to identify and clarify a sexual problem. But after about two months of weekly visits, you should begin to see improvement.

A good therapist will work with you to determine whether the problem is organic, psychological, or related to some other nonsexual problem. You may be given standardized tests and interviews.

It takes courage to go for help. But look what you have to gain. A competent sex therapist is equipped to help you find solutions.

Money Muddles

Since money is so important to the smooth functioning of a household, consider focusing on it early in the courtship. A little bit at a time. What matters is your mutual comfort and your ability to come to a resolution that satisfies you both. It is good to learn early on whether you share money values or have a potential mine field for conflict. If there is the underlying potential for conflict, you might as well work on it early. when you have a chance to resolve it on an intellectual basis. Don't wait until after you have pooled your money.

Children, His and Yours

By now the potential for conflict with children should be clear in your relationship. If there is such a potential, address it. And if you cannot solve the problem through discussions with each other, consider going to a counselor together. Or by yourself. Sometimes the calm voice of a neutral person who listens, questions, and helps set up some rules for negotiating can be an enormous asset to promoting your potential for a good marriage.

Parents and Siblings

As your courtship begins to flourish, parents and siblings enter your cocoon. Holidays, weekend rituals, annual picnics, and other elements of family history come into the personal spaces of courtship. Ideally, you will love his parents and they will love him. Ideally, he will love your parents and they will love you. The same goes for siblings. As the potential for marriage grows, the connection to each other's families just naturally evolves. Hopefully, yours is warm and adds layers of good feelings to your life. Whatever your family situation, if you place each other as number one, you will be well on your way to incorporating family life into your courtship and later your marriage.

Fair Play/Fair Fighting

Adults are going to have differences of opinion. If you find yourself with problems of fighting fair, recognize this problem and take some action to rectify it. Fighting fair means attacking the problem, not the person. It means learning to listen and truly hear what your friend is saying. Fighting fair means being able to repeat what your friend tells you before you tell him your reaction. It often happens that when your

317

friend can hear that you can understand what his position is, he becomes more receptive to hearing yours. Sometimes when you check your perceptions, you discover you misunderstood; he didn't say or think what you thought he did. Or vice versa. And when you both know his and your own true starting positions, you can begin to negotiate for compromise. Fighting fair means dealing with a problem when it is current and you are upset, not harboring grudges and then bringing up all the previous problems (solved or unsolved) while you are trying to resolve the current one.

There are wonderful seminars taught at adult-school education programs, churches, and counseling centers that teach people how to fight fair. Look for announcements in newspapers, community bulletin boards, churches, and temples. Consider making the investment of a few evenings or one several-hour stint to provide a basic structure for building fair play into your courtship. Career Track is one of the companies that sends speakers around the country offering a several-hour seminar for a fee of about forty-five dollars per person. What a great way to go out for an evening with your buddy and learn how to identify your personal mine fields, then find how you can build into your friendship a method to deactivate them.

Use a Light Touch

Your erotic attraction and blooming friendship can and should overpower and trivialize the problems that will inevitably occur between you. But only temporarily. Do not focus too much energy on problems, just enough to minimize their impact in the years that will follow. During the dance of courtship most of your time ought to be spent enjoying each other and the world out there. Whether you go dancing or dining, walking or wining, courtship is a very special time in the life of a woman and a relationship. As the courtship stage draws to a close, you will either be back to setting lures for new candidates or engaging in discussions of permanence.

DISCUSSIONS OF PERMANENCE

Courtship moves through intimacy, to reality testing, to the possibility of marriage. And as biology seems to demand, a proposal of marriage is a man's role. *He* must declare it first. While he must get up the energy to assert it, *you* have tremendous power in activating his declaration. From what I have seen, when a woman verbalizes her desire to marry first, she finds herself in trouble. But when she maximizes her feminine role of receptor, she can precipitate his declaration.

When you have positioned yourself in an intimate relationship by following the Code of Courtship, *you will have the power* to promote a declaration just about whenever you feel ready for it. You do this by exercising restraint and withdrawal. Your objective will be to position yourself, like a magnet, so that you draw him to you. If your force is inadequate, the relationship will end. If your force is overwhelming, it will repel. This truth can hurt. But the truth will set you free to resume your search for a fruitful match. The more truth you can handle, the more power you will enjoy and the sooner you will find your mate.

The dance of courtship involves the wonderful erotic process of sensual connections, coming and going from each other's homes, being each other's Number One, becoming emotionally vulnerable to each other's feelings and judgments, and establishing availability to each other. When the dance is conducted gracefully, you both come to see that you have an ability to face and to solve problems. Even if a man loves you and cannot bear the thought of living without you, he still needs to know that the underlying mine fields can be gotten over without too much stress.[3] Until this time he will probably be unable to comfortably propose marriage. But once, as a couple, you have discovered your problems and have started to develop skills and to find solutions to them, he will approach readiness. In the search for courtship the man's proposal of marriage sets in motion his mental process that will enable him to come to the altar. It's something like body building; the work is necessary to build the strength. This may take some time.

When a Man Seems Reluctant to Propose

There is no formula, no set time period before a courting couple is ready for marriage. Whether you should wait six months or three years or just until it feels right depends on you and your man. It also depends on your ages, needs, and other alternatives. A man who has been divorced will probably have an understandable fear of commitment. The terrible cost that most people endure at the end of a long-term

---

[3] If a girlfriend tells you, "I can't live with him and I can't live without him," advise her, "Live without him." The pain will diminish and she can resume her search.

relationship, particularly a marriage, inevitably leaves scars. From divorce, one of the great scars is usually a long, drawn-out battle over property. If you are in a stage of courtship where this consideration is irrelevant, count your blessings. If either you or your man have endured that kind of breakup, the extra baggage has to be packed away before you will be able and ready to risk that kind of vulnerability again. Besides, you don't want to marry a man "on the rebound."

If you are dealing with a shell-shocked man who is afraid to propose marriage, wonderful erotic connections can help provide a salve to such stress. Still, be alert. Too much salve can reduce the stress but dispel the proposal. If this is the case, you may have to withdraw. If your absence makes his heart grow fonder, you can use his sexual attraction for you to generate a proposal.

Withdrawing to Come Together

He loves you. You love him. Yet there is no proposal in sight. It may be that until you leave him he will not believe that he needs to marry you.

Perhaps he is in his sixties and he is telling you he doesn't intend to marry again. Or maybe he is thirty and saying he is just not ready. He may even cause you to doubt the rightness of wanting to be married. Have faith in yourself and know that a good marriage is better than good singlehood. When you find a partner with whom you can build a beautiful life and you make that commitment, the roots you put down nourish the garden of love. Marriage is wonderful when it is done well. You have every reason to go for it.

If your man is afraid to commit, you may have to take decisive and courageous action to trigger his proposal. You should prepare yourself for the possibility. Consider this action the feminine equivalent of a man's getting up the courage to propose marriage. If you ask him to marry you, you may blow it. But if you take the feminine part, you will permit him to play his natural biological role. Consider Flora's story.

Flora had been involved with Reggie for two years. They had moved from friendship to intimacy and were monogamously connected, spending every weekend together. Reggie suggested living together, but Flora wisely resisted it. (When women who want to get married live with men, they compromise their negotiating power. When you have the appearance of marriage, it is hard to negotiate for the reality.) Flora wanted to get married and put down roots. She wanted an economic partnership and children. She and Reggie had discussed these issues in a tentative way during the last two years, but she wanted to move ahead.

Flora decided to take action. She bought a ticket for a trip out of town—solo. She didn't tell Reggie about it until she was ready to go. Then she sat him down, told him that she loved him and knew he loved her. She told him she was distressed that he had not proposed marriage to her and that she had decided to take some time to think for a while so that she could discover what she wanted to do with her life. She was leaving that afternoon and would be back in a week. No, she would not tell him where she was going or give him the phone number. She needed to be alone to think. She said good-bye, gave him a soul-searing kiss, and left.

Flora took a trip to the seashore, but the place she went is not what mattered. What mattered was that she went away. She used the time to walk on the beach, read, and consider her life and what she wanted from it. It was the longest week she ever spent. She did not call Reggie. But she wanted to. She had entered a dark tunnel and hoped that at the end of it she would find him waiting for her and proposing marriage. But she knew he might not. He might try to argue with her that they should continue as they were, that he "wasn't ready." But she also knew that her own life was passing by, and since she wanted to start having children soon she needed to take action. If he did not want to marry her, she recognized that she *could* get on with her life. If he did want to marry her, he might as well make his decision now. Her waiting and hoping was not making things better.

Flora came back from her trip to a man who had had a chance to recognize what he was risking if he didn't propose marriage. She hadn't demanded anything, but she had communicated what she wanted. Reggie proposed, and she accepted. They got married and lived happily afterward.[4]

This drastic method has variations. Flora might have disappeared for two days. She might have gone for two weeks. The critical point is that she *left* and made herself inaccessible to him. When she returned, her position was much stronger. She had made clear what she wanted, and had demonstrated that she was capable of leaving and getting on with her life. Now he knew he was either going to have to propose marriage or risk losing her. Since we become what we do, not what we say, it is much more powerful to *show* your independence than to discuss it.

[4] Until Reggie invited his mother to move in with them. But that's another story.

Whether a woman is twenty-five and wanting to start a marriage that will later become a family or forty and wanting to have children immediately or sixty and wanting to grow into her older years with a committed partner, when she wants marriage, she should take action and go for it. She needs the courage to leave, and she needs to show him her courage in a civilized, nonthreatening way—no arguments —as an adult, not a dependent supplicant. I do believe that a man must declare his intention to marry. He needs that much courage to show up at the altar. And you can help him by the actions you have the courage to take. What have you got to lose? Think about that carefully.

Next let us focus on you, the winner—the woman who has followed the Code to the prize: a loving man who courted you. By now he has proposed marriage and you are setting the date and working together to negotiate the terms of your marriage.

TEN

Moving to Marriage— The Light at the Tunnel's End

African lovebirds, also known as "inseparables," practice monogamy. The partners feed each other throughout the year. Usually the male feeds the female, especially when she is brooding and stuck on the nest for days at a time. However, the male continues to bring food even when the brooding stage has ended.

And now to plant your Garden of Eden
To prepare the soil before you plant the seeds.
Test your sense of fair play as a couple.

Moving to marriage is the final step along the courtship journey. With you is a man who is your fast friend. And he is clearly courting you.

Having lived the Code of Courtship, you *will* reach your goal: a man you love who asks to marry you. I have seen so many women who employed the Code get married. And they did it without wasting their single months and years pining and waiting. In fact, I went to the showers and weddings of ten women in their forties and fifties during one two-year period. You, too, can experience this joy. It may take subtle skill, but it isn't very difficult to master. The goal is a valuable one, a loving marriage based on commitment and honor.

DON'T LIVE TOGETHER FIRST!

If you have strong religious values and believe that sex is only appropriate in marriage, your suitor will wait. If your values are different, you may have enjoyed sexual intimacy before he proposed marriage. In either case, your potential for a good marriage is better if you restrain the impulse to live together. Although the arguments for it seem persuasive, I firmly believe that living together is counterproductive, leading to a higher likelihood of a dead end for a woman who wants marriage. I've seen this happen many times, and the research findings support it. Love is a growing process. You can love many but should make love with few. Only one man is your candidate for marriage at a time.

If you both want to live together, the bond of matrimony is most fruitfully negotiated *before* you move in together. Marriage is usually the wisest choice for cohabitation because you forge a committed future when you lay down roots. Commitment is better than instability. Be decisive, not tentative. Commitment sets you on a path geared toward permanence through marriage. Emotional and physical health is the reward of a good marriage that is lived as high art.

THE MARRIAGE BOND

Marriage has both legal and spiritual dimensions. On a down-to-earth level, marriage is a contract, a written agreement between man and woman that is legally sanctioned by the government. It establishes a variety of rights and responsibilities for its partners. The government gets involved because the stability of family life affects the social order. Marriage is also a spiritual commitment sanctioned by one's religious community.

In its legal role, marriage protects a man and a woman. It defines, and insists that both parties honor, fair play. It invests them with "standing." Money is only part of the contract, but an important one. Consider the fact that in 1991 women earned about seventy cents for every dollar a man earned for comparable work. This means that men earn 42 percent more than women earn, for the same job. Consider further that *only* women can bring forth the young that perpetuate the species. When one looks at these realities, the legal obligations of marriage begin to make sense. The economic realities are unfair to women who haven't taken the safeguards available through marriage.

Marriage provides economic recourse mainly for women because women and men are biologically different. Once a woman is pregnant, she needs levels of financial support beyond those of a nonpregnant person. Once a woman gives birth, the attendant financial, physical, and emotional responsibilities require a monetary contribution from the partnership. Likewise the older woman experiences other financial inequities. Often she has not enjoyed the time in the job market or the mentorship that would have allowed

327

her access to earn as much as her partner. The contract of marriage addresses these inequities, provides legal rights, and attempts to protect the safety of women and their children. Although we hope never to have to invoke them, the safety provided by the marriage contract protects a woman's best interests by providing legal enforcement of fair play. Just as a courteous person would not force sexual intimacies on a woman who isn't ready, he should not ask her to risk her safety and the security of her children by forgoing the legal and spiritual privileges of marriage. For many couples, the spiritual commitment to honor these responsibilities is far more important than the legal one.

MARRIAGE AS A GARDEN OF EDEN

The emotional contract of marriage is the one most highly prized, but adult partners who make a commitment to marry recognize the ever-changing nature of love and passion and the inevitable ups and downs of an intimate relationship. As with any lovely landscape, they acknowledge the need to plant, to water, and to nourish their garden—and to remove the inevitable weeds and pests that will threaten its life. The parties promise to protect and support each other. They agree that the stronger will care for the weaker during the inevitable swings: "For better or worse; in sickness and in health." In the long run, to be able to bring forth and nurture the next generation is the greater strength. In the short run, childbearing results in special needs and privileges, times when the financial support of the male partner provides the family's economic security.

Marriage supplies the framework that acknowledges these different contributions of men and women. It honors both partners. Each is serving the team when one provides most of the money while the other provides the ambience. Marriage has specific legal and spiritual meaning—status.

Both government and religious communities recognize that a married couple enjoys a different status than unmarried individuals. Respectability. Economic privileges. Open and acknowledged, not secretive or covert.

In making the commitment to a marriage partner, individuals transform their self-centered developmental journeys into a team effort. We become what we do. Making a commitment is the way two separate people merge to form a partnership. Once joined, their separate energies can combine. They can create a lush garden. Just as when you plant seeds, nourishing them with water, sunshine, and nutrients, a marriage commitment establishes the time and the space to put down roots, grow them, and cultivate a lush environment. Your attitudes and actions plow the fields, preparing the fertile ground in which you can cultivate your personal Garden of Eden.

Winning Qualities

As you move toward marriage certain qualities of being are worth cultivating in order to grow the relationship with greater strength.

Dignity, awareness, tact, and joy.   Make these four qualities part of your life. Practice them. Live them daily. And you will be on your way to a confident way of living that can get you what you want. And your fiancé will love giving you want you want.

Dignity should be cultivated so your fiancé (and his relatives) will think of you at the level of being you project. A woman's dignity determines the respect she will get from her man and his family. Establish and develop your ongoing standards. In marriage you can be treated like a queen—a queen who consorts with a king—when you conduct yourself with regal dignity.

Awareness is the ability to focus on what is happening outside yourself. One way to cultivate this quality is to take time to *look at* your man, to really see him as a separate being. Watch the expressions on his face. Imagine (but do not assume to know) what he is feeling. These actions can broaden your perspective. Also pivotal to living deeply is another kind of awareness. Perceiving the shortness of your own life and your power to direct it can dramatically change your experience of a relationship. Awareness of the value of humor, love, and gentleness in relationships will add to your lightness of being.

Tact involves a sensitivity to the feelings of others. A kind of grace. Tact has magnetic quality. People are drawn to those who are sensitive to their feelings. You cannot fake it. But you can cultivate the quality. As you magnify this quality of sensitivity to feelings, your recognition of the sensibilities of other people will grow. And with this, your skills at negotiating will expand. Tact is a quality of giving consideration to others; it gives those who practice it a richer life.

Joy is the capacity to appreciate all the good things that currently fill your life. Joy puts a smile on your face, humor in your spirit, and generosity in your heart. Cultivate joy, and the power of your magnetic attraction will stun you with its greatness.

Nourish these four qualities, and you will be prepared to fight the weeds in your garden.

The Weeds

In moving to marriage, there are new challenges, obstacles to overcome, problems to be recognized, focused on, and solved. When you design a garden and lay out its plan, proper spacing of plants gives the roots the room they will need to grow. And this enhances the vitality of your plantings. As it is important to take time to plan before you plant a garden, it is crucial that you plan before you move in together or commit to each other. Weed your garden early.

When a man and a woman love the nearness of each other and look forward to a future together, the time is ripe for solving problems. This is the time to assess the thorns and weeds facing you. Address them with humor and prepare to enjoy your garden without thorns scratching up your skin or undergrowth choking out your flowers. The first plan is your prenuptial agreement.

THE PRENUPTIAL AGREEMENT

One way or another—written or verbal, spelled out or un-spoken—a man and a woman negotiate their own prenuptial agreement. They look at their problems and either avoid or address them. When they avoid them, they are making a prenuptial agreement to buy now and pay later. You can be sure that this lack of agreement will exact a great price in later years. When men and women make a conscious decision to prune their thorns, they are on their way to removing them. They are less likely to get scratched and bruised.

For the most useful prenuptial agreement, I suggest that you use pen and paper. Address your problems *and* agree on solutions. Whatever you agree upon, the written word will serve as a clear reminder. If you are able to write something down and agree that this writing is what you both mean, you will reduce the potential for difficulties later. Sometimes people forget what they agreed on. Other times they only think they are in agreement. When it comes to writing down what that agreement is, they discover they really haven't spoken the same language. The beauty of the written word is that it focuses both of you on the same message. Moreover, something written can be preserved. Years later you will both see the same agreement—even as you may be surprised to discover the way memory plays tricks on perceptions.

Your Marital Insurance Policy

Think of a prenuptial agreement as an insurance policy. Many people buy fire insurance. Usually they don't buy it because they expect to have a fire. They buy it to prepare against its devastation should they be so unfortunate. When an insurance company considers selling the insurance, they often help the purchaser to fireproof the property. The prenuptial agreement is a test of the couple's ability to define what they believe is fair play. Since it is *not* done in anger, it is generally pretty fair. Take a look around at the women and men you have known. Take a look at how many times a divorce leads to a reduction in the standard of living of the woman but not the man. This true story illustrated one common scenario.

Henry and Mildred had a lovely courtship. They married, started their family, and for Mildred life was hectic but pretty good. Sex was infrequent, in part because she felt so harried so often. With two children under seven and a part-time job, she figured that this was pretty much to be expected. She knew she wasn't taking the time to keep up her appearance, but she assumed Harold would understand. After all, the kids were growing and soon would be in school all day. Then she would have time for herself once again.

It didn't work out that way. In the eighth year of marriage, Harold met Sarah and became involved with her. Since Mildred was tired most of the time and sex had taken a nosedive, he figured he would have a secret affair to save the marriage. He would meet his needs without bothering his wife. A few months later his perspective had changed; he was in love with Sarah. The romance was terrific. He had almost forgotten how wonderful it was to wine and dine and take time for slow and sensuous loving. He wanted a divorce; and he really didn't want to have to give up half his income because he wanted to spend the money he earned on his new life and on his new wife. Meanwhile, Mildred was on a fifteen-year track to support and raise their children. Thanks to marriage, financial remedies were available. Mildred had to live with her emotional pain, but she had some rights too.

Community property rules, which exist in many states, and no-fault divorce have caused enormous problems across the United States. Many different kinds of inequities have resulted from the attempt to say that after many years of marriage, a man and woman are exactly equal. The fact is that if a woman has been raising children, her capacity to earn a living is not equal. That kind of financial devastation is preventable when people negotiate fairly. The couple is forging a *social* contract, not just a legal one.

Prenuptial agreements have been getting bad press lately. They help to provide protection and stability to a marriage. If a couple cannot talk about these issues, that fact is a signal that there is a problem, one that would be more easily handled if it were focused on now. Let's look at what happened to the Starter family.

Mrs. Starter was the mother of Susan, a school chum of Lisa. The children attended elementary school together, and Mrs. Starter often chauffeured the girls around town. The Starters were well-off. They had a beautiful home, lovely gardens. They sent Susan to an exclusive private school. Mr. Starter was a member of some of the important societies and clubs in his city; he was well respected and quite attractive. By the age of six or seven, Lisa would often spend afternoons and occasional overnights at her friend Susan's house, and she was shocked by what she saw. She told her mom that she saw Mr. Starter punching Mrs. Starter, that when the yelling started, she felt scared and didn't want to stay there. And she described how afraid she was for her friend Susan.

Mr. Starter's sudden death, at age forty-six, from a stroke seemed like a deliverance—especially as the story began to unfold. Mrs. Starter had come into the marriage with a great deal of money. She had signed it over to him under the romantic notion that he would take care of her. His will had left "her" money to be put in a trust fund to support her only as long as she did not remarry. In the event of a remarriage, the money was to be forfeited and given instead to a charity. Their daughter Susan was to receive a stipend each year but was never to see the principal.

If that had been the only story I had ever heard of its kind, I would have written it off as a fluke, but the sad fact is that the story is common. Variations of it emerge all the time. It's called:

"Don't you trust me?"

When a woman is asked this question, a healthy response would be:

"Yes, I trust we can talk it out. Let's see what our values are and if we can come to an agreement."

We trust that those who sign contracts will honor them, that those with whom we negotiate will honor their agreements. The true trust is that we become dependent on the goodwill of those with whom we negotiate an agreement. If he doesn't want to negotiate an agreement, starts to express anger, and asks again, "What's the matter? Don't you trust me?" a good answer would be:

"Yes, I trust that you are a man of your word who would not hesitate to put it in writing."

In trying to come to an agreement, remember that you are acting as equal partners in the journey of marriage. Negotiation is for equals. Passive dependency is for children. People change, violence happens, unanticipated events alter life courses. A prenuptial agreement makes sense as a kind of insurance policy. It also clarifies values. It describes the plan for the marriage, and it describes the terms in the event that one or the other wants the marriage to end. Since yoking a man to a woman *permanently* when either wants out is the equivalent of involuntary servitude, a divorce clause recognizes the ultimate freedom of each partner to leave the marriage. It discourages a litigious atmosphere should such a sad outcome occur. Prenuptial agreements can be as varied as the individuals who negotiate them, but negotiating them before marriage will save stress and distress. Every partnership agreement can benefit from acknowledging the potential for change and defining what is fair.

Prenuptial agreements do not necessarily take the romance out of the marriage. Not *all* the romance. Let's face it: A prenuptial agreement is not romantic. Neither is taking out the garbage or buying a life insurance policy. Adults recognize that romance is one of the lovely aspects of courtship, and that providing for stability and security is another important value—not necessarily romantic but definitely health promoting. Think of it as your final barrier to learning how equitable your intended life partner really is. Lawyers are the only beneficiaries of the naïve assumption that "this cannot happen to us and we do not need to plan." Romance can be enhanced when you discover the sense of fair play your intended believes to be correct. Moreover, the very discussion of what is fair will elevate your joint perceptions and help you build a good foundation for your marriage.

The negotiation of a prenuptial agreement is a test. It's one more step in illuminating each other's character. A very important step because you will learn, early on, what you might otherwise not learn for years. You will have an opportunity to consider whether you still want to go forward as you learn more about your partner's character. If your partner is excessively secretive and not forthcoming about his finances, you should weigh that behavior very carefully indeed. A well-drafted agreement, with the advice of attorneys, should disclose assets the partners bring to the marriage.

Negotiating a prenuptial agreement is an important mountain to climb. Once you have completed it, your marriage should be built on a solid foundation. This thoughtful discovery process establishes shared ethics and values. It helps cement the team.

Creating a Formal Document

If neither of you has property or children, you may choose to write out an informal agreement. Sign this and make duplicates so you both have a copy of what you agreed on.

If you have property, or children with former partners, a formal document will preserve your rights and honor what you have negotiated. When people are trustworthy, they

- Should be willing to come to a mutual agreement rather than leave things to chance
- Should be willing to write down the nature of their understanding

337

· Should be willing to commit their agreement to a formal signing

The legal system in the United States recognizes marriage as a legally enforceable economic agreement. If you fail to draw up your own agreement and the two of you separate, the state will decide how to divide your property. In doing so, it will cause you to spend an enormous amount of money and time, not to mention the aggravation, to reach an agreement you could have made yourselves in happier times with much less expense and stress. If you cannot resolve what is fair when you are at the height of your love, how can there be fair play when you are in bitter disagreement? Take charge and decide what you want. You're not looking for trouble, just minimizing its capacity to devastate.

Deciding together on a prenuptial agreement lets you find out before your marriage how much respect and trust you have for each other. And it's good practice at problem solving. You will learn that you can meet as equals, talk things out, and come to a mutual agreement of what would be fair under different circumstances. If you cannot do this, it's better to know that before you bind yourself legally and spiritually. Think of this test as your final hurdle to marriage.

What's in a Prenuptial Agreement?

The issues involved in a prenuptial agreement generally fall into two categories: the agreement for the marriage and the agreement for the rights and privileges in the event of the dissolution of the marriage. Both parts are valuable in defining your shared values, and you should consider both in order to produce a complete agreement.

The topics to review and negotiate for the marriage usually revolve around the following issues:

- *Money:* How it will be spent, who will manage it, how frequently the plan will be renegotiated, and a process for allowing exceptions.
- *Children:* If either of you has children from a previous marriage, what involvement will they have in the marriage? Who comes first? Who supports them? What must they do as part of the team family effort? How often will they be staying over? Who will impose discipline when they create a mess, argue, or create chaos in the marriage?
- *Values and goals for adult children:* Do they pay their own way? Are they to develop financial responsibility? Are the parents to continue to support them? Are they to live within their means? Are the parents to alter their means? How does the marriage change the inheritance plans?
- *The will:* What are your intentions for your wills? Remember your last will and testament is separate from and not obviated by a prenuptial agreement. A will is unilateral and can be changed and revoked as often as its author wants.

The Gray Areas

A prenuptial agreement secures your financial equity in a marriage and preserves your dignity so that you feel good about your partner. Because he has made this commitment to you, you enter the marriage feeling good. The agreement can be as creative as you wish. And it can cover a lot of the gray areas. For instance, it could be designed with punitive features or without. It could say that in the event of infidelity, that person will suffer economically, while the faithful one will not. It could say if either one wants to end the marriage, the terms will be the same. No fault. It could define a "cooling-off" period in such an event.

Whatever the two of you in your most rational moments decide makes sense should be drafted to serve as your insurance policy—insurance against the legal system taking control of your lives and insurance that your future partner is really on the level. An equitable prenuptial agreement will serve both of you well as you enter into marriage. When you have worked out the details, a good investment would be a formalized rendering by a lawyer. The two or three hours it takes to do this is very economical. Don't do it yourself—even with how-to forms. Lawyers are trained to identify what you might miss. (He or she might note that you forgot to say, for example: "if pre-existing debts become *marital* debts . . .") They know the *laws* of your state government that might render your plans unenforceable.

Two Women's Stories

I'd like to share with you two women's experiences that illustrate why I take such a strong position on prenuptial agreements. First consider Jill's story.

> Jill was forty when she met Peter, a divorced man eighteen years her senior. She had been single only six months, and he swept her off her feet. She was madly in love and pining for him long before he decided he was in love with her. Using her restraint, she waited till he was ready. Eventually, he did generate the energy to court her.

After a two-year courtship they began to discuss marriage. But they weren't very good at confronting the reality of their condition. Peter had had two failed marriages before Jill and was a bit gun-shy. A wealthy man, he had four children and owned two houses (his and one for his aged mother). He employed a staff of seventy in his very lucrative business.

When it was time to redecorate his beach house, he asked Jill to do it. He told her he would like her to make all the selections as though it were her house and she was going to live in it. Money was no object. She was to choose according to her taste, only stopping to show him for approval. Six months of her efforts produced a very beautiful seashore house. But during those six months she was driving from the city to the seashore (a two-hour trip each way) at least once and often twice a week.

She couldn't imagine charging him for her energy, although the project meant cutting back on her own self-employed work hours. It was a labor of love. He kept intimating that it was going to be her house and she just proceeded faithfully.

Eventually Peter did propose to Jill and they set a wedding date five months hence. She was in a state of romantic bliss. For the next couple of months she was busily planning their wedding—a gala affair involving complex arrangements. As the wedding day came closer, she started to have some anxieties. They had never really discussed how money was to be managed, and although she owned her house from her first marriage, her alimony would end as soon as her new marriage began.

Two weeks before the wedding Peter handed her his proposed draft of a prenuptial agreement. She was flabbergasted. They had never discussed one. And she had rather naïvely assumed it was not going to be necessary. She had not considered her property or his, her children or his, but *he* had. He suggested she take this document to her attorney so that it would be valid (enforceable) on signing.

The nightmare that unfolded could be the storyline of any soap opera. She reluctantly took the document to an attorney. She learned that although he was leaving her a modest sum on his death, the seashore house and the bulk of his estate were going elsewhere. He was planning for them to live well as long as they were together, but she worried that when he died she would experience a dramatic reduction in lifestyle. Jill was forty-two; Peter fifty-nine. Her lawyer was enraged at the document.

She began to consider the implications of his proposal and became very upset. She had been happily planning to devote the remaining youthful years of her life to him. But once widowed, according to his plan, she would be unable to continue living in the style she would be accustomed to as his wife. In the marriage her time would be devoted to helping him. He was frequently calling upon her to entertain his clients, travel with him, and be available when he needed her. She enjoyed the lifestyle, but worried about her later life. Between the decorating assignment and the entertaining for him, she found herself working less than one day a week at her own business.

The days were passing, and the wedding was scheduled. She did go through with the wedding—on his terms, but with great trepidation. I have not heard about the outcome, but I worry for her. Because she accepted a commitment she felt was inequitable, she had ignored a weed that was bound to grow.

When women do not secure their own protection with an equitable prenuptial agreement, they compromise their confidence and well-being and probably enter a marriage at an economic disadvantage. A woman who makes such an error submits to an imbalance of power that is detrimental to dignity and independence. I strongly recommend that at every stage of man/woman relations, women maintain their dignity and power. It is important to allow a man to dominate in the bedroom, but he should not be permitted to dominate at the bank.

Marriage should secure your safety. Consider a prenuptial agreement a form of fire insurance. If you are securely insured, your search for courtship will launch you into a warm and loving future with your new husband, and you will be ready to build a remarkable marriage between equals who respect each other.

Consider Valerie's courtship. She had a tough set of problems, a wonderful man, and a sure sense of her own need for a fair prenuptial agreement.

> In Giles, Valerie found a warm and wonderful man with great character and a good sense of humor, a man who made her glow just to be near him When he asked her to marry him, he made it clear that Valerie was to be his Number One. But there were problems: Giles did not manage his money well, could not say no to his children, and his children were hostile to her. Valerie was uneasy about the potential conflicts. She knew how much he loved his children and how much they disliked her, the woman who was coming between them. But she trusted Giles, especially when he worked with her to form an agreement on money, courtesy from stepchildren (they each had children), and rules for family visits—and then put it in writing.
>
> They created their new family budget. They agreed to

reserve a stated percentage of income that could be spent each year on each child by the natural parent without any joint consultation. They agreed that the debts their children created were not going to be the debts of their marriage; therefore they would not countersign loans for their children. (All their children were young adults accustomed to "coming home for help.") They outlined what they agreed to do, then took this outline to an attorney, who showed them where their ideas could be invalidated by law and drew up a formal agreement.

With the prenuptial agreement in place, the bookkeeping details became trivial and Giles and Valerie were able to focus their marriage on romance and building a good life together. In the sixth year of marriage now, both believe that their prenuptial agreement was crucial in helping them consider and prevent many potential mine fields.

Sample Prenuptial Agreements

To help you get started on creating your own prenuptial agreements, two variations are outlined below. Part A considers couples that do not have substantial assets. Part B considers those that do. Use the outline to spark your thoughts for setting up your own agreement.

OUTLINE
Prenuptial Agreement between
MARY WIFE and JOHN HUSBAND

This Prenuptial Agreement, between MARY WIFE ("Wife") (address) and JOHN HUSBAND ("Husband") (address), made this _____ day of May _____.

WITNESSETH

WHEREAS, Wife and Husband shall be married *date* at *place*; and

WHEREAS, with full disclosure of each other's assets, liabilities, and prior legal commitments, disclosed in Exhibits A and B, attached hereto and incorporated herein by reference, they desire to execute this Prenuptial Agreement covering the subjects of divorce, and spending values;

NOW THEREFORE, in consideration of marriage, the parties, after receiving independent legal counsel, intending to be legally bound thereby, agree as follows:

1. A. *DIVORCE* [Where neither has substantial premarital property and only one will work]

    a) *Intent of the Parties* The parties intend, insofar as is practicable, in the event of divorce, to divide the marital property to equitably reflect the respective contribution whether homemaking, childbearing, or income producing.

    b) *"Marital Property"* As defined in [relevant state] law. The parties agree to exclude from "marital property" all premarital assets including [list].

    c) *Ratios of Equitable Distribution—Wage-earner vs Homemaker*

      (i) If homemaker never worked outside home, couple had no children to raise, and homemaker never was involved in supporting wage-earner's career, then perhaps 40% to homemaker, 60% to wage-earner is fair.

      (ii) As above, except homemaker *was* directly involved, then 50%–50% might be fair.

      (iii) If homemaker was helping partner *and* raised children, 60% for her/him and 40% for income producer might be fair.

    d) *Alimony & Support* [Enough to train "homemaker" to be wage-earner? Maintain lifestyle?]

    e) *Child Support* [Describe] Private or public schools, college? Graduate school, too?

1. B. *DIVORCE* [Applicable where either has substantial— $20,000 + —pre-marital property and both will work]

    a) *Intent of the Parties* The parties intend, insofar as is practicable, in the event of divorce, to restore their economic status quo ante of [date before wedding] without the marriage having caused substantially disproportionate economic loss or gain to one party compared to the other.

    b) *"Marital Property"* As defined in [relevant state] law. The parties agree to exclude from "marital property" all pre-marital assets including [list]. Also excluded: expected inheritances from Aunt Harriet to Wife, from Uncle Harry to Husband.

    c) *Equitable Distribution* As of the date of separation, the parties shall equitably divide and distribute marital property as defined by this contract in the following manner:

        (i)   Total the sum of cash contributions of each, to the marriage relationship, and divide that sum in one half.

        (ii) Total the contributions of each party.

        (iii) The party whose contribution was less than half shall pay the difference to the other to achieve parity.

    d) *Alimony and Support* The parties, to the extent permitted by law, waive and renounce their claims to alimony and support from the other.

    e) *Child support:* [Describe]. Private or public schools, college? Graduate school, too?

2.   *SPENDING VALUES*

    a) The parties have created a plan for the marital relationship reflecting their agreed-upon spending values and recognition that certain assets remain their individual property not commingled with marital assets.

    b) The principles are mutually acceptable values for the interpretation of this Prenuptial Agreement as clear expressions of the intent and priorities of the parties for the marriage relationship. They are as follows:

        (i)   Husband's salary goes, in order, to alimony to his ex-wife [amt], accumulation of [amt] per year for four years to his son Joe's college education, then balance to the marriage.

(ii) Wife's income goes to her invalid Aunt Harriet [amt], balance to marriage.

(iii) Values and goals for adult children: pay their own way; develop financial responsibility, i.e., consume assets they have earned; live within means; learn to invest part of their earnings to "build a nest." When valid needs arise, the children can borrow from marital unit and schedule payment so that other children will have a resource to do the same.

3. *SEVERABILITY* The parties intend that invalidity of one portion of this Prenuptial Agreement shall not nullify the remaining portions.

4. *AMENDMENTS* Amendments must be in writing signed by both parties.

5. *GOVERNING LAW* This Agreement shall be governed by [Pennsylvania] law.

6. *ARBITRATION* The parties shall submit material unresolved disputes over this Agreement to binding arbitration either to the American Arbitration Association in [Philadelphia] or by each choosing an individual who shall jointly choose a third party as impartial arbitrator. Arbitration costs shall be shared equally by the parties.

IN WITNESS WHEREOF, the parties have executed this Prenuptial Agreement the date first written above in [Pennsylvania].

MARY WIFE	JOHN HUSBAND	(WITNESS)
		(ADDRESS)

EXHIBIT A
TO PRENUPTIAL AGREEMENT of
Mary Wife and John Husband
WIFE'S ASSETS & LIABILITIES

LIABILITIES: MORTGAGES $
              INSTALLMENT LOANS $
              CREDIT CARDS $
              OTHER (DEFINE) $
                                 Total $ _____

ASSETS: REALTY $
              INVESTMENTS $
              SAVINGS ACCOUNT $
              CHECKING ACCOUNT $
              PERSONAL PROPERTY:
                 Automobile $
                 Clothing $
                 Jewelry $
                 Furniture $
                 Other (define) $
                                 Total $ _____

SPECIFIC EXCLUSIONS [for example, potential inheritance from Aunt Harriet]

                                      (INITIALED)
                                      MW   JH

EXHIBIT B

TO PRENUPTIAL AGREEMENT of

Mary Wife and John Husband

HUSBAND'S ASSETS & LIABILITIES

LIABILITIES: ALIMONY AND PENSION LIABILITY TO EX-
WIFE PURSUANT TO DIVORCE ORDER $

MORTGAGES $

COMMITMENT OF FOUR YEARS OF
COLLEGE @ $ PER YEAR TO SON JOE $

INSTALLMENT LOANS $

OTHER (DEFINE) $

Total $ _____

ASSETS: REALTY $

INVESTMENTS $

LIFE INSURANCE $

PENSION $

SAVINGS ACCOUNT $

CHECKING ACCOUNT $

PERSONAL PROPERTY:

Automobile $

Clothing $

Jewelry $

Furniture $

Other (define) $

Total $ _____

SPECIFIC EXCLUSIONS [for example, potential inheritance from Uncle Harry]

(INITIALED)

MW   JH

Prepared by Thomas E. Quay, Esq., General Counsel, Athena Institute, 30 Coopertown Rd., Haverford, PA 19041. (215) 642-3073.

SUMMING UP

Your search for courtship is an activity as important as anything you will ever undertake in your life. It is worthy of your intelligent focus, your discipline, and your strength of restraint.

The prize—a man you love who courts, proposes, and enters into a marvelous marriage with you—is worth all this effort. As adults recognize, it is in the act of working, of thinking, and of accomplishing the deed that the days of our lives move forward and the gardens we cultivate come into full flower.

Here's wishing you a luxuriant bloom—one you will deserve when you have achieved the levels of self-awareness and compassion that an active search for courtship will have given you. What a great woman and wife you will be, and how well you will be treated. Best of luck!

Acknowledgments

I would like to acknowledge and thank individuals who directly contributed to *Searching for Courtship*. First, Loretta Barrett, my friend and literary agent, who initially convinced me that the ideas expressed herein belonged in a book of their own. Both for the impetus of the idea, and the extraordinary quantity and quality of interactions, Loretta Barrett is greatly appreciated.

To Stephanie Young, the health-and-fitness editor at *Glamour* magazine, my grateful appreciation for this, the second book we have worked on together. For inexhaustible good cheer, marvelous feedback, and great editing.

To Thomas E. Quay, Esq., I am grateful for help in reviewing the entire contents of the book, many thoughtful comments, and particularly for his work in drafting the prenuptial agreement outlines in Chapter 10.

I also thank Pamela Sinkler Todd for her beautiful artistic renderings in this book.

To Martha Mockbee Drake, Tracy S. Kramer, Theodora Ashmead, Suzanne Galloway, Jodie Cutler, and Theresa Walsh, for feedback on the early drafts and developing ideas of the search. To Celso García, M.D., for his enthusiastic support.

To Sandra Leiblum, Ph.D., for her thoughtful comments on locating a sex therapist. To those who, while working at the Athena Institute, have helped me with the manuscript typing and editing and provided feedback: Kate Paffet, Jennifer Almquist, Christine Hufschmid, Sara A. Rubin, Jill Kempenaar, Kelly Chon, and Lori Lerner.

To the librarians at Ludington Library, particularly Pat Rayfield and Sandy Naydock, for retrieving references when I needed them.

I am grateful to the wonderful people at Villard/Random House for the consistent high quality and professionalism of their guidance of this book: particularly Diane Reverand, an editor without peer, Melanie Cecka, and Gail Siragusa.

About the Author

WINNIFRED B. CUTLER founded the Stanford Menopause Study and cofounded the University of Pennsylvania's Women's Wellness Program, serving as its first scientific director before establishing the Athena Institute in Haverford, Pennsylvania. She earned her doctorate in biology from the University of Pennsylvania and has published over thirty scientific papers in biomedical journals. Dr. Cutler holds patents for her codiscovery of human sex pheromones.

Because she believes that a search for courtship is an activity as important as anything a woman will ever undertake, she brings her scientific logic to this enterprise.